FOR THE LOVE OF MONEY

74-year-old Elaine Witte of Indiana had no children of her own. But she loved her stepson Paul as much as any mother could. And after he died in a tragic shooting, Elaine opened her home to Paul's widow Hilma "Marie" and their two sons, Eric and Butch.

When she disappeared in the winter of 1984, everyone was concerned. Everyone, that is, except her family. Marie and the boys gave conflicting stories about her whereabouts, and then fled town. When they were finally arrested in a San Diego trailer park, they confessed to something more gruesome than simple murder.

Greedy for Witte's social security checks, Marie had convinced her teenage son Butch to kill his grandmother with a crossbow. Then together they butchered the old woman, running parts through a food processor, dissolving parts in acid, and crushing the skull in a trash compactor. But even more startling was the revelation that the shooting of Paul Witte had been no accident: Marie had induced her other son, Eric, to kill his own father!

BLOOD MONEY recounts the horrifying true story of a woman who, without passion or remorse, turned her sons into murderers and destroyed her family out of nothing more than raw greed.

**GOOD VERSUS EVIL. HEROES TRAPPING MONSTERS.
THIS ISN'T FANTASY. IT'S LIFE.
CAPTURE A PINNACLE TRUE CRIME TODAY.**

JEFFREY DAHMER   (661, $4.99)
By Dr. Joel Norris
Everyone knows Dahmer's name, but how many of us know the man behind the
headlines? Renowned psychologist Dr. Joel Norris sheds light on the dark forces that
compelled Dahmer to butcher and consume the men he loved. Based on unpublished
facts about the killer's lifestyle and background, it features extensive interviews with
his friends and ex-lovers. Readers may never fully understand Dahmer's behavior or
find him sympathetic, but Norris's book outlines how a seemingly normal man can
degenerate and lash out while silently passing among us.

ARTHUR SHAWCROSS: THE GENESEE RIVER KILLER   (578, $4.99)
By Dr. Joel Norris
Despite his parole officer's warnings, child killer Arthur Shawcross was released from
prison early. He headed to Rochester, New York, to begin his next chapter.
Shawcross's second chance at life spelled death for eleven women. He conducted a
horrible slaying spree, reminiscent of Jack The Ripper, that targeted prostitutes and
denizens of Rochester's red light district. Strangling them in remote wooded areas, his
insane bloodlust drove him to butcher their naked bodies and to devour parts of their
flesh before disposing of them. Ironically, police arrested him by luck when he was
observed casually eating his lunch while the nude corpse of his latest victim floated
past him in the Genesee River.

CHOP SHOP   (693, $4.99)
By Kathy Braidhill
Generations of mourners brought their "loved ones" to Lamb Funeral Home. They
trusted the sincere staff, appreciated the sympathetic directors, and knew without
question that their relations were in capable hands. They were wrong. Grotesque
mutilations and sadistic practices flourished at Lamb's. Like a ghoulish twist on a
vampire novel, here the living merrily preyed upon the dead. Fingers were severed to
claim expensive rings; teeth were forcefully pulled out for the ounces of gold filling;
and organs were fiercely removed to be sold to research labs. The crematorium fires
blazed fiendishly around the clock as multiple bodies were stuffed into the chambers
for mass burnings. It was a scenario worthy of the Holocaust. *Chop Shop* recounts
how unspeakable acts of horror were perpetrated against the ultimate victims: dead
men who can tell no tales. Thankfully, Kathy Braidhill broke this case and gave a voice
to these victims.

SEX, MONEY AND MURDER IN DAYTONA BEACH   (555, $4.99)
By Lee Butcher
Florida's society set always makes a splash in the papers: debutante balls, charity
auctions, MURDER. Beautiful heiress Lisa Paspalakis surprised her wealthy family
by marrying for love. She wed Kosta Fotopoulos, a waiter, after a whirlwind court-
ship. This fairytale union was ripe with villains and greed. Fotopoulos and his mistress
had already laid plans for Lisa's cold-blooded demise. This is an explosive indictment
of greed, decadence, and amorality.

BLOOD MONEY

Clifford L. Linedecker

PINNACLE BOOKS
WINDSOR PUBLISHING CORP.

PINNACLE BOOKS are published by

Windsor Publishing Corp.
475 Park Avenue South
New York, NY 10016

The P logo Reg. U.S. Pat. & TM Off. Pinnacle is a
trademark of Windsor Publishing Corp.

First Printing: December, 1993

Printed in the United States of America

To Don Benn and Forbes Julian
for their patience and their time and effort
teaching the journalistic ropes to a tenderfoot.

"Never trust a woman or an automatic pistol."
— John Dillinger,
Indiana Bank Robber and Public Enemy #1

Author's Note

This is a work totally of nonfiction. Nothing has been made up, there are no composite characters, no liberties have been taken recreating conversation, and no names have been changed. Quotes are taken from the recollections of law enforcement officers and other participants, or directly from testimony during the trial and related proceedings. In a few instances accounts of the trial and other events are presented slightly out of chronological order for the purposes of smoothing out the narrative and moving the story along. Many times the stories of participants conflict with each other, and in most instances I have used the account which is the most plausible based on my knowledge of the people and events involved. In other instances I have recorded different versions, pointed out the sources, and left it up to the reader to determine whose story is the most believable.

Acknowledgments

Too many people have had a hand helping me in the research and preparation of this book for me to name all of them individually.

But I would like to express special thanks to Don Benn, my former mentor and colleague at *The LaPorte Herald-Argus,* for his eager and cheerful support. Don and others at the *Herald-Argus* generously opened their files and shared important personal recollections of the case with me.

Bob Wellinski also deserves special mention for taking time out from his busy schedule as a *Herald-Argus* photographer to dig through ten-year-old photo files and provide me with most of the illustrations for this book. When file photographs of some of the participants in the story were unavailable, Bob went out and took his own or rustled them up from other sources.

Laporte County Prosecutor William F. Herrbach, former Porter County Prosecutor Daniel R. Berning, Defense Attorney Scott L. King of Gary, and Trail Creek Town Marshal Eugene "Skip" Pierce and many others including some who preferred not to be publicly identified, generously shared their insider's knowledge with me. The book couldn't have been written without their cooperation.

Efforts by the friendly folks at the American Sunbathing Association's American Nudist Research Library in Kissimee, Florida, provided information that was critical to sorting out some of the early years of various participants in the story. Employees of the National Archives and Records Administration in Washington, D.C.; Indiana Department of Corrections; the Lafayette (Indiana) City Health Department; the Florida Department of Vital Statistics; Palm Beach County Historical Society and the Palm Beach County Library in West Palm Beach, Florida, and the Michigan City Library, Valparaiso Library and Chesterton Library—all in Indiana—were also most helpful to me in pursuing my research.

A big thank you goes to my cousin, Norma Jean Wolfe, of Monticello, Indiana, who called on personal contacts who made it possible for me to tie up some especially perplexing loose ends.

To Paul Dinas, my editor at Pinnacle, my thanks for bearing with me when I strained his patience over the deadline, the classic bug-a-boo that pesters editors as well as writers. And as always my thanks to my agent, Adele Leone, for her support which I have come to expect as "a given" but is much appreciated anyway.

Finally, I would like to thank "Debbie" of the Indiana State Supreme Court's microfilm division in Indianapolis for her swift and efficient response to my last-minute request for a copy of the transcripts of Marie Witte's trial in Michigan City.

Contents

Introduction

Ever since I began my first daily newspaper job with *The LaPorte Herald-Argus* in Indiana, I knew that the police beat was the assignment for me.

Murder and other serious crimes fascinate me now as they did then. I love being a ringside observer to the challenging jigsaw puzzle of emotions, motivations, and police investigation that solves murders and brings killers to justice.

Obviously, I'm not alone in that. Some psychologists claim that only sex preoccupies Americans more than murder.

In LaPorte thirty-five years ago there weren't many local murders for a young police beat reporter to write about. During the six years I was with the newspaper I covered only two: one of an old woman beaten to death by burglars who broke into her home in the city; another of a minor

Democratic party official who lived in the rural LaPorte county area and was shot to death by his wife when she became fed-up with his tom-catting ways.

But my editor, Don Benn, kept my imagination fueled with wondrous stories of other events and characters in our circulation area. Eventually I met many of the people he had told me about. There was a former mayor who stopped to direct traffic while a baffled crowd of citizens waited impatiently blocks away for him to present the key to the city to a celebrity; the young man who primed one of the Civil War-era cannons on the courthouse lawn with powder, stuck a concrete cannon ball inside and shot the deadly missile down the deserted main drag; an eccentric little fellow from Chicago who showed up in town every four years dressed like Robin Hood to campaign for the presidency of the United States.

But the character Don spun tales about whom I would have most liked to meet was Diana of the Dunes. There was no chance of that because Diana had already been dead for about thirty years, but there were still old-timers around who remembered her.

There is no question that Diana was the most exotic, intriguing and tragic historical character who ever inhabited the gently sloping and ever-shifting hills of sand that border the southern tip of Lake Michigan and are known as the Dunes.

The Dunes themselves are fascinating, for many reasons, including their sometimes sinister past. They have been the site of robberies, murder, inexplicable vanishings and of rum-running by Prohibition-era gangsters and smugglers. Stretching east from Lake County, Indiana, at the south edge of Chicago, they continue east through Porter and LaPorte counties and have been used more than a few times as a convenient dumping ground for the victims of both professional and more random killers.

There was nothing really ominous about Diana, whose real name was Alice Mabel Gray. She grew up as the pampered daughter of a Chicago physician before hiking into the Dunes to live by herself at about the time World War I was beginning to flare in Europe. Diana attracted her celebrity, or notoriety, for becoming one of the first streakers.

Beginning in the spring of 1916, she went for daily swims during the warm weather in Lake Michigan, and she didn't bother with a bathing suit. She didn't think much more of towels than she did of swimwear. When she emerged from the invigorating waters, she sprinted, danced, and cavorted along the beach until the drying off process was completed naturally by the lake breeze, her own exertions, and the sun. Then she would flop down on the sand to sunbathe, still nude.

Inevitably, the petite and pretty lake nymph was spotted by fishermen, who began gathering on the beach in the mornings to enjoy the show. When the wife of one of the fishermen heard of the scandalous naked frolics, she stalked across the sand and pounded at the door of the hussy's shack. Alice, as she was still known at that time, emerged with a gun in hand and chased off the intruder.

The outraged wife went to the newspapers, and Alice became a sudden celebrity. She also acquired the moniker Diana of the Dunes from enterprising newshounds who finally came up with the descriptive nickname after trying out and abandoning several others.

The publicity firestorm had finally died down when she became involved in a fateful romance with a man of mystery.

Diana's lover was a handsome, rawboned, blond hulk with a nasty temper, rough ways, a jealous mind, and quick fists. His name may have been Paul Wilson; to this day no one is sure. Area historians never determined how the oddly-matched pair first met, or where Wilson came from, although there appears to be a good chance he was a wandering rattlesnake hunter from Texas.

They lived together only about a year before tragedy intruded in the form of a man whose rapidly decomposing body was found on the beach near their shack. The dead man had been strangled, apparently battered with a club, then burned. It was early June 1922.

Rumors circulated that Diana's jealous lover was the killer. When Paul and Diana confronted a man who guarded cottages on the Dunes and blamed him for spreading the stories, violence flared. Moments later Diana was unconscious, her skull fractured by a pistol butt. Paul was shot in one foot.

Although Diana was hospitalized and in a coma for days, she survived and Paul was eventually able to take her home to their shack. But she never recovered her previously robust health. Three years later on a cold wind-driven night in early February, she died in Paul's arm of uremic poisoning.

The day after the funeral Paul burned the primitive little home he had shared with Diana of the Dunes. Then he dropped from sight.

In 1930, five years after Diana's death, a new inmate named Paul Wilson, was admitted to the Indiana State Prison at Michigan City. Was the convict, sentenced for a stickup in Porter County, the former mate of Diana of the Dunes? No one ever learned the answer.

But a half-century later, the sons of another man named Paul, who was linked to violence and tragedy, would attend schools in Michigan City. And later, like Paul Wilson, they would acquire firsthand knowledge of Indiana prisons.

While roaming the Dunesland area researching their story, the story of their mother, grandmother and other relatives and acquaintances whose lives they helped alter in such a violent way, I often thought about Paul Wilson — and about Diana of the Dunes.

Clifford L. Linedecker
July 1993
Lantana, Florida

Prologue

Elaine Witte put a high value on her friendships, her neighbors, and her family, although at seventy-three, she not only had outlived her husband, but her siblings and most of her close relatives as well.

Grandma Witte was widowed in early September 1967, when her husband, Leonard, died. The death of the longtime employee of the Michigan Central and of the Chicago South Shore and South Bend railroads occurred just about the time he had planned to retire.

After Leonard's death, Elaine's last remaining sibling, a sister, Mildred Moran, moved in to keep her company. But Mildred died in 1981. That was the same year that Elaine's stepson, Paul, was killed in a tragic shooting at his home in the nearby town of Beverly Shores in neighboring Porter County.

Elaine had no children of her own, but was always a loving stepparent to her husband's son, Paul, and had watched with pride as he grew into manhood. She was also especially fond of Paul's half sister, Barbara. The women had known each other since 1962 when Barbara was twelve years old and spending the Christmas holidays with her older brother, who took her to the home of his father and stepmother a few times.

Through the years the two women kept in touch by telephone and through the mail. The close relationship continued after the younger woman married and settled down with her husband to begin raising a family near Oswego, Illinois, a small farming community a few miles southwest of Chicago's lakeside suburban sprawl. Barbara Valencia telephoned Elaine every month or two, drove to Trail Creek with her family to visit her as often as they could, and the women regularly exchanged greeting cards. The older woman became "Grandma Elaine" to Valencia's children, and she never neglected to send them cards for their birthdays and the holidays.

Early in 1982, several months after Paul's death, Elaine opened her own home to his widow, Marie, and their two sons. Elaine was glad for the company. There was more than enough room for the newcomers in her carefully maintained two-story wood-frame house at 320 Johnson Road in the town of Trail Creek.

The white house sat on two-and-a-half acres of

land and had a full-sized, detached garage; an additional one-and-one-half car drive-through garage; a large basement with several rooms; enclosed rear and front porches and five bedrooms. There were enough bedrooms that Elaine, her stepdaughter-in-law, and each of the boys had their own room, with one left over for guests.

The oldest of the two boys, Eric, attended Elston High School, closer to the center city area. His younger brother, John, who was called Butch, was enrolled in classes at Krueger Junior High School.

When her late stepson's family first moved in with her, Elaine doted on the boys and their mother. She was happy to have the company and was pleased that the big house was filled with the sounds of young people. In some of her letters to Mrs. Valencia, Elaine wrote that the boys were a big help to her keeping up with the yardwork.

Initially, it appeared, Grandma Witte's affection for her new housemates was returned, especially by Marie. In 1983 when Grandma Witte's seventy-fourth birthday rolled around, Marie telephoned several of the older woman's friends and invited them to the house for a party. Marie and John, though not Eric, joined in the festivities.

Even then, however, cracks had begun to develop in the older woman's relationship with her permanent houseguests. It wasn't long before they were constantly involved in some squabble or other. Elaine was disappointed in Marie and the boys.

When Elaine Witte got together with her chums from the Indiana Bell Pioneers for the group's monthly luncheons, the slender five-foot, four-inch woman listened politely to her friends' stories about their grandchildren and shared in their pride. But she no longer bragged about her own stepgrandsons as she once had.

Nevertheless, the spry gray-haired woman seemed to be enjoying her life, her home, and her friends in the Pioneers. Elaine had been a member of the club for almost twenty years following a long career as manager of the Bell Telephone office in Michigan City that culminated with her retirement in 1964.

Except for some arthritis in her knees which at times caused her to walk with a slight limp, she was healthy and active. She readily accepted the responsibility when she was elected president of the little group of approximately twenty-five telephone company retirees who lived in the sprawl of cities and towns near the foot of Lake Michigan.

Until early 1984 Elaine never missed a meeting as president of the Pioneers. Eschewing dresses and skirts for snappy slacks and jackets, she was always one of the first members to show up for the luncheons and parties. Inevitably, it seemed, the beige, two-year-old car that she treated almost as if it was a personal friend would already be parked outside the restaurant when her chums arrived.

The happy retiree was basically a homebody. She loved her house and yard. When she left her house, it was usually because she needed to shop, to get together with members of the Pioneer club, or to visit with others of her small circle of close friends.

But she seldom ventured far, and usually confined her traveling to LaPorte and Porter Counties, with an occasional drive across the Michigan state line that was only a few minutes away. When it was time for bed, however, she was usually tucked snugly into her own home.

She didn't take out-of-state vacations. She preferred to spend the pleasant warmer months puttering with the flowers in her yard, raking leaves in the fall, and visiting year-round with neighbors and other acquaintances. Grandma Witte was especially proud of her peonies. The double-blossomed perennial is Indiana's state flower, and its bright pinks, reds, yellows and whites were splashed in brilliant rainbows along the edges of her lawn where she lovingly nurtured it in patches and beds.

Despite the bitterly cold winters and the bone-chilling snow and sleet storms that sweep in off Lake Michigan, she didn't flee to Florida or Arizona to avoid the bad weather as so many other retirees chose to do. She sat out the harsh winters, as she did the pleasant summers, in the security and comfort of her longtime home.

The last time any of her friends from the Pioneer's saw her was at the club's annual Christmas party a few days before the 1983 holiday. One of the neighbors also received a telephone call from her on Christmas Eve, wishing her a happy holiday. Elaine apologized to her neighbor, a friend of thirty years, for not having visited for awhile. She explained she had been busy with Christmas shopping and other activities, and promised to stay in closer touch.

Then Grandma Witte dropped mysteriously out of sight!

When the neighbor she exchanged Christmas greetings with telephoned back several days later, Elaine's stepdaughter-in-law reported the older woman was in bed and too sick with the flu to take the call.

The neighbor tried once more to get in touch with Elaine a week later. That time she was told her friend was away on a long vacation. The neighbor asked Marie to have her stepmother-in-law give her a call when she returned home. But she never heard from Elaine again.

One

Alarm

Trail Creek was a nice place to live.

About a twenty-minute drive southeast of the Indiana Dunes National Lakeshore and the 1,180-acre Indiana Dunes State Park, the town straddles LaPorte County's Michigan and Coolspring townships. Once roamed by mysterious mound builders, then by Indians of the Algonquin nation, including Pottawattomi, Miamis and Chippewas, twentieth-century Trail Creek is surrounded on three sides by Michigan City.

It is a quiet suburb of attractive tree-shaded homes set among a pleasant sprinkle of hills and ravines. There are ranch homes, neat red-brick cottages, and three and four bedroom bi-levels with huge picture windows opening up on broad lawns landscaped with trees, bushes, and shrubs. A few rustic wood and stone houses with redwood railings are also scattered along the sides of steep ravines that cut through the community. Firewood is stacked by the cord at the sides and backs of many of the houses, to be burned during the winter in real indoor fireplaces.

Maples, oaks, pines, willows and other trees with their thick canopy of leaves stretch along the main thoroughfare, Johnson Road, and along most of the other streets, helping to keep the homes in Trail Creek refreshingly cool, even during the hottest days of summer. Only a handful of houses in the town have sidewalks in front of them, but traffic is sufficiently sparse so that it is generally safe for pedestrians to walk along the sides of the roads and streets.

Most residents, even in the many families where husband, wife, and teenagers all hold outside jobs, don't bother to hire a yardman; it is an opportunity to get outside for some healthy exercise and fresh air. They cut their own lawns and trim their shrubs and bushes in the summer; rake their own leaves and mulch flower beds in the fall; shovel snow in the winter; and uncover the flower beds and plant gardens in the spring. And when they do hire help to keep their lawns and shrubbery trim, it is usually a neighbor's son called in for a few dollars in mad money.

The town is a solid middle-class refuge where some residents still drop off to sleep at night with their doors unlocked, although even there it is becoming somewhat of a rarity. Teenage girls still sit with the babies or older children of neighbors and often walk the block or two home by themselves.

The tranquil village is small enough to be patrolled by a town marshal's department whose total staff consists of only four men. During a typical tour of duty they might be called on to corral a stray dog, chase a raccoon out of a garbage can, mediate a family quarrel, arrange for a drunk to be driven home, or investigate a fender-bender traffic accident.

Only rarely is there a violent or other felony crime to investigate, and most of the few criminal acts marshals are called on to deal with are minor burglaries and thefts.

Trail Creek is small-town friendly, a community where householders elect their own neighbors to the town board, and many of the roughly twenty-five hundred residents know each other by sight. They are middle Americans who have found the American Dream.

The town is a bedroom community to Michigan City, a medium-sized town of about forty-thousand people. Michigan City is the largest community in LaPorte County, although the county seat is in the nearby city of LaPorte, which is more centrally located in the primarily rural county than Michigan City.

There are a few businesses in Trail Creek, including a combination bar and restaurant and a couple of gas stations and convenience stores. But most of the town's residents work, shop, and conduct much of their business in Michigan City; or they drive there to take advantage of its parks, excellent library, and other cultural and recreational facilities.

Michigan City is known in northern Indiana and southern Michigan for Washington Park, for the Washington Park Zoo, and for the fine sandy beach that stretches along the lakefront. Also, each year, Michigan City is host to the Miss Indiana Pageant, where a candidate is selected to compete in the Miss America contest in Atlantic City.

A feature of Michigan City less likely to be publicized by the local Chamber of Commerce and other community leaders is its role as the longtime home of the Indiana State Prison, where Paul Wilson, the known stickup man and possibly the mystery lover of Diana of the Dunes, once served time. The grim gray monolith on the city's west side is the oldest prison in the state. It also houses the Indiana Correctional system's electric chair and is considered to be the state's toughest and most secure penitentiary. Nevertheless, escapes have occasionally occurred.

Notorious Hoosier desperado John Dillinger served nine years in the penitentiary and at Indiana reformatories for a bungled stickup and escape attempts before being paroled. Then he masterminded and helped ten convicts break out of the prison by smuggling guns to them. Several of the escapees remained with him to form the nucleus of his bank robbery gang that raged through the Midwest for fourteen violent months in the mid-1930s.

But the kind of violence and danger associated with the men who inhabit the prison seemed to belong to a different world than the one inhabited by residents of Trail Creek. Perhaps that was one reason why Grandma Witte's sudden disappearance was so baffling.

Her chums in the retirement club of the telephone company, where she worked for thirty-four years, hadn't heard from her or seen her in months. Neither had her neighbors.

That simply wasn't like Elaine. She was a woman who never forgot to acknowledge a birthday, a holiday, or an anniversary with a card and a note or a telephone call.

The retirees were among the first of her small circle of acquaintances to become seriously concerned about Elaine's curious absence. Although the Pioneers didn't have official meetings during the first three months of the year, members regularly met with each other two-or-three-at-a-time for lunches and other informal get-togethers.

But Elaine hadn't contacted any of the Pioneers to suggest luncheons, and none of her friends had been able to get in touch with her to set up meetings. There were no telephone calls from her, no excuses or word of explanation to her friends. The woman who had been so devoted to the Indiana Bell Pioneers simply wasn't available to her friends anymore.

At past meetings of the Pioneers the talk had ranged widely over chats about families, soap operas, current affairs and various activities. Suddenly, members realized, a single subject had come to dominate their thoughts and conversations when they got together: Where was their friend, and club president, Elaine Witte?

One of the Bell Pioneers telephoned her home to ask about her. Then another club member called. Family members at the house told both callers variations of the same story about Elaine being away on an extended vacation.

Marie Voisenette, a Pioneer who also lived in Trail Creek and knew Elaine for more than thirty years, called the house more than once to inquire about her friend. The women exchanged cards on holidays, birthdays and other occasions, and Mrs.

Voisenette became concerned after the cards from Elaine stopped.

The first time she telephoned to ask about her friend, Elaine's stepdaughter-in-law told her the old woman was sick. Later calls brought reports that Elaine was touring the country, visiting places she had never seen before; then she was in California. It was difficult for Mrs. Voisenette to believe the stories that her friend was vacationing or in California. She asked Marie if Elaine was in a nursing home. Marie said she wasn't; Elaine was merely away for awhile.

Lucille McCarten, another Pioneer who was in the habit of lunching with Elaine about once a month regardless of whether or not club meetings were scheduled, tried four or five times during the early weeks of the new year to telephone her friend. She never managed to reach Elaine and usually talked with Marie. One time, however, she talked briefly with one of the boys.

Marie told her Elaine was on an extended vacation in the South, traveling by car from state-to-state and it was uncertain when she would return. Elaine wasn't doing the driving, Marie added. But she didn't say who the driver was.

When Mrs. McCarten asked Marie to tell Elaine to write, the young woman promised to pass on the message. During a later call, Marie told her that Elaine's arthritis had spread to her hand and she wasn't able to write.

The elderly woman's concerned chums tried to get more specific information: Where was she vacationing? When had she left? When was she coming home? But the questions brought only vague replies. The stepdaughter-in-law and the boys either didn't know or simply wouldn't tell.

Neighbors were also puzzled at Elaine's disturbing absence. When a couple of schoolgirls who lived a few doors away from the Witte home asked Butch about his grandmother, he told them she was on vacation. The teenagers inquired three or four times about the old woman and were always given the same basic story. But sometimes Butch said she was at one location, sometimes at another.

By March, nearly three months since Elaine had been seen outside the house, her friends and neighbors were in general agreement that she had been on vacation or suffering from the flu for an almost unbelievably long time.

In Illinois, Barbara Valencia was also worried about the woman who she considered to be almost like a mother. Mrs. Valencia had lost touch with Elaine after December 1983, when she wrote Barbara a note on a card decorated with pictures of cats, which she knew the younger woman was fond of. Elaine also sent a card with a cash gift to one of Barbara's sons whose birthday is just before Christmas, and she sent a holiday card with a chatty letter to the family.

Barbara had last spoken with Elaine by telephone in November, and there had been no talk by the older woman of poor health or plans for extended trips anywhere. Then, after receiving the three cards, all communication with Grandma Witte ended.

When Barbara tried to reach her by telephone just after Christmas, Marie took the call and repeated the same story she had told other people: Elaine was away on a long vacation. So Barbara wrote to Elaine, several times. None of the letters were answered.

After awhile it began to appear that the only people who knew Elaine and weren't worried about her uncharacteristic absence were Marie and the boys.

As the heavy winter snows melted, flowers bloomed and trees budded then developed leaves, Grandma Witte still hadn't shown up. Spring was one of her favorite times of the year, and normally she would have been bundled up and outside in the brisk morning air sweeping old leaves from flower beds, raking lawns, and sprucing up the yard.

But as the weather began warming in early 1984, it was obvious that the yard was being neglected. The flowers were left on their own. If they were hardy enough they pushed through the cover of old leaves and grass and bloomed. If not, they rotted under the smothering cover of old mulch.

A few weeks into the new season, the yard that Grandma Witte had previously cared for so lovingly and diligently was sprouting with weeds. The exterior of the house itself was also beginning to show disturbing signs of change.

The house was Elaine's pride and joy—and along with her pension checks, Social Security, and modest savings which she and Leonard accumulated over the years—it was her sanctuary and the safeguard of her independence in her old age. She had been as finicky and careful about the upkeep of her house as she had been about her own health.

Neighbors used to exchanging pleasantries with the retiree as they worked on their own lawns or rubbed shoulders with her at shopping centers continued to fret. One neighbor, who was a fellow Pioneer club member and had known Elaine Witte for thirty-five years, later recalled how unlike the old woman it was not to be puttering around in her yard.

Another Pioneer recalled months later that she

never did believe the story about Elaine being on a vacation. In all the years she had known her friend, she never recalled Elaine taking a vacation away from her Trail Creek home.

So far as the Pioneer club members and other neighbors knew, Elaine had no surviving close relatives except for Marie and the boys. There was no one else for Elaine's friends to ask about her mysterious absence. However, months after Elaine was last seen by her friends, the mother and sons who lived at 320 Johnson Road still hadn't gotten their stories straight. Sometimes they said she was on vacation. At other times she was said to be sick. They couldn't seem to make up their minds.

Then in late spring, Marie contracted with Jerry's Construction company to do some work at the house. A middle-aged woman paid Gerald Gallion with cash and two checks, one for $1,500, the other for $200. Although Gallion was never introduced to the older woman, both checks were signed with the name of Elaine Witte. Curiously, there was still no contact by Elaine with either her friends from the Pioneers or with her neighbors.

The disturbing sense of unease among her friends and neighbors was rapidly turning into outright fear for the old woman's safety. They suspected something was dreadfully wrong.

Early in April one of the Pioneer club retirees telephoned the house on Johnson Road to ask if Elaine would be attending the monthly luncheon. Marie said her mother-in-law was away on a year-long trip. Then another former colleague telephoned to ask about Elaine. She was told Elaine was in California, and planned to do some additional traveling before returning home.

Elaine's friends were becoming desperate. A couple of them continued to speculate that she might be in a nursing home, but no one really believed that. They were afraid something much worse had happened to the chipper little woman they hadn't seen for so long. A couple of the Pioneers decided it was time to approach police about their fears.

In May 1984, Elaine's neighbor, Max Trout talked with a friend of his, Roger Bernard, who was a deputy with the LaPorte County Sheriff's Department. Trout was employed at Memorial Hospital in Michigan City, and Bernard worked there part-time as a security officer. Trout told his colleague that he had been talking with friends and neighbors of Elaine Witte and they were worried about her. He explained that she hadn't been seen outside her house for several months, and recounted the story Marie was telling about

Grandma Witte being on an extended vacation. It wasn't at all like the missing woman to leave without telling any of her friends when and where she was going, he said.

Bernard promised to look into the situation and see what he could do. Then he telephoned Sergeant Eugene "Skip" Pierce at the Trail Creek Marshal's Department and said he wanted to meet with him.

There seemed to be a good chance, Bernard disclosed at the meeting, that an elderly resident of the little community had met with foul play.

Two
Hilma Marie

If Hilma Marie Crist's childhood wasn't miserable, at the very least it was outlandishly peculiar.

The little girl born in a Pittsburgh hospital on April 20, 1948, made her appearance on the first day of the sign of Taurus. According to many astrologers, that meant she was almost predestined to develop personal characteristics of patience, determination, stubbornness, and devotion.

Her birthday was also the same as Adolf Hitler's, who had committed suicide only three years earlier after plunging most of the world into destructive and terrible war.

But the thoughts of her parents, Albert Russell Crist and the former Mary Margaret O'Donnell, were focused on more pleasant matters as they took their daughter home to join an older sister, Margaret Lee.

Despite the presence of two healthy babies, however, the Crist home wasn't a happy household for very long.

The frayed emotional health, alcoholism, and bizarre behavior of their mother, was called Marcie, was at the heart of their unorthodox childhood.

Marcie O'Donnell grew up in Duquesne, Pennsylvania, a small factory town where the huge U. S. Steel Corporation plant spread along the serpentine Monongahela River just outside the southeastern city limits of Pittsburgh. She was a troubled child, who was high-strung, nervous, and prone to mental problems. Her tenth year was especially difficult. That year her tonsils and adenoids were removed, a growth was taken off her back and she was admitted to Children's Hospital in Pittsburgh with a nervous breakdown.

She seemed to improve for awhile when she and Albert Crist married. But when she was pregnant with Hilma Marie, her mother died. Marcie took it hard, bawling for days, and eventually the family had to call on professional help to assist her over her depression.

After her treatment and recovery, she and her husband once more became parents, this time of a boy they named John. He was the last child they had together. To outsiders the young family, with three healthy children and a means of earning a comfortable living, may have seemed to be blessed. For awhile they owned a restaurant, and Marcie also operated a thrift shop.

But she was a terrible parent. She screamed at her husband and at her girls. When the girls were still too young for school, Marcie would fly into rages and hit them without any apparent reason.

A few hours or a few days later, she couldn't even remember the attacks. There were also other memory lapses which grew more frequent as she began to drink heavily. She made the family's homelife a hell. Her husband finally packed up a few belongings and found himself a job in California.

Marcie didn't go with him, but she didn't seem to mind being left behind. She didn't have the slightest bit of trouble attracting boyfriends from among the steelworkers and other men she met at local bars and other hangouts. Soon after her husband relocated, she moved herself and the girls in with one of the men she had attached herself to. By that time she was showing more interest in beer and vodka than in the responsibilities of parenthood. With their father gone, the children often had to fend for themselves.

One day when the girls were left alone in the apartment, Margaret trudged off looking for their mother. She left five-year-old Hilma Marie with a neighbor, who sexually abused her.

* * *

Child welfare authorities and the courts eventually stepped in to remove Marcie's custody rights, and the girls were sent to Saint Paul's Orphanage. Soon after losing custody, Marcie suffered another one of her periodic breakdowns and attempted to commit suicide by swallowing an overdose of pills. Her stomach was pumped and she was committed to a psychiatric hospital.

The girls remained at the orphanage until Hilma Marie was about eight years old, when her father obtained legal custody and took them to live with him and their brother in California. The years in California represented some of the most pleasant times of Hilma Marie's childhood. But the idyll ended when her father was injured in a work accident.

Late in 1959, a grandmother and an aunt picked the girls up in California and returned them to Pennsylvania. Hilma wasn't quite twelve years old when she and her sister moved in with their grandmother in the town of West Holmstead on the south side of the Monongahela between Pittsburgh and Duquesne.

By that time, Marcie had left the hospital and remarried a man named John E. Dawson. The couple lived for awhile in South Carolina, before picking up stakes and moving back to the Pittsburgh area. Marcie's brood continued to grow and she and her second husband became the parents of two more girls, Marianne and Regina Elyse.

43

But Marcie also wanted her older daughters with her. She petitioned in court and was granted day-visitation rights. She began picking her daughters up, spending the day with them, then returning them to their grandmother's house.

One day she picked the girls up and told them that they were going on a vacation to Florida with her, their stepfather and their two young half sisters. The Dawsons took the girls to a nudist camp near Tampa. A week or two later, Marcie and her husband loaded the children into their car and drove almost directly across the state to another nudist camp.

Marcie and John were the managers of Sunny Acres Farms, a seventeen-and-a-half-acre retreat a few miles northwest of the town of Delray Beach on Florida's Atlantic coast. Located in southern Palm Beach County just off the Sunshine Parkway, the rustic resort was fenced in and surrounded by barbed wire.

John Dawson was a dedicated man who believed so firmly in naked living that he was national secretary-treasurer of the American Sunbathing Association. Marcie told her daughters they had to live at the camp as nudists. Years later she claimed it was only her husband who was devoted to nudism, and she consented to live at the camp and adopt his chosen life-style in order to

44

keep the family together.

Whether or not that was the case, the timing for settling in to life at the Sunny Acres Farms probably couldn't have been much worse for Marie. She was at an age when children are usually painfully self-conscious about their bodies, and the passage to puberty is stressful enough without being required to walk around naked in front of friends and strangers.

But at Sunny Acres the girls were permitted to wear clothes only when attending classes at school or when they were otherwise away from the camp for travel, shopping, and other activities. Adults and children ate their meals nude, slept nude, and worked, played or simply relaxed nude while they were at the camp.

Hilma Marie and Margaret Lee spent the summer at Sunny Acres, then were sent back to Pennsylvania to stay with their father who had returned there. But Albert Crist had never recovered the good health he enjoyed before the accident, and near the end of the new school year Marcie showed up once more and took the girls back to Delray Beach.

The two sisters remained at the camp for several months, then about the time the new school year began they ran away. They didn't share their stepfather's affection for nude living, and they didn't like the isolation. Sunny Acres was seventeen miles from Delray Beach, the nearest town.

The flight from the camp wasn't well planned however, and the sisters didn't get very far before their mother and stepfather caught up with them. Margaret Lee and Hilma Marie were walking along a highway when they were picked up, hustled into a car, and driven back to Sunny Acres.

But the runaways had created such a ruckus that three or four weeks after their aborted escape from the nudist camp they were sent back to Pennsylvania. They moved in with their father once more. But again, the reunion was a short one. A few months later Marcie showed up at her former husband's apartment, told Hilma Marie that he was too sick to take care of two girls, and took her back to Florida. Her older sister Margaret Lee stayed behind.

Marcie and her husband were having marital problems that had much to do with the girls being shuttled back and forth between Florida and Pennsylvania. At one point Marcie left her husband and filed for a divorce, accusing him of extreme cruelty. She claimed he left their trailer more than a year earlier and was living by himself in the clubhouse. She accused him of insulting her, hitting her in front of the children, and failing to support the family.

Palm Beach County Circuit Court Judge Russell O. Morrow refused to grant the decree, and declared that Marcie's case was extremely weak. He also issued a court order to remove the two younger girls, who were five and six years old at that time, from Marcie's care. Marcie packed up her daughters and headed for Pennsylvania. That flight north accounted for one of Hilma Marie's breaks from her life in a nudist camp, but it was only temporary until her mother and stepfather reconciled.

In his ruling on the divorce petition, Judge Morrow came down hard on what he called the immorality of raising children in a nudist camp. Both the plaintiff and the defendant had come into court "with unclean hands," he declared.

"The moral degradation and human degeneration of a nudist colony is not only a violation of the law, but a fertile spawning ground for juvenile delinquency, and the court is shocked that the parties . . . would permit their minor children to be exposed to any part of such environment," he said.

Dawson responded to the scathing denunciation of the family's life-style by announcing he planned to invite the judge to personally inspect the camp. He also issued an angry nine-hundred-word statement to the press branding the judge as "prejudiced," "bigoted," "misinformed," and the judge's remarks as an "unfounded travesty of truth." He added: "The one really outstanding contribution of nudism is to the moral betterment of children.

47

There has never been a case on record of a child from a nudist household in court as a delinquent."

The Dawsons' personal marital squabble had burgeoned into a public debate over the morality of nudist camps. It was a titillating mini-scandal that drew attention of the conventional and nudist press.

It did appear to many observers of the debate that a nudist camp was a difficult environment for preteens and teenagers to be raised in during that time of cold war and family bomb shelters. It was long before anyone had ever heard of hippies, flower children, Woodstock or wife swapping. Nudity was still something that was primarily confined to the shower stall, the bathtub, or the bedroom.

Most Americans were more concerned about the rapidly burgeoning commitment of troops in Vietnam following Congressional passage of the Tonkin Resolution and a destructive race riot and looting spree in Harlem that was one of the first of many that quickly flamed across the country. At Sunny Acres, residents acted as if they hadn't heard about those problems — or they didn't care. Male members who lived or visited at the camp strolled around wearing only a pair of black socks and shoes to hold a comb and billfold, or casual flip-flops. Most of the women, if they wore anything at all, also confined their dress to shoes and socks or sandals. Life at the camp was casual and unencumbered. There was almost always at least one match of volleyball going on. Residents and vacationers also played shuffleboard, swam, picnicked, and visited.

Delray Beach is only a few miles north of Fort Lauderdale, and it can be a pleasant place to grow up and live. But children are often cruel, and it probably wasn't easy being known among other preteens and teenagers as the girl from Sunny Acres.

Despite all the traditional nudist talk about a healthy, relaxed life-style and the pleasures of sunbathing, passing from childhood to puberty in a nudist camp was a trying process. And it had its dangers for a young girl left with little or no supervision.

Shortly after Hilma Marie's return to the nudist camp in 1964, she was married to Charles Dennis Narrow, a twenty-three-year-old U.S. Coast Guard yeoman from Miami whose ship was home-ported in Key West. A graduate of Dade Community College in the Miami area, Narrow had known Marie for two of the three years he was a practicing nudist. The young man, whose friends and fiancée called him "Chip," revealed that his bride's wedding ring would be a solid gold band he had found

49

five years earlier while he was working for Western Union.

Although news accounts of the wedding referred to the bride as Hilma Marie Dawson, or Sissy Dawson, she was never adopted by her stepfather. Her last name was properly recorded on the marriage license as "Crist."

On one hand, John Dawson seemed to welcome publicity, but he also complained about the press. In an effort to control coverage of the story, he established stringent rules, including a stipulation forbidding reporters from asking last names of other guests at the ceremony.

Several days before the wedding Dawson was already complaining that the press was blowing the approaching nuptials way out of proportion and treating it like a football game. He declared that his Sissy was going to have an old-fashioned wedding.

Describing the bride, Dawson remarked: "She's exceptionally mature and intelligent. Most parents raise their children in ignorance and hypocrisy. She has the judgment of an adult. Sissy was raised in a nudist camp." Hilma Marie had observed her sixteenth birthday less than a month before the scheduled May 9 wedding. Florida required parental consent for girls to marry before they were eighteen, and Marcie signed her approval.

Hilma Marie had her heart set on a traditional wedding, so there were actually two sets of nuptials. She wore a borrowed wedding gown and veil and carried a bouquet for one set of nuptials.

It was the other ceremony, which featured the bride and groom and most of the rest of the wedding party in the nude, that excited the attention of the press and the public. There was a brief scare a few minutes before the ceremony was set to begin, when Dawson dashed from the clubhouse with a rifle in his hand. According to some later news accounts, he took the weapon with him to check out some people who had just shown up at the main gate. Other stories indicated he waved the rifle at a low-flying airplane that was slowly cruising over the resort.

Whatever the reason, it didn't bother the naked groom. "You don't need that. I'll marry her anyway," the quick-thinking sailor quipped as Dawson snatched up the rifle.

When the ceremony at last began, the slender brown-haired bride's total trousseau for the occasion consisted of a wedding veil and a pair of white patent leather high heel shoes. She also carried a traditional bouquet. The groom wore a pair of rubber flip-flops on his feet. Paul Kwitney, a Miami Beach lawyer and notary public who conducted the civil ceremony, was the only member of the wedding part who was fully clothed.

Three bridesmaids, three ushers, two flower girls, the matron of honor and the best man were naked. The matron of honor was publicly identified as "Aunt Cecelia," a seventy-year-old longtime nudist who was attending her third naked wedding. The nude eighty-six-year-old best man was identified at "Uncle Dick."

Members of the three-piece orchestra, who played "Here Comes The Bride" and "I Love You Truly" on an accordion, guitar, and drum, were also bare. Even the tiny images of the wedding couple atop the four-tiered cake were naked.

Appropriately, the late Saturday afternoon nude nuptials were conducted outdoors at a makeshift altar set up next to the Flamingo Country Club's swimming pool. A short time before the wedding, Sunny Acres had been given a new name.

Professional and amateur photographers flocked to the Flamingo to record the nuptials, and admission was charged at the gate. But male reporters for newspapers, radio, television, and the wire services were permitted to attend only if they were accompanied by a female colleague who agreed to share the total skin experience. Dawson was so pleased with the plan, he confided that he hoped it would become a rule for dealing with the press at all nudist weddings.

* * *

The local media was divided in its response to the stark all-nude conditions established by Dawson, who explained it was his way of trying to obtain objective news coverage of the event. Some attended; some didn't. Those who did elect to attend were easily identified by nudist camp regulars as reporters because of their lack of overall tans.

The now defunct *Miami News* snorted in a four-paragraph story after the wedding that it didn't cover the event because editors decided the condition restricting attendance to naked pairs of reporters was in bad taste. The story added however that "the newspaper understands" the event was held as scheduled.

Even then, journalists weren't permitted to photograph the naked wedding couple. Dawson ordered the cameras to be confiscated from everyone except photographers for nudist groups and publications.

Despite Dawson's outspoken reservations about the press, the nude wedding developed into a titillating media event that attracted international attention. Writeups included not only the area pages, but also a story in *The Baltimore Sun*, and page-one coverage in the combined Sunday-Monday edition of an English language newspaper published in Rome for Americans in Italy and the Middle East. A Spanish language newspaper which covered the event headlined the story: "*La Novia Estará Desnuda y el Novio También.*"

Roughly translated, the headline read, "The bride is nude, and so is the groom."

Conventional newspapers and television both at home and abroad, however, had to make do with photos of the bride dressed in a traditional wedding gown which she slipped on after the ceremony. The confiscated cameras were then returned, and Sissy posed prettily next to the cake with her wedding ring, which was a perfect fit. But no photographs were permitted to be taken of the groom.

Accounts of the wedding and photographs of Sissy appeared in the major nudist magazines still published at the time. In the middle 1960s when the wedding occurred, the high-circulation nudist magazines were already on the way out. Even *Sunshine And Health*, for decades considered to be almost the Bible of the movement, was gone. Grainy photographs of nude women playing volleyball or seated at picnic tables simply couldn't compete with the likes of the naked beauties in *Playboy*.

Despite Marie's stint in the limelight as a nude bride, the marriage was brief. Marie remained at the Flamingo for a couple of weeks until her husband moved into an apartment in Miami Beach, where he was stationed. According to Hilma Marie's later account, about four months after she and her new husband set up housekeeping in Miami Beach, her stepfather took her back to the nudist camp.

By that time she was three months pregnant, and a week after returning to the Flamingo she miscarried. When Narrow showed up at the gate to the camp to see his wife, her mother and stepfather refused to allow him inside. Soon after that Narrow filed for divorce. The marriage that had drawn worldwide publicity—and shocked gasps of disapproval from outraged moralists—lasted approximately six months.

Hilma Marie wasn't left alone for long to grieve over her failed marriage. Paul J. Witte had been keeping an eye on her for weeks before she and Narrow were married. He could hardly believe his good luck when he learned that Hilma Marie was a single woman again.

Witte was a muscular steel mill worker and former Navy sailor from northern Indiana, who was spending an extended holiday at the nudist camp when he got his first look at the pert and vivacious wood sprite. Hilma Marie was a delicate beauty, with a trim body, fingers that were slim and white, full pink lips, and bright inquisitive eyes that always seemed to have an exciting hint of mischief in them. For Paul, at least, it was love at first sight.

The rugged steelworker spent his remaining time at the nudist camp courting the winsome teenager. Marcie thought the broad-shouldered vacationer was handsome and charming, and made it plain she welcomed his interest in her daughter.

Paul was totally enamored by the nubile Lolita when he returned home to northern Indiana, and after a few weeks he telephoned Marcie and told her he was in love with her daughter. Marcie turned the telephone over to Hilma Marie, and she talked with Paul.

Hilma Marie enjoyed the attention. After the first call, Paul telephoned at least once a week, and mailed long love letters to her. Finally, during one of the telephone calls, he asked her to marry him. She wasn't in love with him, but she was ready for a change. Hilma Marie agreed to become Mrs. Paul J. Witte.

Late in 1964 she boarded a bus for Indiana. Marcie's life was careening out of control again, and she eagerly grabbed at the opportunity to transfer responsibility for Hilma Marie to the enamored steel mill worker. Marcie was drinking heavily, experiencing blackouts, and having trouble keeping up with the responsibilities of helping manage a popular nudist camp while watching over three young girls. Paul met Hilma Marie at the bus station in Michigan City and drove her to the family home in Trail Creek to meet his father and stepmother.

Elaine seemed to be almost as taken with the fetching teenager as Paul was, but the older woman was concerned that Marie was too young to be taking such a big step into adulthood as marriage. Paul was twenty-seven and his intended bride wasn't even seventeen yet. Elaine suggested it would be a good idea for the young couple to wait awhile. She pointed out that Hilma Marie had already been married once and it didn't work.

Elaine told the teenager that if she didn't want to get married right away, she could stay at the house on Johnson Road and finish high school. Leonard Witte was an easy going man and he was agreeable to the suggestion.

But Paul wasn't interested in his intended bride finishing high school. He insisted on going ahead with the marriage plans, and she agreed with his wishes. Elaine had little choice but to go along with their decision.

Paul and Hilma Marie were married on December 19, 1964. The nuptials were quiet and private, a far cry from the young bride's headline-making first marriage. Only a few members of the family were present and everyone wore their clothes as the couple was united in wedlock by an Evangelical minister, the Rev. A. H. Vaughan of the Grace Bible Baptist Church in Springfield township. The newlyweds set up housekeeping in a duplex in the lakeside town of Beverly Shores across the city from Trail Creek.

* * *

Although she was disappointed that the couple hadn't accepted her suggestion to wait awhile before getting married, Elaine put her misgivings aside. She cheerfully concentrated on being a good mother-in-law to the young girl Paul had chosen as his bride. Hilma Marie quickly became the daughter that Elaine never had, and the two women developed a close friendship. In fact, the older woman often referred to Hilma Marie as her daughter, not as her daughter-in-law. Hilma Marie called the older woman "Mom."

In return, Elaine cheerfully passed on housekeeping tips, cooking secrets, and favorite recipes to Paul's young bride. She was careful not to be too pushy when the women teamed up in the kitchen, however. Although Hilma Marie learned the basics of cooking, an acquaintance would later recall that she never liked working in the kitchen.

About a year after renting the duplex, Paul and Hilma Marie moved to an unfinished house and a couple of acres of property in Beverly Shores. The structure was little more than a shell when they moved in, but Paul was a skilled craftsman who was good at everything from carpentry to electrical work and plumbing. Marie was young, healthy, and energetic, and she helped out as her husband

58

virtually built the house from the ground up.

Beverly Shores is part of the sprawl of cities and towns that hug the southernmost shoreline of Lake Michigan and stretch along the dunes from Michigan City west, past the steel cities to Chicago. It was still primarily rural; a flyspeck-sized Dunesland hamlet of approximately eight hundred people about a twenty minute drive west of Trail Creek. The rustic village was close to Paul's high-paying job as a millwright at the United States Steel Corporation in Gary. Yet it was a world away from the grim, ash-coated steel city, with its runaway crime and warring street gangs.

Paul was willing to put the trouble-shooting skills he had learned as a teenager and as a pipe fitter during four years in the Navy to work at the mills. But he refused to settle his wife and raise a family in Gary or in the neighboring cities of Hammond and east Chicago. In those industrial towns, there was a soaring crime rate, and air-borne ash from the huge smokestacks at the mills constantly covered houses, cars, and lungs with sticky coats of grime.

The grim, gray mills dominated industry in the tri-city area of northern Lake County. But Paul preferred the healthier atmosphere of Porter and LaPorte Counties, with their trees, unpolluted lakes, and fresh air. His home in Beverly Shores

59

was a half-hour drive from his job, and its rural location also provided an opportunity for him to begin acquiring Siberian sled dogs. Eventually, after several years of marriage, raising and breeding Siberian Huskies became his favorite hobby.

When he wasn't running the dogs, dozens of area lakes, as well as inviting tracts of fields and brushy woods offered all the opportunity he needed for fishing and hunting. If he was in the mood to fish, a short drive would take him to Pine Lake, Clear Lake, Stone Lake, Fishtrap Lake, and Horseshoe Lake, which were all located in or around the edges of the county seat town of LaPorte. Dingler Lake and Oahms Lake in Porter County were even closer.

During the spring, summer and fall, the surface of the lakes were sprinkled with fishermen in rowboats angling for perch, crappie, bluegill, sunfish, pike, or bass. In the frigid northern Indiana winter months, ice fishermen took over. Paul loved the winter when he could climb into a warm deer-hunting outfit, cover his feet with felt packs and waterproof outerboots, bait his hook with fathead minnows, maggots, or mealworms, and drop it into the chill water through a hole in the ice.

Lake Michigan also draws a share of area sports fishermen who angle for lake perch, coho and steelhead salmon, and in the spring when the smelt are spawning, net thousands of the small silvery fish while their hormones are running amuck. Cooked crispy in beer batter, heads, tails, guts, fins and all, the smelt provide especially tasty snacks and meals for patrons at local taverns during the season.

Paul could also take off with one of the little Brittany Spaniels he kept as hunting dogs, and seek out birds and other small game, including ducks, quail, grouse, pheasants, rabbits and squirrel — as well as the rapidly proliferating white-tail deer — in local fields and woodlands. He liked to shoot and eventually collected five or six rifles and shotguns and a pistol.

In July of 1966, Hilma Marie gave birth to Eric. Although he was born a bit premature, Eric August Witte was a healthy, happy baby, and Paul couldn't have been prouder of his son. The devoted outdoorsman, who loved camping, guns, hunting, and motorcycles, could hardly wait until the boy was old enough to join in his activities. Paul had wanted a son, but he had no desire for additional children. The three of them were all the family he cared for.

Nevertheless, three years after Eric's birth, another son was born. Hilma Marie was twenty-one. Paul and Marie named the new baby Hans Dieter Witte, but by the time he was a toddler most people were calling him either by the Anglicized version of his Germanic name, John David, or simply Butch. His mother didn't care much for her first name either. So she dropped it as eagerly and easily as she had abandoned the nickname Sissy, her stepfather and others at the nudist camp had used. Her husband, other relatives, and friends in Indiana called her by the name she preferred, Marie.

Despite his macho nickname, however, Butch Witte was a sickly and fussy baby. He was asthmatic, prone to upper respiratory infections and troubled with allergies. The little boy cried often, and by the time he was three he was throwing terrible temper tantrums, and continued to wet and mess the bed. He broke things, and when he was old enough to experiment with matches, he set fires.

Paul ignored the troublesome baby when he could, and didn't spend any more time around him than he absolutely had to. When Butch tried to climb up on a couch to sit by his father, Paul pushed him away. When Paul was walking around the house and Butch happened to be in the way, the child would get a smack from his father instead of a hug. Understandably, Butch's behavior didn't improve. Finally when the boy was three years old, the family doctor recommended that the couple take Butch to the Michigan City Child Guidance Center for tests. He was diagnosed as being hyperactive.

Doctors ran a battery of tests and made several recommendations, including counseling to deal with Butch's nighttime incontinence and daytime misbehavior. Paul wouldn't even consider following through on the recommendation. He was convinced psychologists, psychiatrists, and any kind of kiddie counseling was a waste of time and money.

As the boys grew older, it became evident that both resembled their slender mother in build more than their solidly constructed, broad-shouldered father.

Of the two boys, Paul clearly favored his older son. He hadn't wanted a second child, and he grew increasingly closer to his firstborn, and farther away from the petulant, emotionally troubled newcomer.

While Hilma Marie was settling into married life with a new and loving family in Indiana, her mother was once more experiencing serious problems in Florida. She suffered a miscarriage, was still drinking heavily, experiencing medical difficulties with her thyroid, and dealing with other troubles.

She emerged on the losing end of a bitter legal

brouhaha over the lease to the camp property, and she and her husband eventually divorced. As her boozing once more veered out of control, she experienced frightening hallucinations, blackouts, and losses of memory. Neighbors reported she was wandering in and out of other people's homes and sleeping in their beds. She screamed and struck her children, neglected their needs, and quarreled with just about everyone around her. A doctor had her admitted to Bethesda Memorial Hospital in Boynton Beach, the next town north of Delray Beach, after she confessed she couldn't remember where she left her children. They were being temporarily cared for by a sympathetic couple and a clergyman.

A few months after Hilma Marie's long bus ride north, Marcie was again committed to a psychiatric hospital for treatment of her mental problems and to dry out. She was declared by the courts to be mentally incompetent but harmless after a doctor reported she was schizophrenic, confused, had memory lapses, and was a suicide risk. Marcie later blamed her latest period of psychiatric treatment on worry over the divorce and a mix-up in her thyroid medication.

But others, whose memories of her behavior at that time were better focused and sharper, recalled different, more ominous behavior including a suicide attempt. During the commitment proceedings, the couple who helped care for Marianne and Regina Elyse indicated they found enough phenobarbital in her belongings to supply a pharmacy. Phenobarbital is a barbiturate, a powerful sedative often used to control epilepsy attacks or convulsions, and prescribed as a daytime sleeping aid. Overdoses can cause fluid to collect in the lungs, and eventually lead to coma. It is especially potent when combined with alcohol. Marcie was a drunk who was known to have previously attempted suicide, and she had been hoarding the medication for months.

Three
Paul

In many ways Paul Witte was probably no worse than most husbands, and he may have been better. In other ways, according to some of the people who knew him best, he was an unholy terror.

Although he was a hard worker who was attentive to his job at the mills, he enjoyed his homelife and always made time to share the outdoor activities he loved so much with family members.

Hirsute and shaggy, Paul looked every bit the outdoorsman he was. A husky, muscular man, he let his brown hair and coarse beard grow long. When he was dressed for the outdoors, he could have easily passed for one of the rugged mountain men: the traders, hunters, and trappers who helped settle the American wilderness during the eighteenth and nineteenth centuries.

He was a man who charged at life headlong

like a runaway rhino, with every inch of he-man gusto that he could muster. And he wasn't afraid of hard work. His father had taught him the character-shaping value of working for a living, and Paul grew up believing that a little sweat and dirt under his fingernails helped define himself as a man.

He also had a gentler, more creative side, however, and sometimes struck out on his own for the Dunes or a nearby woodland with a sketch pad or canvas to draw and paint scenes from nature. When Paul returned home with a new painting, it was usually a dunescape or a depiction of some wild animal that was native to the area.

As Paul's wife, Marie learned to feed and care for the growing brood of Siberian Huskies; she and the boys joined him in wilderness adventures; and they cheered him on when he directed the Huskies in dog-sled races.

A family man, Paul enjoyed sharing his skills and knowledge of boating, camping, target shooting, hunting, dogs and dog-sledding with his wife and older son. By the time Eric was seven, his father had already taught him to sail their boat. Thereafter father and son frequently took off on sailing excursions on Lake Michigan or on the smaller lakes dotting Porter and La-Porte Counties.

Paul was a skilled forager who knew where to

look for wild berries, when the paw-paws were ripe and ready for eating, and which roots were edible and where they could be found.

But dog-sledding was his real love. In his mind there was nothing better than pulling on a pair of long johns, warm trousers and sweater, gloves, thick woolen socks, boots, a parka and scarf and heading for the outdoors with a half-dozen or so bushy-tailed Huskies. He loved cold weather and thrilled at the sight of his own breath freeze-dried and visible in the chill air in front of his face.

Paul sometimes talked to friends of how he would love to move to Alaska or the Yukon in Canada and live the wilderness life full-time. He admired the hardy dog-sledders who competed in the annual Iditarod race across 1,049 miles of rugged Alaskan wilderness from Anchorage to Nome, and sometimes fantasized aloud to friends about entering his own team.

But being a good dog-sledder, he once explained to a friend at the mills, takes the support of the whole family. If he was serious enough about moving, he could have relocated his wife and sons to Alaska. But the rest of his close relatives were firmly settled in the Midwest. His mother, Mary Bowyer, and a brother, Charles Bowyer, lived in the central Indiana town of Logansport; a half-sister, Barbara Valencia, lived a few miles outside Oswego, Illinois; and his stepmother, Elaine Witte, was in Trail Creek.

At least twice a year, Paul and Eric struck out together with a dozen or so of their hardy gray dogs for a few weeks of camping and sledding in Michigan's snowy wilderness. When Eric was twelve and again when he was thirteen, the father and son spent the entire month of February in the Manistee National Forest that stretches roughly from Muskegon to Cadillac, racing the dogs, hunting and living off the land.

Paul ran his dogs in sprints of five to seven miles, thirty-six-mile runs, and in 1980 in a week-long contest farther north in Michigan's snowy Upper Peninsula in an exhausting two-hundred-fifty-mile trek. Trained to pull a load of five-hundred-fifty pounds, his top fifteen-dog team was once clocked at four hours, twenty-nine minutes over thirty-six miles. Like other serious dog-sledders, Paul eschewed reins and directed his dog team with voice commands.

During their campouts in the national forest a few miles inland from the Lake Michigan shoreline, the man and the boy were usually up before dawn and toiled around their camp and worked their dogs until after the sun set at night. Most days they were up and out of the camp running

their dogs before the moon had set, and took
only a few ten-minute breaks during the frigid
cross-country odysseys. At their camps they lived
inside an authentic Cheyenne Indian tepee and
warmed themselves with heavy layers of clothing,
blankets, and a wood-burning stove Paul constructed, while temperatures outside sometimes
plummeted to thirty degrees below zero.

The campers lived primarily on potatoes,
bread, and meat. Before heading into the woods
they provisioned themselves with about two hundred pounds of meat, including one-hundred-
twenty pounds for the dogs. Each member of
the fifteen-dog sled team ate about two pounds
of beef each day. Paul and his son baked their
own bread and ate two loaves each, every day,
with gobs of butter.

Paul was skilled in first aid for both humans
and for his dogs. He saved the life of one of his
Huskies after the dog tangled with a porcupine
and wound up with a throat that was painfully
skewered by quills.

Paul often took both boys to dog shows. And
he gave Butch a little hunting dog, then took the
boy and the animal into the field for training.

Paul also set up a few campouts that were
family affairs so that everyone went along, even
the sickly younger son. They would load up the

truck, select a few favorite dogs and take off for northern Michigan for a few weeks of roughing it in the wild. During those backwoods adventures, they would shoot deer, rabbits, and other game animals, and do their own butchering and curing of the meat.

They learned how to remove the hides with a sharp knife and to separate bones, cartilage and sinew at the joints, while carving up a fresh carcass. Paul demonstrated how to slice open the stomach of a deer, remove the steaming entrails and viscera, chop off the head and legs, and reduce a large carcass to smaller, more handy chunks of meat in minutes.

It was a butcher's skill that would come in handy a few years later for Butch and Marie. Paul was proud of his ability to live off the land and to support his family the old-fashioned way by foraging and shooting and butchering wild animals for food.

When the outdoor adventures ended, the family usually left for home with huge packages of salted, smoked, or frozen venison and other wild game for the freezer.

Neither of the boys was a match as woodsmen for their robust father, although Eric was by far the better of the two. And he was healthy. As an elementary school student, and after entering junior high, Butch was still sickly. Reed thin and pallid, he suffered from a dreary cornucopia of allergies. The youth was also troubled by asthma, and cold weather would bring on attacks that left him helpless and pop-eyed while he wheezed and struggled for breath.

Furthermore he continued to wet the bed long after most other children had outgrown the problem. And he had trouble controlling his bowels. This led to angry blowups by his father, who railed that he wasn't going to take him along and allow him to stink up the tent. Butch stayed behind with his mother during most of his father's and older brother's major sledding and survival adventures.

There was no question that Paul preferred Eric's company to that of his weaker younger son. Even when Butch was still a toddler, Paul seemed to have given up on him. As Butch grew older, Paul clearly resented the fact that the wan, anemic-appearing youngster didn't take to or couldn't tolerate the outdoorsman's life as readily as his sturdier older brother did.

Butch didn't drift away from his father—he was shoved. Predictably, he was much closer to his mother and during most of his free time he hung around with her at home. The elder Wittes didn't go out of their way to encourage either of their sons to make many outside friendships. Butch, especially, never managed to attract a large coterie of neighborhood pals or school chums.

He wasn't good at athletics or the rough-and-tumble games that most school-age boys square off in. And he was such a poor loser when he did get involved in games and other play that other children began to avoid him. Consequently, he often trailed along after his mother as she did household chores and other activities. She was especially protective of her frail son and coddled him.

While other neighborhood boys Butch's age were scrambling together and skinning knees and elbows on paved driveways under basketball hoops attached to their garages, Marie took her youngest son along on her shopping trips for groceries or to the mall. Mother and son watched afternoon movies together, skated at a roller rink, or visited the Franklin Park Zoo. But most often of all they took long walks past the comfortable homes and orderly wooded lots in Beverly Shores, chatting quietly or merely enjoying each other's company.

At times Paul was an attentive father, but the affection he showed his boys was uneven and often marked by cruelty and violence, according to family members.

When he was crossed he was quick to yell at

73

the boys, especially his disappointing youngest son. He wasn't the kind of father to easily tolerate a mama's boy, and he and Butch continued to drift farther apart.

Marie stood up for both her boys, but most often found herself defending her frail younger son to her critical husband. She showed less devotion to her housekeeping than to her responsibilities as a parent, although she may not have been totally at fault. It seemed that one or more of Paul's huge dogs was always wandering in and out of the house.

When Paul wasn't fooling with the Huskies, riding his motorcycle, or at work, he was often busy in his role as a fireman with the Beverly Shores Volunteer Fire Department. The family never knew when he might receive a telephone call in the middle of the night, slide out of bed, race for his truck, and head off somewhere to fight a fire. Often he beat the fire truck to the scene.

Paul never felt better than when he was on one of his wilderness trips or with a group of men fighting to put out a fire somewhere. He liked the exhilaration of pushing himself to his physical limits while sharing the camaraderie of other men like himself.

When the boys were in elementary school, an

accident occurred that would later be blamed for helping change the lives of everyone in the family for the worse. Paul was riding his motorcycle when the front wheel hit a pothole in the road. The bike spun out of control, and Paul was thrown to the pavement. It was a nasty fall.

As he tumbled and skidded head over heels over the pavement, he banged his head, suffering a concussion, broken ribs, and had the skin sheared from most of one leg. Although he survived the crash, he lost weeks of work and never fully recovered the vigorous health he formerly enjoyed. He was in almost constant pain, and his back caused him special trouble. It made him irritable and easily angered.

The ailing man did his best to keep up his active life, but he paid for his efforts in pain. As he learned to live with his disability, he spent more and more time with his dogs. He finally put up a sign advertising the Wind-O-Lakes kennels. Sale of sled dogs contributed to the family income.

Soon dogs were all over the property. At least thirty bitches and pups were allowed to roam through the house, and another fifty to seventy were kept outside. Their constant presence added to the stresses that Paul's injury had already placed on the marriage.

* * *

Thrown so closely together in the house, what were formerly small quarrels between husband and wife swelled into big quarrels. And they occurred more often. Paul and Marie fought over the dogs; they fought over the boys; they fought over money.

Marie was feisty and strong-willed, with a determination to get her own way, and she held her own in the nasty give-and-take of the bickering. But Paul was often cranky and mean-tempered, and he didn't easily back off from the arguments.

The couple quarreled most bitterly over Butch, who had never stopped throwing tantrums. Paul's temper was as bad or worse. He once snatched up a copy of his youngest son's birth certificate and snarled that the boy was a mistake who never should have happened. With increasing frequency, Paul referred to Butch in front of other family members as "a mistake." The blunt-speaking man hadn't wanted a second child, and he still resented the fact Marie had gotten pregnant again after Eric's birth.

There were also quarrels over Marie's mother. Marcie was released from the hospital in Florida after psychiatrists determined that she wasn't dangerous to herself or to others. But that wasn't the end of her troubles. She had lost her second husband to divorce, her thyroid to the surgeon's knife, and her job at the nudist camp.

For awhile she resumed her rolling-stone wanderings through the South, occasionally supporting herself by traveling and working with a carnival. She lived for awhile in Georgia, New Orleans, and Texas before returning briefly to Pennsylvania. Then she moved south to settle once more in Georgia with a boyfriend named Harold. As she usually did, even though they didn't bother to marry, she adopted his last name.

Shortly after Butch's birth, Marcie traveled to Beverly Shores to stay with the boys, house-sit and care for the dogs while her daughter and son-in-law took a vacation. After the vacation, she returned to Georgia where she stayed until 1975.

Marie was at a friend's house recovering from minor surgery when Marcie telephoned Beverly Shores and said she and her boyfriend were broke, didn't have jobs, and had been evicted from their trailer. Paul drove to Georgia to pick them up and bring them back to Indiana. They moved in with Paul, Marie, the boys, and the dogs at the house on Beverly Drive.

Both Paul and Marie were working outside the home, and Marcie was expected to help out by taking care of Eric and Butch, cooking and doing the laundry and housework. But she and her companion spent much of their time boozing and quarreling, according to later sworn statements by Marie. Paul eventually got fed up with their behavior and ordered the boyfriend out of the house. He told his mother-in-law she could go with Harold or stay behind; the choice was up to her.

Marcie elected to stay . . . for awhile. But one day Marie and Paul drove her to the Marquette Mall to do some shopping, with instructions to telephone when she was ready to return home. A couple of hours later Marcie and her boyfriend drove up to the house and she announced she was leaving. They moved into an apartment in Michigan City, then resettled in the Haven of the Rest Motel, and finally moved to the Pines Trailer Park. Marie brought the boys to her mother to baby-sit with during the day, until Marcie and her boyfriend moved once more, this time a few miles across the state line into southern Michigan.

Paul's temperament improved for awhile after his mother-in-law left, but it wasn't long before the family tensions once more caught up with everyone. And Marcie continued to drop by the house frequently.

Then she moved back in to stay. She telephoned one day, blubbering, slurring her words, and moaning that she had been beaten up. Paul and Marie drove to the motel she was staying in, brought her home and sobered her up. But Paul laid it on the line to his mother-in-law. He told her that if she returned to Harold she couldn't come back. She could stay with them if she wished, but she had to stop shuttling back and forth, control or quit her drinking, and get a job to help support herself. Marcie elected to stay. She vowed to dry out, get back on her feet and find work.

There weren't enough bedrooms to go around, and she had to sleep on the living-room couch. Marcie agreed. She didn't want to go back to Harold. She also knew better than to openly take sides in the quarrels between her daughter, son-in-law, and their boys. She concentrated on staying out of Paul's way, and tried her best to avoid being put in the middle during the family fights.

Despite her promise, however, she failed to find a job. And she continued to drink staggering amounts of vodka, beer, and any other alcoholic beverages she could lay her hands on. Instead of leaving the bottles and cans lying around in the open, she hid them. Marie found vodka bottles stuffed in the back of cabinets, under the bed, and stuck behind furniture.

And despite her boozy efforts to stay out of Paul's way, she had trouble steering clear of his explosions of temper. He screamed at her, threatened to toss her out of the house, and once threw a chair at her. Eventually, disregarding his ultimatum, she again moved out and went back to Harold. A few months later, however, she returned to Beverly Shores. For awhile, Marie hid her mother inside the house so that Paul wouldn't know she was living there again.

Marie and her husband also fought violently over sex. If she wasn't in the mood for lovemaking and he was, he would rip her clothes off and rape her, she later claimed. Marcie also stated, under oath, that there were times when Marie would lurch out of her bedroom and collapse on the floor of the hallway. Marcie said when she asked her daughter why she fell, Marie replied only, "He was rough!"

By the time the accusations were made by Marie and her mother of brutality and spousal rape, it was too late for Paul to defend himself.

But there is no question he became especially irritable and abusive after his accident. He yelled at Marie and the boys when he felt bad, which was most of the time. A nasty stomach ulcer, prostate troubles, and blinding headaches added to his misery and contributed to his short temper. He took pills for his pain, for his ulcer, and for his prostate. He simply wasn't the robust man he had formerly been, and he hated being sick.

When he was displeased with something his sons did, he swatted them on their backsides. Sometimes he used a wooden paddle, at other times a leather belt. He sometimes beat their bottoms so severely with a leather belt that their mother and grandmother would sit them on blocks of ice or in tubs of cold water to alleviate the swelling. Understandably, they drew farther away from their father and closer to their mother. Butch sometimes talked back to his father, but Eric was quieter and seldom stood up to him.

The Witte household resembled an armed camp with two factions, Marie and the boys pitted against Paul with Marcie as a bumbling spectator. The situation had deteriorated into a domestic stalemate, and it was ready-made for catastrophe.

By the mid-1970s while most Americans were reading and watching news reports about the fall of Saigon, the forced resignation of an American president, and the kidnapping of heiress Patty Hearst, the Wittes were concerned with a more mundane and personal matter.

Marie was talking about divorce. She later claimed she told Paul she wanted out of the marriage because of the spousal rapes and his abuse of the boys.

Paul responded by advising her that he would never pay child support or alimony. He added that if he was ever put into that position "we would end up dead," according to Marie. At other times Paul threatened to leave. By that time, Marie was working in the ticket office of the Chicago South Shore and South Bend Railroad, where her father-in-law had been employed for so many years. But she had developed health problems and had to take a disability leave. After awhile she was placed on permanent disability and began collecting Social Security. Being abandoned without a means of support for herself, two boys, and a dependent mother had to be a sobering and frightening thought for Marie. The idea of living the rest of her life on disability payments wasn't pleasant.

But there were times, increasingly frequent, when Paul seemed almost impossible to live with. He screamed and yelled at his wife and the boys, and one time he became so angry that he rushed out to the car, picked up a brick, and threatened to pitch it through the windshield.

Curiously perhaps, there were long periods of time when Paul got along better with Marcie than he did with his wife and sons. Despite his own violent treatment of the boys, however, he objected when Marcie tried to discipline either

Butch or Eric. So did Marie, Marcie would later claim.

Neither Paul nor Marie filed for divorce, although she continued to make threats about a split-up. But only she knows if she backed off because of fears for her own and her children's safety or if she was more concerned about losing her source of support.

Marcie was also continuing to cause problems for the family. Marcie and Elaine had been thrown together by Paul and Marie's marriage, but they never became friends. Elaine barely tolerated her stepson's eccentric mother-in-law, in fact. Eventually, Elaine barred Marcie from the house on Johnson Road. Valuables were being stolen and Elaine blamed her for it.

Elaine told Paul's sister, Barbara Valencia, about one incident when Marie surprised her by turning several rings over to her. Marie explained she found them stuffed into a sock hidden in the clothes dryer at the house in Beverly Shores. Elaine hadn't even known they were missing from her porcelain jewel box until her daughter-in-law gave them back to her. They were good pieces of jewelry and she only wore them on special occasions. Marcie was living with Marie and Paul at that time.

* * *

As the turbulent 1970s ended and the new decade began, Mount St. Helens erupted in Washington state, John Lennon was assassinated, and President Reagan was shot. In Beverly Shores the family quarrels were still raging. Marie continued to talk about divorce. Paul remained dead-set against it, although he also continued to grumble an occasional threat to walk out and leave his family to fend for themselves.

The national tragedies that helped usher in the new decade were about to be reflected on a smaller but grimly personal scale at the house on Beverly Drive.

Four

A Terrible Accident

After years of quarreling, the relationship between Paul and his family was becoming worse instead of better.

Eric, who was his father's favorite, was wilting under the constant stress. He was going to a doctor three or four times a year because of injuries or illness he blamed on the stress and violence in the family.

One time when he confided to his doctor about his father's abusive behavior, the physician treated the matter as a joke, Eric later complained. According to him, the doctor telephoned Paul and reported the conversation, while making a remark such as, "Boys will be boys."

Eric didn't bother trying to seek out any doctors, high school counselors, or other authority figures for help after that. It was a family problem that apparently would be kept within the family and resolved by the family. But it was a sick family, where love and anger, and hurt and greed were all mixed up together in a toxic witch's brew of conflicting emotions that were about to explode in tragedy.

Sometimes when she or Marcie were preparing a meal, Marie would sprinkle some Valium in Paul's food to calm him and keep his temper down. Before adding the medication to her husband's food, Marie carefully peeled the purple coating from the pills. The Valium apparently helped, but when Paul wasn't drugged it seemed that just about any little thing that happened could set him off and cause him to fly into one of his rages.

At other times, low-grade marijuana harvested from fields and roadsides, where it grew wild and was called "ditch weed" by local teenagers because of its poor quality, was ground up and sprinkled into Paul's food.

Huge amounts of marijuana were planted in Indiana during World War II so it could be harvested and made into rope while supplies of hemp were cut off elsewhere by the Japanese and Germans. Carried by wind and animals, the seeds spread to unprotected fields and ditches, and in the last few decades the plants have become a handy source of cheap marijuana throughout the state. But the ditch weed ground up for Paul's meals wasn't potent enough to have much, if any, effect on the unsuspecting man's temperament and behavior.

By the middle of 1981 Marie had already begun talking to her mother and to the boys about a more permanent solution to the family problem. It wasn't a problem that was going to be solved by a divorce or mediated by a marriage counselor. Paul didn't believe in those types of solutions.

She had pretty much given up on the idea of divorce, anyway. Marie was aware that even if Paul wasn't serious about threats to kill his family over a divorce, he could probably make it difficult for her to support herself and the boys.

But if Paul died she would be left with his pension from the mills, Social Security payments, and all their property.

Marie began to talk to her mother and her oldest son about the best means of killing Paul. They discussed different pills and how he might be made to overdose on a large amount or on a combination of medicines that would make his death look accidental.

Finally, Marie decided poisoning might be the best way to get rid of her husband. In selecting poison as a method to deal with her domestic problems, she was following a classic pattern for females who murder husbands or other family members. Women, after all, traditionally cook and care for family members, preparing their food when they're hungry and nursing them when they're ill.

Cyanide, strychnine and arsenic are all deadly potent poisons capable of killing in seconds, and each is still used today to get rid of an occasional unwanted husband, parent, or business partner.

Cyanide, which is a natural vegetable acid found in small amounts in many leaves and fruits, including peaches and almonds, kills by smothering its victims. It prevents the blood from carrying oxygen, and paralyzes the respiratory center of the brain.

Strychnine has lost some of its popularity as a poison for murder because of its difficulty to obtain and the necessity of masking the bitter taste. But once it is put into use, the effect is rapid and devastatingly painful. Like cyanide, it causes difficulty breathing, but also affects the central nervous system and produces horrible convulsions.

Arsenic appears to be the substance of choice for most poisoners today. When administered in small doses, as it usually is, arsenic produces an especially slow, drawn-out death.

Three recent American female killers are classic poisoners. And each used arsenic, which has been so popular with poisoners that it is sometimes referred to as "inheritance powder."

Margie Velma Barfield, a churchgoing grandma who became the first and so-far only woman executed in the United States since California gassed Elizabeth Ann Duncan in 1962, was a poisoner. She killed at least five people, including a husband, her mother, and a boyfriend by lethally doctoring their food and drinks. Appropriately, when she died at the Central Prison in Raleigh, North Carolina, on November 2, 1984, she was put to death by lethal injection.

Anniston, Alabama, housewife Audrey Marie Hilley was another who fed poison to trusting family members. Her husband died in horrible pain; she poisoned her mother; she was hard at work poisoning her teenage daughter when she was at last stopped. Marie died of hypothermia early in 1987 after walking away from a prison furlough and hiding out in the woods during a cold rain.

Much-married Nannie Doss, who killed at least eleven people including four husbands, four children, and her mother, is another notorious American female poisoner. Nannie's thirty-year murder spree finally ended with her arrest in Tulsa in 1954. When she died of leukemia in 1964, she was still known by her nickname, "Arsenic Annie."

Death by arsenic is especially cruel and painful. When arsenic is administered a small amount at a time, as it usually is, it causes weakness, vomiting, diarrhea, devastatingly painful stomach cramps, and can lead to paralysis. Victims suffer a long, lingering death.

One of the reasons arsenic is so popular with killers is its ability, when carefully administered, to mimic other illnesses such as hepatitis and viral infections. For this reason, and because it is so difficult to detect, it has been called the great pretender of poisons.

Marie told Marcie that she had settled on arsenic as her poison of choice. She began sprinkling a mysterious white powder on Paul's food, in addition to the occasional doses of Valium and ditch weed. At other times she emptied some of Paul's vitamin capsules and replaced the original contents with the white powder. Paul dutifully swallowed whatever she handed him, never giving any indication that he suspected a plot against him.

Paul was a firm believer in the benefits of vitamins and minerals, especially since his motorcycle injury. He gulped down pills and capsules by the handful and talked often about what he believed were their near miracle power to restore his good health. He talked to his wife and family about vitamins, and he talked to his friends at the mills and with the fire department about them. He seemed convinced that they would someday help him regain his old vigor and strength.

Marie had other plans. She still didn't like cooking and her mother was handling most of the kitchen chores for the family. So she enlisted Marcie's reluctant help in doctoring Paul's food and drink.

One evening Marie ground up some pills between two paper plates. Then she told her mother to hold one of the plates which had been filled with Paul's food. When Marcie took hold of the plate, Marie grabbed her hand and turned it, causing the ground-up powder from the pills to spill into the food.

"There, now you're in it as much as we are,"

91

Marie told the older woman.

Another time Marie gave her mother a concoction she had whipped up and told Marcie to put it in Paul's food. Marcie did as she was told. Marie later said that the concoction was rat poison, and she was lucky it hadn't killed Paul, Marcie eventually claimed. Many rat poisons have a heavy arsenic base.

Paul got sick from the repeated lacing of his food and vitamins with poisons and drugs. Sometimes he doubled over with excruciating stomach pains, vomited, or experienced exhausting spells of diarrhea. Even he blamed his stomach troubles on his ulcer, however.

Marie passed the experiences off to her husband as an upset stomach caused by his food. She blamed the sickness at various times on tomatoes, sauce, or an especially rich dish she or Marcie had concocted.

But Marie never became an "Arsenic Annie." She didn't succeed in killing her husband with poison, even though she experimented with it. Probably only Marie knows why she abandoned that scheme and began pressuring her oldest son to kill his father. Perhaps she simply didn't have the patience or would have persisted if she were a better cook.

* * *

It was the summer of 1981 when Marie first brought up the subject of murder with her oldest son. She suggested he either shoot his father or beat him to death with a hammer. She insisted it would be better for Eric to carry out the killing than for her to do it. Marie selfishly reasoned that if something went wrong and her son was caught, the penalty wouldn't be as stiff for him as it would be for her if she was convicted of murder because he was still a juvenile and she was an adult.

Despite his mother's reasonings and urgings, Eric resisted the scheme. But Marie was persistent. She kept after him, insisting that if there was ever to be any happiness again within the family, Paul had to die. Sometimes she talked to Eric about shooting Paul in the presence of her mother. At other times she talked privately to Marcie about her wish for Eric to shoot his father. The subject was discussed as casually as if she were planning the family menu for the next day. Once, the mother, the grandmother, and oldest son gathered around the dining-room table to carry on the murder discussion.

Despite all the food doctored with pills and poison, soft drinks laced with Valium or arsenic, and talk of murder, the weeks and months dragged on and nothing changed. Paul still woke up grumpy and drove off to work in the morning, and returned home grumpy and feeling bad at night. The quarrels continued, and Marie still fretted, schemed, and pressured her oldest son to kill his father.

Finally, she threatened to commit suicide if Eric didn't carry out the murder, and once pointed out to him that she had just refilled a prescription and had enough medicine on hand to overdose herself.

The pressure on Eric was becoming intolerable. The teenager and his father had enjoyed good times together since Eric was a little boy. When they were in the woods or on some other outing and no one else was around, Eric felt like they were a team. But there were other times when the father-son bond was strained to the breaking point. There was simply no denying that Paul had turned mean since his motorcycle accident, and the whole family was miserable.

Eric's parents seemed to be fighting all the time. They screamed, threatened each other, and argued about the boys, money, the dogs, and divorce. Paul had long claimed that raising the dogs would help out the family finances and provide a means of catching up on the bills; perhaps even putting some money into the bank. But it wasn't working out that way. Bills for feeding the dogs, seeing to their health needs, and keeping up the kennel were staggering. The

Wittes were spending more money on the dogs than they were earning.

That didn't help Paul's temper at all. Increasingly, he took out his disappointment and anger on Eric and Butch. He whacked them with his belt or a leather strap he kept to break up dog fights, slapped them with his hands and kicked them. He used almost anything he could lay his hands on in a hurry for the beatings. Marie didn't try to stop the beatings by getting between her husband and the boys, but she was usually there to comfort and treat their bruises and welts when the beatings were over.

At last, Marie's insistence that Paul had to die to restore peace to the household, began to make sense. Or at least it must have seemed so in Eric's troubled mind.

On Tuesday night, September 1, 1981, four days after Paul's forty-fourth birthday, the murder scheme finally came together.

Outside the Witte home it was a typical northern Indiana late summer evening. Leaves on the maples, oaks and elms that thrived in the area were still a week or two away from beginning to turn from the deep green of summer to the rich yellows, reds, and browns that signaled the changing of the season.

Although athletes at local high schools were already training for the new football season and last-minute preparations were being made at the Porter County Fairgrounds in Valparaiso for the kickoff of the fifth annual Fall Farm Festival and Steam Show on Labor Day weekend, Dunesland communities were still sweltering under a late summer heat wave.

Inside the Witte house, temperatures were also high. Paul had been in another of his nasty moods for several days, and just about everyone in the family was upset.

One recent evening Paul had been angry and started yelling after Marie and her mother came home late from visiting with a friend of Marcie's in Michigan. After that agreed-upon point, serious differences later developed in accounts of the event by Marie and her mother. According to Marcie's recollections, Marie got him calmed down by telling him she had found a wood-burning stove, which he wanted, and some other valuable antique furniture, as well. Paul wound up agreeing to get a $2,000 loan from a bank so they could buy the furniture, which Marie said she could resell for a good profit. She never bought the furniture, however, and instead used the money to pay household bills that had piled up on the family.

The furniture was never delivered, and Paul

angrily demanded to know why. Marie stalled. Although she assured her husband the antiques would be delivered soon, day after day he returned home and there were still no antiques. At last he told her she had until September 2 to get the furniture delivered, or she would be in big trouble.

Early Tuesday evening it appeared there was going to be a showdown and another angry blowup when Paul got home. When he walked in the house he was feeling terrible. He had been working in the fierce heat at the mills, then driven home in the sweltering temperatures of the late summer day. He grumbled that he had one of the agonizing headaches that had bothered him ever since spilling his bike. He threatened to make his wife and the boys sorry if the furniture wasn't delivered the next day, and he confirmed his suspicions they had been lying to him.

Marie remembered the affair differently. Her mother came up with the story about the wood stove and the antique furniture, she claimed. And although she and Paul did take out a loan, it wasn't to buy the antiques with, but was used to pay for dog food, other kennel bills, and sledding equipment. Marie said she eventually told

Paul her mother had lied about the furniture, and he agreed to let the matter drop.

Marie and Marcie weren't the only ones who had conflicting recollections of the events that led to the tragedy that occurred on that early September night.

According to Eric, he was the only member of the family to suffer physically from his father's anger that night. Father and son were in the driveway at the side of the house when Paul accused him of failing to properly train one of the dogs. A few minutes later Paul reached for the heavy leather strap he used on the dogs and began beating his son with it.

But Butch eventually said it was he who was beaten. The boy claimed he left the door open to a cage and his pet bat escaped, leading his father to reach for the strap. Eric countered that Butch had a ferret as a pet, not a bat, and wasn't beaten at all that night.

Family members agreed on a few things about that night, however. For one, they agreed that Paul at last calmed down a bit and ate a sandwich Marie made for him. Then she fixed him a root beer float. Marcie claimed later that her daughter mixed some clear liquid from a small bottle in with the root beer and ice cream before carrying the drink into the front room to her husband. She said the liquid didn't mix completely with the rest of the contents and remained on the bottom of the glass.

Paul sipped at the drink as he began pulling off his shirt and stepping out of his pants. At last he stretched out nude on top of a sleeping bag that had been put over the sofa. Paul hadn't changed his mind about nudity in the years since he first met Marie at Sunny Acres and still liked to relax without the encumbrance of clothes. He insisted on sleeping naked, whether or not he was in his own bedroom or on the living-room sofa. As the boys grew up they were used to seeing their father nude, and bare male skin—including her son-in-law's—was nothing new to Marcie.

While her husband was nursing his headache and allowing the feeling of drowsiness to creep over him in the quiet room, Marie had another of her mother-and-son talks with Eric. She told the boy she couldn't stand any more abuse. If Eric didn't kill his father that night, Marie threatened, she was going to commit suicide. She also brought up the possibility that she might wind up in jail.

The fifteen-year-old boy was confronted with a ghastly choice between his mother and father. He mumbled that he would do what he had to do.

Then Marie left the house, explaining she was going to the grocery store to pick up a couple of items. She took Butch with her. While Marie was gone, Marcie talked with Eric. Marcie spent much of her time in an alcoholic haze and sometimes had trouble figuring things out or keeping them straight. But she realized there was something seriously wrong with the direction things appeared to be headed that night, and she was scared to death. She told her grandson that they all had other options more sensible than murder. Marie could get a divorce, or everyone could simply leave Paul alone in the house. There was no real reason that he had to be killed.

When Marie returned from the store, Paul was lying on his back on the sofa, slumbering. He had set the empty glass on the floor beside him before dozing off. Marie peered at her husband, then went looking for Eric to have another talk. She was more insistent than ever that Paul had to die that night.

Then she walked out of the house once more, climbed into her car and drove away. Eric had been given another chance to be a dutiful son. He walked into Paul's bedroom and unlocked a cabinet over the bed. Leaning over the bed in the silence of the darkened room, he reached inside the cabinet and took out his father's .38-caliber Smith & Wesson Police Special. Standing quietly by the bed, he loaded the weapon. At last he turned and walked toward the front room where his father was sleeping. A moment before stepping inside, he cocked the weapon.

Still, the teenager couldn't bring himself to point the gun at his father and pull the trigger. With the loaded revolver in his hand, he sat down on a rocking chair a few feet from the naked man slumbering on the couch.

Marcie was in the kitchen brewing a pot of tea when she heard the loud crack of the pistol discharging. There was a biker hangout nearby and the occupants of the house on Beverly Drive were used to the sound of backfires. Marcie desperately wanted to believe that the sharp report she had just heard was only another backfire from a motorcycle or a passing car.

Then she saw the headlights in the window above the sink and moments later Marie had parked her car, and was running into the kitchen.

"Get some towels. Paul's been shot," she screamed.

Eric had dashed outside the house to the car as she drove up, and babbled that his father was shot. Then he ran back inside the house with his

101

mother, and unlocked Butch's bedroom door. Butch was in his room at the back of the house playing with his dog when Eric had twisted the knob of the door handle locking him inside before walking into the bedroom to get their father's gun. As Marcie lurched from the kitchen, Butch had reached the hallway and was also hurrying toward the living room.

Inside the room, Paul was dying on the sofa, with his shattered head resting in a sticky splatter of blood and bone. A single bullet had smashed through his skull and shredded his brain. Blood was gushing from the bullet hole, his nose and his mouth, and soaked through the towels as quickly as they were pressed to his head and face.

Marie snatched up the telephone and dialed 911. They needed an ambulance, she blurted out. Her husband had been shot.

Then she hurried back into the living room, grabbed up a pair of Paul's shorts, and began stuffing his legs into them and pulling them up over his hips. She didn't want him naked when the ambulance arrived.

Paramedics who arrived at the Witte home with a LaPorte County ambulance from Michigan City a few minutes before 9:00 P.M., attempted to revive the victim. Marcie later claimed they dropped him as they were attempting to move his body off the couch.

But Paul was beyond help. Less than an hour after the outdoorsman was shot, Porter County Chief Deputy Coroner John Evans pronounced him dead at the scene.

Beverly Shores Police Chief Gary Alban, along with Detective Sergeant Arland "Arley" Boyd and Investigator James Bonfield, both from the Indiana State Police Post at nearby Lowell, investigated the shooting along with other local town officers. Chief Alban was casually acquainted with Paul. Beverly Shores was a small village, and the two men occasionally crossed paths while Paul was helping out in his volunteer fireman duties.

A few minutes after investigators arrived at the house, Marie, Marcie, and Butch were separated from Eric, and ushered into a bedroom where they were told to wait. Police officers talked with Eric in the living room.

Chief Alban and his fellow cops were almost immediately suspicious of the story the teenager told in response to their questioning. After police officers have investigated a few fatal accidents and homicides, most of them develop a perceptive knowledge about such things that is part intuition and part deduction. Their feeling was that the reputedly accidental shooting simply didn't smell right.

Although the occupants of the house at 159 Beverly Drive told basically the same story to police that night, later accounts varied greatly.

At the scene, Eric told investigators he was reading in the rocking chair when he got up and went into the bedroom to look for a book. That was when he found the pistol hidden under a pile of magazines in the bookcase and picked it up to show to his father. He claimed he was holding the pistol in one hand and bringing it into the front room when he tripped. There was an explosion, and his father's body jerked upwards off the sofa.

At the request of investigators, the boy nervously reenacted the accident, repeating what he said were his movements as he came into the room, stumbled, and fired the gun into his sleeping father's head. Eric said he didn't know what caused him to trip.

Even though Marie was outside the house and her mother was in the kitchen when the shooting occurred, they stubbornly backed up Eric's story. They insisted the shooting could only have been a terrible accident. It was a cruel and capricious act of fate.

As Marie, Marcie, and the boys were questioned, and their replies written down on notepads, other detectives moved methodically through the front room, their eyes carefully scanning the floor, walls, sofa, and other furniture near the dead man. Occasionally one of the police officers scribbled a note onto a small pad of paper.

Bonfield quickly recovered the shell casing ejected onto the floor when the .38 Smith & Wesson discharged. Despite a careful inspection of the sofa, walls, and floor, however, he couldn't find the slug. The death scene had been disturbed by attempts to revive or help the victim, and conditions weren't ideal for investigators.

Some of Marie's behavior appeared downright weird. A woman who had been so suddenly widowed would normally have been expected to be in tears, more likely in hysterics. But Marie didn't behave that way at all. For long periods she was curiously calm, while at various other times she would laugh or break out in a fit of giggles. There were none of the uncontrollable tears and grief police more commonly observed on the part of relatives at the scene of a sudden, unexpected death.

Police didn't believe the account of Paul's shooting, and investigators did their best to figure out any legal maneuver that would give them some leverage in getting the truth from the boy and his family members. They suspected that he and the others were holding something back that would shine a very different light on the shooting. Eric was no streetwise gang member who had been questioned by police before, and it was reasonable to suspect he might break and change his story if he was approached just right. He was a slender, shaken boy whose frightened, darting eyes stared out from a round, Charlie Brown face balanced on a head that looked too big for his skinny neck.

But the investigators never got the break they were looking for. And faced with Eric's firm declaration that the shooting was an accident, backed up by the two women, there wasn't much they could do to change the situation.

Some of the officers present that night apparently tried, although it would be years before details of the incident were brought up in court. There were claims that three policemen grabbed the boy by the shoulders and made him stand over his father's body while they ordered him to tell how the shooting occurred.

The unorthodox interrogation was reputedly stopped when Marie and Marcie intervened and forced the officers to release the boy. Even if it were true that Eric was so roughly treated, however, anything he may have blurted out, as well as other evidence collected as a result of a forced confession, would more than likely have been disallowed at a trial.

The old third degree under bright lights is a relic of popular old movies, not a part of modern American police work. Suspects today must be handled with kid gloves, and good interrogators have become skilled psychologists. Violence, or the threat of violence—any coercion—must be avoided, no matter how frustrated police become during an investigation.

Various state laws and state and federal court rulings have severely restricted police during questioning of suspects over the years. During the past five or six decades a number of confessions have been thrown out by the U. S. Supreme Court because of illegal tactics by police interrogators. Any competent defense attorney would have challenged a confession made under such circumstances.

* * *

Marie made an official statement to Chief Alban and other officers a few minutes after midnight. One of the lawmen who was an acquaintance of the victim said he knew Paul had been rough on the boys when they were younger and had thrown them around at times. He asked Marie if that was true. She confirmed it was, but quickly added that he hadn't done anything to discipline the boys for about six years other than grounding them. He had changed, she said.

"All right. You feel that in your opinion from what you've said here this evening, it was an accidental shooting, with no doubt in your mind." the lawman asked.

"No, not at all," she replied. "It was an accident." Marie signed the statement.

It was past 1:00 A.M. before police finished their on-the-scene questioning of the women and the boys. Eric was so shaken and upset after the trauma of the evening that Marie drove him to the emergency room at St. Anthony's Hospital in Michigan City for treatment. The sixteen-year-old boy simply couldn't handle the shock and stress of what had occurred without medical help.

Investigators were far from satisfied that they had learned everything there was to know about Paul's death, when his body was at last loaded into an ambulance to be taken away for autopsy. Indiana statutes, like those in most states, require autopsies whenever someone has died a suspicious or a violent death, either by homicide or by accident.

Before leaving, Bonfield asked Marie to make sure that nothing was disturbed in the house until he was able to resume his inspection and search for clues the next day. But when he returned in the morning, the house had been cleaned up. The incident even further bolstered police suspicions that something was wrong with the story they had been told of the shooting.

Chief Alban and Detective Sergeant Boyd took another statement from Marie on September 10, and again asked if her husband whipped his sons.

"Paul was an old-fashioned man. He believed the children should be taught respect for adults," she replied. "He paddled them like most fathers would."

"Did he paddle them abusively at times?" she was asked.

"Not abusively. No!" she said. And she denied that he beat them so severely that their bodies were bruised. "The only place Paul ever paddled those kids was on their backside."

The lawman asked about another story he had heard, of a different kind of abuse. He wanted to know if it was true Paul had sometimes locked the boys in dog pens. "No," Marie said. "When they misbehaved?" he persisted. "No," she declared once more.

Marie stubbornly stuck to her story. Investigators realized they weren't going to prove that Eric deliberately shot his father on the basis of any statements from his mother. They ran a records check on Eric, but the computer failed to reveal any previous brushes with the law. There was no rap sheet. No other members of the Witte family had felony records, either. Nevertheless, police weren't the only ones who were suspicious about the events surrounding Paul's tragic death.

In Oswego, Illinois, Paul's half-sister, Barbara Valencia, was also having difficulty accepting his shooting as accidental. But Mrs. Valencia had no proof, nothing to go to police with that could be used to challenge the story of the people who were in the house the night he died.

One mystery surrounding the shooting was cleared up during the autopsy. The missing bullet was found in shrapnel-like chunks where it fragmented inside Paul's skull and ripped his brain to pieces. The slug didn't pass all the way through his head.

The brain isn't the soft porous tissue that many people believe it is. "The brain's pretty tough," explains a Vietnam veteran and former mercenary soldier who knows about such things. "It can stop a bullet. It's like shooting into a telephone book."

In addition, hollow point bullets are fashioned to begin opening up when they leave the barrel of a gun as soon as the air hits them. On impact, they usually fragment and break into deadly chunks.

Even if a physician had been on the scene when Paul was shot, the former steelworker's chances of survival would have been almost nonexistent.

During the autopsy, samples of Paul's blood, bile, and gastric contents were also obtained and later analyzed at the Northwest Indiana Criminal Toxicology Laboratory in Lowell. The tests revealed the presence of acetaminophen, the chemical component of Tylenol and other similar painkillers. But toxicologists failed to turn up any trace of narcotics or dangerous drugs in the dead man's system. The Porter County Coroner ruled the shooting was an accidental death.

One of the investigators telephoned a deputy prosecutor at the Porter County Courthouse in Valparaiso and informed him about the shooting. But the matter was not taken up with Prosecutor Daniel R. Berning. There was no reason to. The telephone call was standard procedure, nothing more.

In Beverly Shores, Chief Alban laboriously transcribed his handwritten notes on the investigation with an old manual typewriter. At the Indiana State Police Post in Lowell, Detectives Boyd and Bonfield also transcribed their notes. Then the notes were filed away in drawers; the gun, the shell casing, and other physical evidence collected at the scene were filed in an evidence locker.

The investigation was shelved. Chief Alban, Boyd, and Bonfield turned their attention to other new and more immediately pressing police matters. Crime doesn't stop occurring just because police are busy, and old cases frequently have to be set aside as new cases pile up. And that's especially so when dealing with a case like the death of Paul Witte. Despite the suspicions and curious circumstances, no one had uncovered evidence that it was anything other than what his wife, sons, and mother-in-law claimed it to be: a terrible accident.

* * *

The day after the shooting a two-paragraph account of Paul's death appeared with several obituaries, hospital notes, and accounts of traffic accidents on page twelve of Porter County's *The Chesterton Tribune*. In the story, headlined, "Accidentally shoots father," Porter County Chief Deputy Coroner John Evans was quoted as saying Eric found a pistol in a bookcase and while showing it to his father it discharged and Paul was struck in the head.

By contrast, the *News-Dispatch* responded to the tragedy by printing a major page-one story and a photograph of Paul's sheet-covered body being carried from the house on a stretcher by a trio of police officers. The victim was referred to in the headline as a "Noted dog-sled racer," but the story also indicated the shooting was accidental.

Paul's body was prepared for burial by morticians at the Carlisle Funeral Home, but there was no visitation. Three days after the shooting, an early evening memorial service was held for him at the Beverly Shores Fire Department.

Eric attended the funeral services for his father. A few weeks after Paul was buried, Marie collected more than $25,000 in insurance payments from a policy at the mill and another from the Chesterton State Bank.

By that time a male friend had moved into the house on Beverly Drive to help care for the dogs. But the family's troubles were far from over. Someone was sneaking around the neighborhood shooting at the house with a rifle. No serious damage was done, and except for jangled nerves no one was hurt, but the mystery gunman was never caught or identified.

According to Marcie, she was more frightened by the behavior of her daughter and eldest grandson than the phantom rifleman. She claimed Marie accused her of talking too much to outsiders about family secrets, and that Eric once threatened her by pressing the blade of a bayonet or sword to her throat.

On April 30, 1982, Marie helped her mother pack up some clothes and a few other possessions. Then she drove Marcie to Chicago and put her on an airplane headed for Georgia. Marcie didn't oppose the move. She was relieved to get out of the house. She settled in Powder Springs at the west edge of Atlanta and found herself a job at a Dairy Queen.

Five

Goodbye to Grandma

Marie and the boys appeared ready to put their troubles behind them and get on with their lives after Paul's death. But they wouldn't be rebuilding their lives in the house on Beverly Drive.

Elaine Witte was sensitive to the shattering loss her stepson's family had suffered, and the two women agreed that Marie and the boys should move in with her. Her sister Mildred had died, leaving Elaine alone in the big house on Johnson Road, and she welcomed the idea of company.

The two women had always gotten along well, and it seemed the new surroundings would be as good for Marie as it would be for her sons. Elaine was sympathetic to the boys who had lost their father when they were still so young and in need of his company and firm, masculine direction.

She realized the loss must have been especially difficult for Eric, who fired the shot that killed his father. She resolved to do what she could to help both the boys and their mother put the shooting

115

behind them so they could move on with their lives.

Marie began moving a few choice furnishings, clothes and other personal items into Grandma Witte's house even before Marcie left for Georgia. And she sold off the dogs, so that there was no longer a houseful of animals to contend with. Then she and her sons moved into their new home.

Marcie stayed in Georgia three or four months before returning to Indiana. Marie and Butch met her airplane in Chicago, and they all stayed overnight in a hotel before driving back to the house in Beverly Shores. The house was a disaster, and it wasn't fit for Marcie to stay in. But she wasn't welcome at Grandma Witte's house, so her daughter rented an apartment for her. Marie told her not to let Elaine know she was in town.

Marie continued to pay Marcie's rent until September, when she found a job as a live-in companion-caretaker for another woman who was disabled with rheumatoid arthritis. She remained there until her employer died the following July. Then she moved into a house at 218 East Eighth Street in Michigan City with a longtime friend, Irma Frye, who was called Jeannie.

The two women first met about 1969 or 1970

when they worked together in a restaurant in New Orleans, Marcie as the cook and Jeannie as the bartender and waitress. They lived in the same hotel. Although Jeannie was married at the time, the women moved in together in Michigan City. Her husband stayed behind in Georgia.

After becoming Jeannie's housemate, Marcie continued to supplement her Social Security payments with jobs as a companion-nurse to invalids and other shut-ins. Jeannie did similar work. There was never any shortage of old or infirm people who needed help from a woman who was willing to do the cooking, cleaning, and laundry as well as serve as a companion. The shut-ins usually considered their helper as their last opportunity to maintain any sort of independence and stave-off the time when they had to move into a nursing home.

About the time Marie and her sons were moving in with Grandma Witte, and her mother was settling in with a new roommate and into a new job, a mysterious fire swept through the house in Beverly Shores. The damage to the house that Paul had worked so hard to build for his family was so complete that it was eventually torn down.

Despite the apparent good intentions of Marie and her mother-in-law, the easy relationship in the

117

newly-formed three-generational household on Johnson Road was probably doomed from the beginning. Wide cracks rapidly began to develop in the new living arrangement, and the honeymoon ended almost as quickly as it began.

In some ways the boys were normal teenagers. They listened to rock and heavy metal music, and watched more television than Elaine thought was good for them. But there were more serious troubles than the problems usually associated with the generation gap.

Grandma Witte did her best to adjust. But Butch was a spoiled brat, and although his brother was less of a problem to Elaine, they also clashed over matters of behavior and discipline. As Marie had done when her sons were at odds with their father, she continued to stick up for them during their differences with their stepgrandmother.

Having just shot his father to death a few months earlier, Eric was, not surprisingly, a troubled teenager. The young man who returned home from the emergency room at St. Anthony's Hospital wasn't much different than the patient he had been when he was taken there for treatment.

Eventually Marie sent her oldest son to the Swanson Center, a state-supported mental health facility in Michigan City, for outpatient counseling and psychological therapy. Eric was nervous, confused, and unhappy.

He nevertheless got along well with other teenagers in Trail Creek and at Michigan City Elston where he attended high school, and made friends more easily than Butch. By 1982 he was dating Tammy Willis, a pretty girl from Michigan City, and she began showing up at the house along with other teenagers.

Eric's grandmother got along well enough with Tammy, but she didn't like many of his other friends. And she complained frequently that he stayed out too late. The boys were told to take their shoes off when they came into the house, to pick up after themselves, and to help with the yardwork. Marie also repeatedly cautioned Tammy and other visiting teenagers not to play the radio and records too loud and to be nice to Grandma Witte. It was the old lady's house, she pointed out.

Eric was an average student, and outside the classroom he spent much of his time playing the popular fantasy game Dungeons & Dragons.

Dungeons & Dragons, or D & D as devoted players usually refer to it, typically appeals to males of junior high, high school, or college age.

119

It is a challenging game set in a mythical medieval world that requires playing out fantasy roles assigned by a dungeon master—usually the most experienced or skillful player.

Basic equipment includes instruction manuals, four, six, eight, and twelve-sided dice, and small figures of such characters as trolls, knights, dwarfs, and dragons. Manuals are also provided for advanced players, as their skills and the complexity of the game increase. There is no board to play on. The dice and the whim of the dungeon master set players off on their adventures.

Roles include thieves, assassins, wizards, clerics, fighters, and other characters who kill their opponents while competing for fabulous treasures. It is a game with monsters and weapons including everything from swords and daggers to crossbows, deadly curses, and magical spells. A dozen or more players often compete at the same time.

Games, which may be set in the present, past, or future in different worlds or different planes of existence, might last a few hours or continue for months. Almost as soon as Dungeons & Dragons became popular, it began acquiring a reputation, fairly or unfairly, for violence and other troubles some of the young players became involved in. It has been blamed by detractors for dozens of suicides, murders, grave robbing, and by some clergy for leading youngsters into Satanic worship.

Critics claim the game causes some adolescents and older players to lose contact with reality when they become too deeply immersed in their characters and the adventures. Outraged parents, as well as some psychiatrists and law enforcement officers, have joined clergy in criticism of D & D and other violent role-playing games. Several times it has attracted considerable attention in trials of young players accused of murdering their parents or other people, and has been blamed for leading to teenage suicides and other misdeeds.

Elaine Witte knew little or nothing of the controversy surrounding Dungeons & Dragons. She knew only that she was uncomfortable with Eric's devotion to it, and all the talk about demons, devils, magic, and killing devices. Eric even had a collection of weapons, including guns, knives, and a crossbow.

Perhaps due to all the attention to magic and monsters in the D & D games, Eric also developed a keen interest in the occult, especially in parapsychology. He experimented with mental telepathy and telekinetics, attempting to read minds and to control the roll of dice and move other objects with only the power of his will.

Predictably, perhaps, he passed on his interests to his younger brother. Butch also began dabbling with pseudo-scientific pursuits that among some circles might be called New Age, but in much of the Midwest are looked upon by clerics and parents as Satanism or witchcraft. Like his brother, Butch put together a weapons collection. He had knives, axes, and martial arts throwing stars.

Butch became deeply involved in D & D. He played at home with his brother, and he played with other students at Krueger Junior High School who had formed a Dungeons & Dragons Club. So Elaine was confronted with not one but two teenagers spouting strange stories about titanic struggles between the fantasy characters whose roles they had taken on.

Even Marie became involved in some of the experiments. She was intrigued by the idea of mental telepathy and joined in trying to project thoughts from one to the other. She tried to convince her boys that she could read their minds.

She played Dungeons & Dragons only once and quit after about a half-hour when her character was killed. Tammy also agreed to play with the boys one time, but her character was quickly raped, attacked by wolves, and killed. Eric was upset with the other players because he wanted her to like the game, but Tammy had enough. She didn't play D & D with them again. Women and girls seldom develop the same obsessive interest in the fantasy game that many males do.

Elaine quickly learned that dealing with Butch wasn't an easy task. Aside from what she viewed as his perplexing and near obsessive fondness for D & D, there were still broad and far more serious areas of conflict between her and her stepgrandson.

Twelve years old when he and his brother and mother moved in with Elaine, he was a handful for the old woman. Like his older brother, he was a troubled boy who had much more on his mind than any child his age should have to worry about. Butch was already a deeply disturbed boy before his father was killed; with Paul's death, the youngster's behavior spun rapidly out of control.

He didn't like school, neglected his studies, got into fights with other pupils, and skipped out on classes whenever he had a good opportunity. He screamed and cursed at his teachers. And once he got into trouble for giving a male teacher the finger in front of other students in a school hallway.

Butch was also suspended from school for several days after pulling a seven-inch knife on the principal. No one was injured in the ugly confrontation, but Marie was called to the school and the principal sternly advised her to find an outside counselor for Butch to deal with his behavioral problems. Marie arranged for counseling with the same psychologist who had worked with Eric, and drove him there. Many times after Butch's mother drove away from the psychologists's office, however, Butch would skip his appointment and use the money she had given him for the counselor to play video games or buy things he wanted for himself.

Later when Marie asked how the counseling session went, he would often reply that it went very well. They were beginning to make real progress, he assured her.

Butch got into trouble another time after school authorities telephoned Marie and said he was giving away money. For awhile she went to school and sat in his classrooms with him. The maneuver embarrassed him in front of the other children and was more effective than other forms of discipline she had tried, such as grounding him and taking away telephone and other privileges. He improved his behavior for awhile, but as soon as Marie got involved in other things and he was left on his own once more, his old bad habits returned.

When he wasn't in school, he often lounged around the house toying with D & D, drinking booze, and smoking pot. Occasionally he hung out with a friend or two at arcades and area parks or listened to music.

Despite his generally outrageous performance as

a scholar, he put together a small personal library which he kept in his room, and took advantage of other books his brother collected or borrowed. Most of the books dealt with parapsychology, spiritualism, Egyptian mythology, and other elements tied to the preternatural and supernatural. One well-thumbed book, *King of the Witches*, traced the religious career of Alex Sanders, an English witch, whose followers perform rituals both robed and nude, or "skyclad," in the lingo of modern witches.

The book was illustrated with photographs of Sander's pretty young blond wife at that time, Maxine, and of other coven members leaping skyclad over a cauldron or performing other rituals.

Eric and Butch also thumbed through a copy of *Psychic Self Defense*, which is a classic for people who take their study of the supernatural seriously. And like other avid D & D players, Butch kept various manuals to be used or consulted while playing the game.

When he did attend school or was around other teens at fast-food restaurants and other hangouts, he told outrageous stories. He seemed somehow always to be just a step or two behind or to the side of reality. The scrawny boy was desperate for respect and attention, no matter how he got it.

Painting himself as an expert in the veiled and arcane world of the occult appeared to be one avenue for attracting the kind of ego-stroking esteem he craved.

Butch asserted that he had developed a host of mysterious skills, including telekinesis, the power to move objects with no more than the prodigious powers of his mind. He spun wild tales about his purported occult powers, especially when he was trying to impress girls.

One fifteen-year-old Trail Creek neighbor recalled that he told her he could draw a circle, stand in it, and make her and her girlfriends fall to the ground. Then, continuing to use only his mind power and knowledge of the occult, without laying a hand on them, he could prevent them from getting to their feet. Butch may as well have been spinning yarns about Paul Bunyan and his giant blue ox, Babe.

If he was hoping to impress the girls with his adolescent hints of mischief and mystery, his efforts were failures. The boy's tall tales were hard to believe, and his schoolmate confided months later that she thought he was weird. So did her friends, she said.

The girls also thought it was strange that he could be so cavalier when he told them once about how his older brother accidentally shot his father to death. One of the girls recalled that he acted as if it didn't bother him at all.

Butch's grandmother was also sometimes treated to his stories of wondrous abilities, extrasensory powers, of witchcraft and magical spells. She wasn't impressed either.

Elaine Witte didn't know much about ESP, witchcraft, or pot, but she understood that Butch was dreadfully neglecting his studies, seemed to have little ambition, and didn't show proper respect for his elders and other authority figures. Elaine wasn't satisfied to put up with that kind of behavior.

Marie was lax and uneven about disciplining the boys, however, and when Elaine stepped in to correct the behavior of her grandsons she was met with resentment all around: from Eric, from Butch, and from their mother.

There were other stresses in the household in addition to the conflict over discipline.

Tensions increased when Elaine began to notice that money and other valuables were missing from the house. Months earlier, she had banned Marcie from the house for stealing, now there was another thief to contend with. Butch was accused at various times of stealing from his mother as well as from his Grandma Witte.

One time after he sneaked some of Elaine's

money from a kitchen cabinet, his mother found out about it and sternly admonished him never to steal from his grandmother again. But Butch had developed expensive spending habits for a boy who didn't have a job. He reputedly handed out money to teenage girls he wanted to impress, and he blew scads of cash in game arcades. Eric estimated that for awhile his younger brother was spending from $50 to $100 a day.

Even though Marcie was sharing the apartment in Michigan City with her friend and had been told by Elaine to stay away from the house, she was an occasional guest there anyway. But the two older women didn't have anything in common except Marie and their grandsons, and they simply didn't get along.

The slender widow who owned the house was quiet, private, fastidious about her dress and surroundings, moderate in her habits, and generally courteous and considerate in her dealings with others.

Marcie was a big, brash, coarse woman with a loud, grating voice, who had a habit of popping Valiums and washing the pills down with vodka or beer. She and Elaine mixed about as well as oil and water.

When Elaine discovered that a prized collection

of fifty-cent pieces and some jewelry were missing, Marcie was an obvious suspect. Elaine didn't allow her in the house again. But she continued to keep her spending money, bank books, and other valuable papers in the drawer of a china cabinet, just as before.

Butch had picked up some of his grandmother O'Donnell's worst habits. He was already in enough trouble over his thievery, but he also drank. Then Elaine found marijuana in his room and threatened to notify the police. Eventually she and Marie began discussing the possibility of sending the troublesome teenager away to a military school.

Money, not just small amounts missing from Elaine's coin collection or from her purse, was a source of serious contention in the household almost from the time Marie and the boys moved in. And it had much to do with changing the previously close relationship between Marie and her stepmother-in-law into envy, resentment, and distrust.

Marie was chronically short of cash, despite her income from the Carnegie Pension Fund which she collected as Paul's widow, the payments from his life insurance policies, and her disability checks. She also collected Social Security payments for the boys.

Even though her disability payments helped make up for her old paychecks from the job in the South Shore ticket office, it was still less than she had earned before. And the checks were missed. There hadn't been extra money to spend before Paul's death, but since then it was worse. There was never enough to go around. She wasn't extravagant; Marie had never been a "shop till you drop" woman, and she wasn't a clotheshorse. She was usually satisfied to putter round the house, do her grocery shopping or visiting in a faded pair of bluejeans and tank top or slacks and a blouse. Elaine even got after her sometimes to dress up more before she went out.

She didn't go out much either, although every so often she drove to Michigan City and took her mother and Jeannie to breakfast. The restaurant was never anything fancy or expensive; just a booth-and-stool, bacon-and-eggs kind of place.

But taking care of herself and two growing boys was expensive. Then the disability payments were stopped. Marie appealed the decision, and was notified that a hearing would be scheduled. She had been collecting more than $630 a month from the checks and the cash cutoff was a devastating financial blow. She found herself increasingly depending on her mother-in-law to make up the difference between her income and what she had come to count on for meeting the family's financial needs.

Grandma Witte helped out as best she could, especially in the early months after the family moved in. She paid for music lessons for Butch, and shelled out nearly $1,000 to buy an electric guitar and amplifying equipment for him. Then she complained that he played it too loud. Butch never did seem to have the talent he would need to become another Eric Clapton, anyway, and he developed other interests.

Elaine made personal loans to Marie, and cosigned bank loans with her. She also sometimes allowed Marie to use her bankbook to make mutually agreed upon withdrawals.

Despite all the help, Marie couldn't seem to manage her finances well enough to pay all the bills every month, and she lapsed into some of the same bad habits she had followed when her husband was alive. As the old saying goes, she borrowed from Peter to pay Paul. And, just as she had done when she was supposed to buy the antique furniture, while she was living with Grandma Witte she accepted money for one thing, then spent it on another.

Marcie was living with an arthritic woman she was caring for when Marie began showing up at the door, desperate for money. Marcie later claimed that her daughter sometimes asked for grocery money, money to pay Eric's doctor, and cash to cover up for funds Elaine gave her for Butch's music lessons that she spent on other things.

Marcie wasn't paid a big salary, and room and board accounted for much of her earnings. She never had much money left over after buying booze and paying for other incidentals, so she couldn't do much to ease her daughter's financial burdens. She helped out when she could, but sometimes there was simply no money to give to Marie.

Elaine was much better off financially, but Marie depended on her too much. The older woman began to worry about her own financial welfare. With Marie and the boys in the house, Elaine's bank account was withering at an alarming rate. She began to rebel at the constant pleas for money.

Although Grandma Witte had indicated she would pay for the family's food when Marie and the boys moved into the house, she eventually reneged on the promise. The cost of feeding two teenage boys and two adult women was staggering. There was just no comparison to shopping only for herself. But when Elaine told Marie she would have to contribute more to the family's grocery bills, the younger woman made it clear she was unhappy with the new arrangement.

The women also clashed over who should pay for remodeling a bathroom that Marie wanted done. Marie eventually paid the bill, but more hard feelings were created.

Marie began mixing a little rat poison in Elaine's food, according to later testimony. And she occasionally dropped poison into the old woman's drinks. The poison had no more effect on Elaine than it previously had on Paul. Elaine's moderate lifetime habits had paid off for her with good health. Although Marie took pills for depression, nerves, and asthma, Grandma Witte seldom used anything stronger than an occasional aspirin or Tylenol for her arthritis.

Marie, obviously, was not cut out to be a successful poisoner. But she didn't immediately give up on the idea of getting rid of Elaine.

Family tensions had become almost as stressful in the house on Johnson Road as they were earlier on Beverly Drive. Eric wasn't getting along much better with his mother and his brother than he was with Grandma Witte. Marie's fretfully uneven treatment of her oldest son kept his emotions on a roller coaster. One day she would kick him out of the house, and the next day track him down wherever he was staying and tell him to come back home. His easiest family relationship at that time was with his Grandmother O'Donnell, but she wasn't living with them.

Early in 1982, Eric at last packed up a few of his favorite possessions and moved out of the house. A sharp difference of opinion would eventually be aired publicly over his reasons for leaving: to escape the carping of a strict grandmother; to get away from a domineering mother who was making demands he couldn't, or wouldn't, comply with; or Marie ordered him to move out.

But there was no question Eric was determined *not* to commit another murder for his demanding mother. He didn't want to be put through another police grilling or a repeat of the devastating emotional trauma he suffered after shooting his father. The troubled teenager was still attending Elston when he moved into an apartment a few doors off Coolspring Avenue in Michigan City. Marie paid the rent.

He wasn't living on his own for long, however, before his mother cut off the rent money. Eric later claimed she stopped the payments because she wanted him to return home. Instead, he moved in with Marcie and her friend at their apartment. Eric got along well with his grandmother's best friend, and once drove to Georgia to bring her home from a visit there.

Marie didn't cut herself off from her son, however. When he graduated from Elston, she obtained a bank loan and bought him a Ford Escort as a present. Marcie helped with the down payment. Earlier Marie sold the family pickup truck and bought herself a gray Chevette.

Eric continued to see a lot of his mother, and when they got together she usually brought up the same subject that he was so anxious to avoid. She kept after him to kill Elaine, he said. She was as persistent as a possum after a road kill, and she reportedly whined that she was going to get into a lot of trouble because of the money she had taken from her stepmother-in-law. Marie confided she was putting drugs in Elaine's food and drink, and was hopeful they might cause the old woman's death.

The drugs and poison hadn't yet worked, however, so Marie asked her reluctant son for his opinion about just how a killer could best go about the task of eliminating Grandma Witte. His mother talked about using Valium, Percodan or nitroglycerine tablets, he later recalled. Eric said he told his mother that none of the medications would kill Elaine.

Eric eventually moved back into the house on Johnson Road. Despite Marie's persistent wheedling, however, he refused to help her kill Grandma Witte. He had committed one murder for his mother and he wasn't going to commit another.

On July 5, 1983, while other local teenagers were water-skiing on local lakes, sunbathing on the Dunes, or picking up summer cash baby-sitting and working at fast-food restaurants, Eric walked into the recruiter's office and enlisted in the Navy. It was the day after his seventeenth birthday.

There was a waiting period before he could begin boot camp so he remained in the Michigan City area for a few months, shuttling between an apartment of his own, Marcie's home, the home of a friend, and Elaine's house. Just about every time Eric returned to 320 Johnson Road, however, his mother pestered him to kill Elaine or wanted to talk about the best way the murder could be carried out. Marie warned that if Elaine wasn't killed, Eric might wind up witnessing his mother going to jail. There was serious trouble over money, she warned.

Butch also confided to his big brother that their mother had been after him to murder Grandma Witte. He said he was wondering if he should do it. According to his brother, Butch concluded at the end of the conversation that he wouldn't.

At last, on December 17, Eric made the 110-mile trip from Michigan City to the Naval Recruit Training Center at Great Lakes, Illinois, a few miles north of Chicago, to begin boot camp. Before leaving, he packed the crossbow, knives, and other killing instruments in his weapon collection into a trunk and slid it under his bed. He had asked Tammy to keep it at her house because he didn't want his brother to get into it, but she refused.

When Eric left, Marie told Tammy not to come to the house unless she telephoned first.

Elaine may have hoped that the Navy would be good for her grandson, as it had been good for his father, and help make a man out of him. He was, after all, born into somewhat of a Navy tradition. No one mentioned it, but even Marie's first husband was a seagoing man.

Despite Eric's absence from the house, Marie's income still wasn't keeping up with the rate of spending she wanted to establish for herself. When Grandma Witte wasn't around, Marie slipped the old woman's bank card out of the drawer in the china cabinet. The younger woman appeared to have found a handy, if temporary, solution to her money problems. Around the end of

November 1983, she began withdrawing money from her stepmother-in-law's savings at the Citizens' National Bank in Michigan City and redepositing it in her own accounts. She usually conducted her banking business with drive-up tellers and through automatic teller machines.

She also began forging Elaine's name on the elderly woman's Social Security checks and cashing them. Marie spent hours crouched over a table with tracing paper and a pencil intently practicing Elaine's signature.

Marie nevertheless continued to worry that the thefts would soon be discovered and traced back to her. Eric had tried to remove himself from the situation, but when he came home his mother kept after him to help get rid of Grandma Witte.

A few days before Halloween the old woman was lured upstairs to help with the fitting of a hooded costume she was told Eric was going to wear to a party, according to a story later told by Butch. Butch said he hid in a closet with his brother's crossbow, and Eric was supposed to clamp some ankle cuffs on Elaine as she stood on a trunk while Marie was supposedly cinching the sheetlike costume around the waist.

Eric couldn't go through with the scheme. Butch said the young sailor just walked out of the room, and the murder plot was called off . . . for the time being.

Marie refocused her attentions on her youngest son. She told Butch she was in financial trouble, and she wanted him to help her by killing Grandma Witte. With both Paul and Eric gone, Butch was now the man of the house.

As mother and son calmly talked of murdering the woman who had taken them in after Paul's death, they agreed that shooting Elaine with a gun probably wouldn't be a good idea because her death would be too similar to Paul's. And police had been openly suspicious about the earlier shooting.

They discussed poisoning, suffocating, strangling, pushing her out a second-floor window or down a flight of stairs, or running her down with a car. Butch once suggested that he could take her down by a nearby creek and karate chop her in the throat or rip out her larynx with his hands. The schemers, however, didn't immediately settle on any definite method.

Inevitably, Grandma Witte learned of the banking withdrawals, which were recorded in her monthly statements. When two of Elaine's checks were returned for insufficient funds, and she discovered her account had dwindled to a measly

139

$8.63, she confronted Marie. At the conclusion of a nasty quarrel, Elaine threatened to go to the bank to straighten things out. There might be some legal action as well, she advised. Grandma Witte began about talking about throwing her daughter-in-law and grandson out of the house.

The younger woman was already in financial trouble, and if she was put out of the house on Johnson Road she would have nowhere to go. Her house in Beverly Shores was only a memory, and she couldn't move in with her mother, at least not for any extended period.

Marie reacted by once more helping herself to the pass book for her mother-in-law's savings account, driving to the Citizens' National Bank in Michigan City and withdrawing $6,000. She redeposited $1,700 in her own checking and savings accounts at the Chesterton State Bank in the town of Chesterton in nearby Porter County, and put the rest in Elaine's checking account at Citizens' National.

That night while Marie worried about the missing money and her troubles with Grandma Witte, Butch was living it up in the basement swilling booze and smoking marijuana. If there was ever any excitement and feeling of good cheer inside the troubled household during the recent holiday season, it had permanently yielded to darker, more sinister emotions.

At about 6:30 A.M. the next morning, on Tuesday, January 10, 1984, Marie padded into Butch's second-floor bedroom. Outside, low-hanging snow clouds had turned the sky a deep, brooding gray. The only light came from the faint, yellow halo of a street lamp about a half-block away and from the multicolored gleamings of a neighbor's outdoor Christmas decorations that were still strung and blinking around the house. It was one of the dreariest days of the winter.

Marie switched on the bedside light, leaned over Butch and gently shook him awake, then perched on the side of his bed to have a little mother-and-son talk. The cold wind sweeping off the lake whirled gritty particles of old snow against the outside of the window as they softly conversed. Marie had been awake since about 5:00 A.M., and there was no longer any time to waste, she said. The time had come for him to kill Grandma Witte. The old woman was sleeping in her own bedroom a few feet down the hall.

Marie warned the boy that if she went to jail for taking the old woman's money, he would be left without his mother and his home. She was so anxious to put the plan in motion she barely gave the boy a chance to brush the sleep from the corners of his eyes, or to slip out from under the covers, to stretch and to scratch.

Butch was told that since he was going to do the job, he could decide how to carry it out. He chose to use his brother's crossbow. He realized that the crossbow, which was a favorite weapon in the imaginary adventures of D & D, was fast, quiet, and simple.

Crossbows are fiercely destructive weapons. They can rip through flesh and bone as easily as most bullets. When they were first introduced into warfare during the Crusades of the early twelfth century, they quickly replaced the short bows and arrows used by archers at that time, which could not penetrate the newly developed chain mail. The wounds they inflicted were so savage that in 1139 the Lateran Council issued an edict banning them from use in warfare. They were the nuclear, chemical, or biological weapon of their day. Despite the ruling, however, they continued to be widely used until development of the powerful and longer-range longbow.

Crossbows have experienced a revival of popularity in recent years by hunters and collectors who admire them for their unique silent killing power, maneuverability, and compact beauty. Newly manufactured crossbows carry model names such as Thunderbolt, XT-2, Demon, and

Ninja. Silent and deadly accurate at short range, crossbows have also become a favorite weapon for murder.

Although Butch left it unsaid, using the crossbow would also eliminate the need for him to come in close body contact with his victim, as he would have to do if he strangled, suffocated, or pushed her out a window. Most murderers, except those who kill for lust and enjoy the feel of the sigh and shudder of life violently leaving a body, prefer to do their grim work at a distance. In the United States where firearms are so easily available, the weapon of choice is usually a gun. But a handgun had already been ruled out, with good reason.

Marie did her part to carry out the nasty job ahead of them by mixing some Valium into Elaine's breakfast to put her to sleep.

In the meantime, Butch settled down with a set of dice and game manuals and began playing Dungeons & Dragons. Later, he explained that he played the fantasy adventure game until he slipped into a neutral state.

While Butch was playing Dungeons & Dragons, his mother bundled up against the fierce mid-winter cold and wind and drove to the bank in Michigan City. She used Grandma Witte's banking card to withdraw yet another $200 from the automatic teller machine. It was only one day after she had withdrawn the $6,000 from Elaine's savings account.

At about noon Butch left his dice and D & D manuals and game charts and walked down to the basement. There, surrounded by black-painted walls, as the furnace hummed in the background, he loaded Eric's crossbow with a single sharp metal bolt.

Then he turned and climbed two flights of stairs to the seventy-four-year-old woman's bedroom, where she had lain down and fallen into a drugged sleep after eating the Valium-laced meal Marie prepared for her. Grandma Witte was dressed in a favorite pair of blue pajamas and was lying on her back when her grandson padded into the shadowed room.

A few moments after slipping into the bedroom, the fourteen-year-old boy aimed the weapon at the sleeping woman and triggered it. The harsh *tung* of the crossbow as it was tripped was followed by the dreadful whisper of the bolt as it cut through the air and slashed into Elaine's rib cage near the center of her chest. She gasped almost imperceptibly as her frail body was slammed back into the bed, then she lurched slightly forward. But her eyes never flickered and there was no other visible or audible sign she was conscious and aware of the agony of her impalement.

Butch walked slowly over to the bed and touched two fingers to the old woman's neck. Calmly he pressed them against the artery which stood out prominently from the elderly woman's sunken flesh, feeling for a pulse.

Satisfied there was no pulse, the teenager straightened up and turned to leave. A dark ooze of blood slowly spread over Elaine's blue pajama top where the bolt entered her chest. It scraped one of her ribs as it buried itself into her flesh.

Butch was on his way to tell Marie that Grandma Witte was dead when he met his mother halfway down the stairs. Before he had a chance to speak up, she began talking.

"Don't worry about killing Elaine. We'll sort the money problems out later," Marie told her son.

"It's too late," the teenager somberly replied.

Marie, followed by her son, hurried into the bedroom to see for herself if Elaine was really dead. She stared for a moment at the figure outlined on the bed in the dim early winter light that was filtering from a window into the darkened room. Marie leaned over the old woman's body and pulled out the crossbow bolt.

A few minutes later Butch carried a large plastic garbage container up to Elaine's bedroom. Marie helped him stuff Grandma Witte's body headfirst into the fifty-five-gallon drum like it was yesterday's trash. Then they placed the cover on the can and made up the bed. Grandma Witte liked things neat.

At last they returned downstairs and cleaned up. Finally they pulled on heavy coats, calmly walked into the garage and got into the family car. Marie was behind the wheel as the mother and son pulled away from the silent house on their way to the South Shore Station in Michigan City. At the station Marie paid for tickets with some of the $200 withdrawn a few hours earlier from Grandma Witte's checking account, and they boarded a train for Chicago. Marie's hearing on her Social Security disability appeal had finally been scheduled, and she was determined not to miss the meeting.

Marie figured they could deal with the body when they returned home. Grandma Witte wouldn't be going anywhere while they were away.

In Chicago, Marie represented herself at the Social Security hearing. She delivered such an impressive presentation that the hearing officer agreed to reinstate her disability payments.

146

Six

A Grisly Cover-up

The murder of Elaine Witte and its immediate aftermath was cold and gruesome. But there was even more horror to come.

When Marie and Butch returned to Michigan City from Chicago she was in a good mood over her success at the hearing. But she realized that dealing with Grandma Witte's remains wouldn't be handled as easily as the problem with her Social Security claim.

Consequently, after stopping at a McDonald's for sandwiches and fries, the mother and son drove around Michigan City for awhile as she tried to figure out just what to do with the corpse. A fierce wind from a cold front sweeping down off the lake from Canada whipped gritty gray snow off the plowed streets onto the windshield, and the tires kicked up a dirty slush that coated the side paneling and doors as they moved through the quiet city streets.

Despite the months of talking about murdering Grandma Witte, Marie hadn't given much serious thought to covering up the crime. There didn't appear to be much chance of convincing police that the slaying was an accidental death; especially in light of what had happened to Paul.

With the lapse of several hours since Butch shot the old woman with his brother's crossbow, there was even less reason to hope that investigators would consider an accident as an excuse for her death. As they drove and talked the rhythmic click of the windshield wipers, it became obvious that there was only one solution left: Grandma Witte would have to disappear.

Marie stopped at a telephone booth and called her mother at a house in Michigan City where she was looking after an elderly woman. After preparing dinner and eating with the old woman, Marcie had just finished cleaning up the kitchen and washing the dishes when the telephone rang and her daughter said they had to talk. Marie was agitated and upset. Marcie told her to drive over to the house.

As soon as they had walked into a room by themselves and were alone, Marie confronted her mother with a terrible story. "Mommie, I need you," she said. "Momma, Elaine is dead."

Marcie began to shake and moan as Marie explained there had been a terrible accident. Marcie usually managed to stay sober on the job, but she was having trouble focusing on what her daughter was telling her. She didn't really want to hear the story. She didn't want it to be true. Despite her agitation, however, enough information sank in to confirm her worst fears.

"Butch was playing with the bow and arrow and it shot. It went off and it hit Elaine and she's dead, Momma," Marcie later recalled her daughter telling her on that dreadful night.

Even though she and Elaine weren't close friends, Marcie had been scared to death the old woman would be murdered. Now it had happened, and she was being drawn right into the middle of the whole affair. Her daughter insisted they return together to the house where Elaine's body had been left after the killing. It was the last place Marcie wanted to go.

She said she couldn't leave the shut-in she was caring for. But Marie insisted that she needed her help. Marcie tried telephoning one of the woman's sons, but couldn't get through. When she called another son, she talked to his wife and concocted a story about being needed in New York to care for a relative who was hurt in an accident. The younger woman gave Marcie a check for the money she had already earned.

Then Marcie climbed into the car with Marie and Butch, and they drove to the house on

Johnson Road. The house was freezing cold because the furnace had broken down. It had been a long and exhausting day for Marie; she was tired and cold. Nevertheless, she was intent on beginning the task of cutting up the body that night.

First, however, Marcie was given a look at the body. Led upstairs, she was ushered into the master bedroom that faces onto Johnson Road. The window blinds were closed, but a nightlight was on. It provided faint illumination which revealed a large garbage can near the foot of the bed. The bed was neatly made and looked as if it hadn't been slept on.

Marie lifted the lid off the closed container, and her mother peered hesitantly inside. Elaine's body was ignominiously stuffed head-first into the garbage can. Marcie was horrified! She shuddered and moaned as images of the old woman's hair, part of her face, and a splash of blue shimmered eerily in the weak light and tickled her consciousness. She gasped, turned away from the ghastly spectacle, and lurched downstairs, pressing one hand against the wall to steady herself.

Marie was determined that there would be no corpse for pathologists to examine. She and her son wrestled the garbage can with the body inside along a hallway and into the closet of another upstairs bedroom.

The walk-in closet would be the abattoir; the temporary slaughterhouse where she and her son would turn the murdered old woman's corpse into more easily and safely disposable chunks of meat. But from the very beginning of the disarticulation process there were serious problems.

Elaine's corpse was bloody, and her bladder had emptied when she died. The odor of stale urine rose and hovered over the body in waves. By the time Marie and Butch returned to the house, the process of rigor mortis was also well underway. Rigor mortis sets in eight to twelve hours after death, and the condition can last for another twelve to twenty-four hours before the joints loosen and a dead body becomes limp and supple once more.

When the amateur butchers began the job of cutting up Grandma Witte, her joints were as solidly locked as if they had been welded together. She was stiff as a board and exceedingly difficult to handle. But they were anxious to get on with the job and began carving up the corpse anyway. At one point they plugged in an electric knife and attacked the fleshy parts of the body as if they were carving a Sunday roast.

Lividity had already turned Elaine's face, head, and shoulders a sickly purplish color. The condition is caused when the heart stops beating and gravity pushes the blood in the body down. That process stops an hour or two after death, however, when the blood coagulates. Lividity can provide valuable clues to pathologists and other investigators in determining the time and other aspects surrounding a death—that is, when there is a body to study.

But Marie and her son had no time for speculation about the esoterics of forensic pathology. They had work to do, and it was a nasty job.

The horror of dismembering the old woman's corpse was overwhelming, but it was also simply too cold to stay in the house that night. Consequently, the two women and the boy checked into a nearby Howard Johnson Motor Lodge and eventually spent four nights there before the furnace was fixed. During the day, they returned to the house and resumed the grisly task that awaited them.

While her daughter and grandson sliced and sawed at the body upstairs, Marcie kept shaky watch downstairs. Marie didn't want the telephone to go unanswered if someone called, and she didn't want anyone knocking at the door and interrupting them while they were occupied with Elaine's corpse.

The day after Elaine's murder, Marie telephoned an order to a Sears Roebuck & Company store at the nearby Marquette shopping mall for a garbage disposal unit. She insisted that it be installed as soon as possible. Ray Cole, a building engineer and part-time appliance installer for Sears, drove out to 320 Johnson Road and put the unit in place under the kitchen sink. Marie, who had an older woman with her, showed him where the unit was to go. Marcie signed the work order with Elaine's name.

Marcie had refused to go along with her daughter's suggestion to rent a motel apartment with a garbage disposal so it could be used in the elimination of Elaine's corpse.

About two weeks later, Marie drove to the Allan Furniture Mart on U. S. Road 20 West and bought a heavy-duty trash compactor. It was a freestanding unit that didn't have to be built in to the kitchen and was one of the best made. Manager Steve Gonzalez, who sold the appliance, nevertheless was mildly surprised when Marie bought a dozen additional white garbage bags. The compactor already came with five bags, each one large enough to hold the normal garbage of an average-sized household for a week.

Marie also purchased a used pickup truck with a camper on the back. Finally she financed purchase of a 1972 Winnebago through Citizens' Bank.

Dissecting the old woman wasn't all that different from dressing a freshly slain buck, except that deer are usually eviscerated and cut into workable chunks of meat in the clean crispness of the outdoors, where the blood and the waste and the odor aren't much of a problem. And the flesh, bones, and other parts that are left over after butchering don't have to be hidden or destroyed.

Marie and Butch made adjustments to facilitate cutting up the cadaver inside the house by hauling huge sheets of plastic and plywood upstairs and lining the closet with it. Marie didn't want any unnecessary blood stains ruining her floors and walls or left behind as possible evidence of a murder.

Despite the efforts at neatness, the cloying odor of death rose from the desiccated corpse as Marie and Butch worked. Although it was a typically fierce Dunesland winter and temperatures outside the house often hovered near zero, it was hot and humid inside the closet after the furnace was fixed, and it reeked with the smell of decaying meat. The odor clung to the walls, and after a few hours of work it saturated the hair, bodies, and clothing of Marie and Butch.

* * *

About the middle of January, Eric telephoned home from Great Lakes. He barely had time to say "Hello," before his mother took command of the conversation. "We've got a problem. Elaine is dead, and I can't tell the police," she blurted out. Marie was terrified that the police would learn their secret. "We've got to hide the body!" she said.

Although Marie didn't immediately explain how the old woman was killed, it was obvious to the young sailor that his mother and brother were in serious trouble. It was too late to do anything for Elaine, and Marie and Butch needed his help. Eric suggested they temporarily stuff the corpse into a large freezer that was kept in the basement. Marie and Butch began stocking the freezer.

For once Marcie came up with a helpful suggestion and refined the scheme even further. Since Elaine's corpse was already dismembered, they could separate the fleshy parts of the body into meal-sized chunks, and cook it before bagging and storing it in the freezer, she suggested. Then even if someone else did happen to stumble onto it, they would probably assume that she was merely using good economical judgment by buying, preparing, and storing meat in large quantities.

Following through on the suggestion, Marie took some of the meat out of the freezer and cooked it in a deep fat french fryer in an effort to further obliterate evidence of Elaine's murder. Marcie watched as her daughter used a knife to saw at a large, thick piece of thigh-sized flesh on the kitchen floor and drop slippery chunks into the appliance. Marie also tried rendering the intestines in the microwave. But the sudden, fierce blast of heat caused them to explode, creating a disgusting mess to clean up.

Marie and Butch didn't dare give up. They continued cutting up the cold greasy flesh; ripping, splintering, and tearing for days.

They grunted, sweated, and snapped at each other in the close quarters of the closet while they worked amid the blood, grease, and bile. They sliced and diced the body into ever smaller bits with skinning and butcher knives, a hammer, chisels, and circular saws. While Marcie nervously roamed the main floor of the lonely house, she could hear the moist thump of cleavers slashing through meat and gristle and the eerie shriek of the saw as it tore apart bones and flesh upstairs. She worried at every moment that a car was going to pull up in the snow-covered driveway or someone was going to knock at the door.

Every so often Marie or her son, faces flushed and glistening with sweat and exertion, struggled downstairs with a bagful of flesh or body parts and stored them in the freezer.

Marie stuffed chunks of Grandma Witte's flesh into the garbage disposal, and set a metal pan underneath to catch the mass of blood and tissue that seeped outside. Butch helped his mother mix the mess with potting soil, then carried it outside to dump. Eventually, however, the meat clogged up in the unit and burned out the motor. Marie didn't want to call a repairman for fear he would become too curious about what she had been stuffing into the device.

She didn't have any better luck when she tried crushing the old woman's skull in the trash compactor, which she had bought specifically for the job. It, too, broke down, and again she was afraid to call a repairman. She tried using a vise to crush some of the bones and found that it worked much better.

One day Marcie was in the sun-room when her daughter walked in and reminded her how lucky she was. "You didn't have to face what I had to face," she told her mother. "I just finished the head." Marcie didn't ask any questions. She simply turned away and mumbled that she didn't want anything more to do with what was going on.

In the meantime, Marie continued to keep in

close touch by telephone with Eric. He had remained at Great Lakes to attend Navy hospital corpsman's school after completing boot camp, and she shared information with him about her problems. She was having special difficulty getting rid of the fingers and long bones.

Elaine had been dead for weeks when Eric suggested trying to dissolve the remains with acid. He had asked some of his buddies at Great Lakes if they knew of an acid that would be good for cleaning concrete and dissolving pebbles or rocks. One of the sailors who had been a good high school chemist recommended trying a mixture of sulfuric acid and hydrochloric acid. It should be strong enough to do the job, he said.

A short time later, Marie obtained some muriatic acid and filled a vat in the kitchen with it. She and Butch began dumping the bones and flesh inside. As Elaine's remains settled, gray foam bubbled to the top of the tub.

Muriatic acid is an industrial name for hydrochloric acid, a powerful corrosive commonly used to clean metal and for processing ores. Throughout modern criminal history, it has also been a favorite, along with quicklime, of murderers anxious to dispose of bodies. It can turn flesh into a nasty slime of jelly.

Even hydrochloric acid, however, couldn't rid the ghoulish mother and son of the old woman's corpse. Bones aren't dissolved as easily as flesh.

Grandma Witte's remains were soaked in the acid bath more than a month, and before they were removed—glistening pearly white but still intact—the sour graveyard stink had swarmed through the entire house. When portions of the body were carried into the motor home, that, too, began to smell.

The odor was dank and wet like old sewer water that had backed up under a house. It had a touch of sweetness, but it was unpleasant, powerful, and ugly.

Marie scrubbed and cleaned, but it seemed that nothing worked. The stink from the closet was especially foul and she ordered Butch to help scrub it out, but he balked. Months later Marcie recalled that Marie was furious at her son's sullen mutiny and snapped: "You got us into this damned mess, and you're going to help us get out."

Marie burned citronella candles and used a strong orange-scented spray both on the house and the Winnebago. Despite all the efforts, however, it was impossible to totally get rid of the odor of death. The gangrenous miasma lingered, as persistently as the "damned spot" in *Macbeth*.

When Eric returned home on a weekend liberty, he asked what was done with Elaine, and was told she was in the freezer. He walked down to the basement to see for himself, and found the appliance was stuffed with bulging plastic garbage bags. He didn't open any of them for a closer look.

Marie eventually admitted to Eric that Butch deliberately killed Elaine after she told him to because of troubles over the old woman's bank accounts.

When Butch talked with his big brother about the motive for the slaying, however, he let his imagination run wild. At least once he ran through the accident story concocted by his mother. Another time he said he was drunk after boozing and smoking pot in the basement for hours. He also said he did it to protect their mother because she was stealing money from Elaine and was afraid of going to jail.

Although there were additional versions, his most outrageous explanation was that he needed a human sacrifice to work a black magic spell. The boys were talking inside the Winnebago when Butch reputedly spun the bizarre yarn and said he expected the spell to make him stronger and cure his medical problems. One of the books Eric had collected and left in his room referred to such a spell.

Eric began bringing buddies home from Great Lakes almost as soon as he graduated from boot

160

camp shortly before the end of February. One of his friends at the base was Douglas Allen Menkel, a husky twenty-year-old sailor from New Jersey who attended boot camp and the hospital corpsman's school with him. Menkel drove to Trail Creek with Eric and another sailor one weekend near the end of May, planning to play Dungeons & Dragons. He had been playing the game ever since he was in junior high school. After his first trip to Trail Creek, he began visiting at the Witte home almost every weekend he was free.

He wasn't a guest there for long before he spent the night in bed with his buddy's mother. Although she was almost twice his age, Marie was still on the light side of forty, and had a fine-boned, elfin face. She was slender and fetchingly seductive. Menkel was no match for the experienced, manipulative, older woman.

Marie's sons didn't appear to be bothered by the easy sexual relationship that developed between their mother and Eric's sailor pal. Menkel quickly assumed an important role in the family; tending to Marie's romantic needs, playing Dungeons & Dragons for hours with Eric and Butch, and helping out with household chores. He was impressed with the Wittes and believed that Eric had psychic abilities. Much later Menkel explained that he was told things about himself by his Navy friend, intimate things, that Eric

161

couldn't have been normally expected to know.

He suspected that Eric not only possessed extrasensory perception, but also had telekinetic powers. Marie and Butch told Menkel they had similar amazing abilities. Sometimes Eric and Menkel squared off and tried to read each other's minds. At other times they experimented with trying to move dice or other small objects with mind power. Butch, Marie, or other sailors who happened to be hanging around the house that weekend occasionally joined in. Marie claimed at times she was successful in reading their minds, and could predict the future. The experiments never worked for the boys, but they continued to try.

Several weeks after the New Jersey sailor first met Marie, she asked him to help dispose of some garbage bags which had been packed into strong black plastic bags, then stored in an old ice cooler. Menkel rode with Butch in the Winnebago to some marshes in an isolated area near the Indiana-Michigan line, where they dumped them.

When the young sailor asked about the foul smell, he was told it was food that had putrefied and been run through the garbage disposal. Marie didn't tell him until about a month later that Grandma Witte had been shot to death with a crossbow. Until then he had believed she was on vacation.

But Menkel was given a carefully sanitized version of the incident. He was told the shooting was a dreadful accident. According to the story outlined by Marie and her sons, Butch was walking up a flight of stairs carrying his brother's crossbow when he stumbled. The weapon accidentally discharged, and one of the metal bolts struck his grandmother, killing her.

The first time Marie told him the story, she said Butch was near the bottom of the staircase when the bolt struck Elaine, who was sitting at the edge of the bed. The sailor was dubious and pointed out that the angle of the stairs would have made it almost impossible to hit her from the bottom. So Marie changed her story. She said Butch tripped as he was at the top of the stairs, and accidentally triggered the crossbow. Marie had been confused.

Menkel also asked an obvious question: Why hadn't Marie simply reported the accident to police?

She replied that she was afraid to, because of the earlier mishap when Eric shot his father to death. Police investigators made it clear at that time they didn't believe the shooting was an accident, she said. And she was afraid they would take the same attitude about Elaine's death. Two tragedies so much alike could have aroused nasty suspicions and led to all kinds of trouble with police and the courts.

Then, according to Menkel's later version of the occurrences, Marie played her ace. She told him that parts of Grandma Witte's body were in the garbage bags and cooler he helped dispose of. If he revealed the old woman's death to police, he could be charged with being an accessory to the crime or with some other serious offense.

By the time the storytelling was over, Menkel agreed to help his friends dispose of other remaining portions of the body. Early in September Marie produced a small glass jar, with Elaine's teeth inside. Menkel cracked them in a vise, one by one, as easily as if they were walnuts. When the dreadful chore was completed and the jar was at last empty, the teeth were reduced to a fine white calcium dust.

Marie had tried unsuccessfully to get rid of the teeth earlier by soaking them in acid, before coming up with the idea of using the vise. She told Menkel a couple of weeks after the teeth were ground up that she and Butch dumped the white powder near a big amusement park in Illinois.

Menkel became deeply involved in the scheme to dispose of the woman's remains almost before he realized what was going on. When he asked questions of Marie, he got conflicting answers.

She changed her version of the events whenever it was convenient or necessary. The few times he tried to get information from Butch, the skinny teenager erupted in anger and smashed a wall with his fist, slammed a piece of furniture with his foot, or flailed his toothpick arms at the bigger, older youth until he was pushed away or grabbed in a bear hug and forced to calm down. Menkel learned that it was difficult getting the truth from any of the Wittes. But he wouldn't be the only Great Lakes sailor who would have that trouble.

As weeks passed while the family was preoccupied with getting rid of Grandma Witte's corpse, Eric continued introducing his mother and brother to Navy friends. There were young sailors at the house almost every weekend, so many that Marcie couldn't remember all of their names. She met one boy she remembered only as Jose, another whom she knew as Thomas, as well as by his nickname, Squirrel. There was even a sailor from the Navy electronics school who shared her grandson's first name, Eric, and was one of Douglas Menkel's pals.

She also knew Jeffrey David Schoonover, who was one of Eric's closest buddies from boot camp. Marie first met the nineteen-year-old sailor, along with Menkel, when she drove

Butch, Marcie, Eric's girlfriend, Tammy, and another teenage boy to Waukegan, Illinois, a few miles north of Great Lakes for a celebration in a hotel after the sailors graduated from boot camp on February 19. Marie used Grandma Witte's car for the trip. Tammy had already been told Elaine was vacationing at the Grand Canyon.

It wasn't much of a party for Tammy. There was a large amount of booze, but not much else to keep the group in a party mood. Eric was jumpy and in a bad mood, and a couple of times Marie told Tammy to leave the room because the boys were picking on Marcie and she wanted to straighten things out. When Tammy had a chance to talk with Eric, she asked him why he was so tense. He said he was sick of having to bail his younger brother out of trouble.

Schoonover also quickly got bored with the party, and only hung around about an hour before leaving to play video games, long before the serious talks that got Tammy barred from the room began. But like Menkel, Schoonover soon began traveling to LaPorte County with Eric to visit in the Witte home during weekend liberties. Schoonover had stayed at Great Lakes to train as a machinist's mate.

Tammy and Eric sometimes quarreled when he began getting weekend liberties and returning to the Michigan City area because he didn't want to spend any time at the house on Johnson Road, even though it was usually filled with his fun Navy friends. Eric preferred to simply ride around in the car or stop at Marcie's house. Usually he gave in to Tammy's pleadings, however, and they wound up at Grandma Witte's house. Tammy never saw Elaine at the house after Eric went off to boot camp.

Marie and Butch made the one-hundred-ten-mile drive to Great Lakes to see Eric and his buddies more than once. One time Marie telephoned Menkel and told him she wanted to visit him at Great Lakes so he could help her dump some garbage. That evening Marie and Butch picked him up in the Winnebago, and the three of them turned around and drove east once more. A few miles west of the Indiana border, they pulled several bags filled with something foul-smelling and dumped it in an isolated marsh.

Marie, Eric, and Menkel also transported bits and pieces of the disarticulated corpse in Grandma Witte's car and dropped them off in isolated areas around LaPorte County and just across the state line in Illinois.

Some pieces of the old woman were dumped between U. S. Highways 12 and 20 among the sandburs, bogs, and scrub brush of the Indiana

Dunes State Park and the Indiana Dunes National Lake Shore only a few minutes drive from her stepson's former home in Beverly Shores. Others were driven past the plywood chili-dog stands, quick shop marts, and pastures with signs offering "Free Manure," clustered in the Dunesland area and dumped in rustic and isolated spots near the Michigan state line.

The putrefying flesh was inside Marie's car just long enough to saturate it with the ugly, cloying odor. She tried spraying the old car to get rid of the smell. One day, Marie, Butch, Menkel and a few other sailors drove the car to Marcie's house on East Eighth Street, where they stripped the interior down to the metal frame, scrubbed the inside of the stripped-down car with ammonia, and put in new upholstery and seats. Marie told the boys the car was sprayed by a skunk.

Marie decided at last that it was time to get rid of Grandma Witte's former pride and joy. She arranged to sell the 1979 Chevy.

Vivian Bentley, a Michigan City woman, drove to the house with her grandson, Kenneth, to look the car over. When she returned a few days later, she bought it for him. He was also a sailor, but wasn't part of the crowd that hung around with the Wittes. Marie handled the business transaction. But Eric was also present, along with another older woman he introduced as "Mrs. Witte."

Like the Witte brothers and Menkel, Schoonover loved to play Dungeons & Dragons. The four youths frequently played the game at the Witte home. Schoonover was impressed with the handsome old house and asked who owned it. Marie explained it had been a present to her from her late husband's mother. When the young sailor was an overnight guest, he slept in Elaine's room, which for awhile was still filled with decorative dolls, bottles of perfume, and other feminine accoutrements.

Like Menkel, Schoonover was eventually drawn into the tragedy that was still being played out. Unlike his sailor friend, however, he never became Marie's lover.

Marcie was also drawn deeper into her daughter's sinister activities, and she was so befuddled by alcohol, Valium, and fear that she was powerless to extricate herself. She hated it when Marie told her to put on Elaine's coat and hat, then drove her to Michigan City banks to cash the old woman's forged Social Security and retirement checks or to make withdrawals from checking and savings accounts. On those trips Marie would look for a drive-up spot as far from the teller window as possible even when close lanes were clear and available. Marcie would sit in the front passenger seat.

At other times Butch or Menkel accompanied Marie when she drove to the bank to cash Elaine's checks. Marcie, Butch, and Eric all saw Marie forging or practicing the old woman's signature or cashing checks at various times. Menkel watched once as Marie used some old documents Elaine had signed to practice the signature. Eric told her she wasn't doing it right, that the handwriting needed to be smoothed out.

One time when Marie was sitting at a table struggling to duplicate Elaine's signature, Eric suggested a better method. He told her to put a copy of Elaine's signature on a light table, so it could be more accurately and easily traced. Eric's system was a big improvement.

With plenty of money to spend once more, Marie redecorated the house with expensive paneling and bought new furniture and carpeting. Almost everyone in the extended family moving in and out of the house on Johnson Road helped with the renovation and cleanup projects that seemed to be constantly underway. When Tammy asked what Elaine was going to think about all the changes, Marie replied that the old woman had sold her the house and planned to move into an apartment.

Tammy was banned from the basement while

she was visiting at the house, and told it was because the kitchen floor had caved in. Later on the upstairs was also put off-limits.

Schoonover did his part, helping get rid of unwanted furniture. Some of it was simply tossed out of the upstairs window. His hosts told him it was old and using the window was easier than lugging it downstairs. He and the brothers tossed the furniture on a pile in the backyard, where it was burned.

Marie refused to allow Tammy to come over when the burning was going on. She said the girl would distract Eric from his job helping out if she was around. Marie and her boys put several other loads of refuse from the house into a truck and drove it into rural areas of the county for burning. The bed Elaine died on was included among the furniture consigned to the burn piles.

One of the burn piles was on a property directly south of Trail Creek a few miles from Waterford. Jeannie worked at the house helping care for an invalid who was a double amputee, and the Wittes burned the material there.

The shut-in's daughter-in-law was there one day when Marie and Butch unloaded some wooden crates and a bucket from their car and burned the material. The woman told them to be sure and clean up the mess after they were through, and an hour or so later drove back to the house to see for herself if they had kept their promise. They had cleaned up and raked the ashes after the fire died out, and it was as neat as could be.

Another of the burn piles was on property owned by Kathy Klosinski just east of Michigan City in Springfield township. Mrs. Klosinski had gotten to know the Witte family through her father, who worked at the steel mills with Paul. And she had met Elaine at Eric's high school graduation ceremonies.

Marie told her that Elaine was vacationing, and she was cleaning up and needed to get rid of a few things. Butch and Marcie helped Marie with the burning. Elaine's clothing, mattress and bedsheets, bloody towels and rags, along with the plywood and plastic used to protect the walls and floors of the closet, a horsehair rug, Styrofoam coolers, and the upholstery and seats the sailors ripped out of the car were dumped on the fire pit. The crossbow, knives, and other articles used to carve up Grandma Witte were also consigned to the flames.

After the fire died out, Marie and her sons sifted the ashes with a shovel and rake. Knife blades and other chunks of metal they turned up were picked up and tossed away. Some of the ashes were dumped in with leftover bits and pieces of Grandma Witte's remains and mixed in the bags of potting soil to be disposed of.

* * *

In April, a few weeks before Schoonover was transferred from Great Lakes to shipboard duty, he helped Marie move a heavy stand-up freezer from the basement to the apartment Marcie shared with her friend Jeannie in Michigan City. The door was removed and a heavy chain was wrapped around the bulky appliance before it was moved. The grisly contents were also removed before it was transported to Marcie's apartment and repacked inside later.

Marie told Schoonover that Marcie needed the freezer. But Marie was having the basement painted and making other major renovations, and didn't want to chance any of the workmen peeking into the freezer. Some of Eric's Navy pals also helped carry various other pieces of furniture to Marcie and Jeannie's home in Michigan City, including Elaine's prized dining-room table, chairs, and pictures from the walls.

When Jeannie asked Marie about the furniture, Marie told her that when Elaine returned from her vacation she planned to move into an apartment by herself and wouldn't need it anymore. Marie gave a rubber tree plant, a rug, and a few other things from the house to Mrs. Klosinski.

About a week after the freezer was moved, Marie answered a telephone call, then hung up and announced that her mother was upset. Eric, Menkel, and Schoonover climbed into the car with Marie for the drive to Michigan City. When they got to the house on East Eighth Street it reeked of booze, and empty beer cans were lying all over. Marcie was staggering and weepy-eyed. The mother and daughter got into a ferocious quarrel. Schoonover and Menkel were in the kitchen while the argument raged in another room. Schoonover heard Marcie screech, "Get it out. I don't want it here!"

Moments later Marcie reeled into the kitchen, her florid face glistening with tears, and grabbed Schoonover. He recoiled and broke away from her as she tried to give him a sloppy kiss. Then she reached for Menkel, but he also headed away. The sailors began a strategic retreat to the living room, but Marcie lurched after them. So the boys moved back into the kitchen. A short time later Marie left with her relieved Navy escort.

The next weekend, Schoonover overheard another argument between the two women. This time he was at the house on Johnson Road playing Dungeons & Dragons with his friends, while Marie and her mother were watching television and drinking in the living room.

"There's a body in my house. Get it out!"

Marcie yelled. When Schoonover asked his pal what Marcie was talking about, Eric replied that she was getting along in years and becoming senile.

In June, Schoonover flew home to Hawaii on leave, and early the next month reported for duty aboard a guided missile cruiser, the *USS Leahy,* at its home port in San Diego.

A few weeks after Schoonover left Great Lakes, Eric was transferred to San Diego to attend an advanced school for hospital corpsmen. He took the last of the body parts with him on the long drive across country. The final earthly remains of Elaine Witte were a disgusting mess. It had been cut and chopped with knives and a saw, cooked, soaked in acid, and frozen, while being reduced to a pitiful oozing and corrupt gray mush roughly the color and consistency of mucous.

But the slender sailor took it along with him, carefully stored in a compact freezer that he packed in the trunk beside his Navy gear. As soon as he arrived in southern California, Eric rented a trailer in an RV park along the Mexican border in San Ysidro a few miles south of the San Diego Naval Station and the Coronado Naval Amphibious Base. He also rented a post office box under the name, E. Witte.

At home, the situation wasn't improving for Marie or for her mother. Marcie's drinking was once more out of control. Already a big woman, her face and body were puffed up and red. She was nervous, haunted by the terrible things she was witness to and party to . . . and she was afraid. Marcie acted as if she was scared to death of her daughter and her youngest grandson.

The pressure was also continuing to build on Marie and Butch. Butch had never cared much for school since he was old enough to attend junior high. He wanted to quit, but Indiana law stipulated that he wouldn't be old enough to drop out until he was sixteen. Marie came up with a solution when she suggested that he get himself expelled. So Butch took his cigarettes to school, and, sure enough, in April he was expelled for truancy and smoking.

Once the mother and son had all day to spend together, however, their stress increased.

As summer approached, a few of Elaine's hardiest jonquils, violets, and crocuses began poking their way through the weeds and yard clutter in a bright sprinkle of yellow, purple, and white. It was becoming increasingly difficult to explain away her absence to friends, neighbors, and police who were asking about the old woman.

Even the house was depressing. Whether or

not it was the indelible memory of the drawn-out and terrible thing that had occurred there, or the actual odor, hardly mattered. It was true, though, that despite all the cleaning, scrubbing, and redecorating, the smell of death still seemed to cling to the closet and the bedroom where Grandma Witte was chopped and cut up.

Furthermore, Elaine's friends and Paul's half sister were continuing to pester Marie about the old woman's whereabouts.

Mrs. Valencia hadn't given up on her efforts to contact her friend by mail and telephone. In February she sent a Valentine's Day card to Elaine; in March, a St. Patrick's Day card; in April, a birthday card; and in May, a Mother's Day card. None of the cards were acknowledged, and Elaine was never available to take any of the telephone calls.

During a telephone call in early June, Barbara talked with Marie, who told her Elaine and some friends had driven to Holland, Michigan, for the Tulip Festival, then returned home and almost immediately left again on a vacation to the Grand Canyon.

On July 29, Mrs. Valencia and her family stopped at the house on their way back home from their own vacation. Barbara hoped to catch the elderly woman at home. Neither Elaine nor her prized 1979 Chevrolet were there. Only Marie, her sons, and some Navy pals of Eric's were at the house. Marie complained she wasn't feeling well and appeared to be recovering from the flu or some other illness.

As soon as she stepped inside the house, Barbara realized it had undergone major redecoration and renovation since the last time she had visited. The front porch was newly carpeted, new flooring had been installed on the back porch and in the kitchen, kitchen cabinets were painted, the dining room was paneled, and some of Elaine's favorite furniture had been replaced by new pieces.

Drawings sketched by Elaine's mother years earlier and a picture Barbara had given to Grandma Witte were missing from the dining-room walls. Houseplants the old woman had lovingly nurtured and fussed over were also missing. Even Elaine's bed was gone. It didn't appear the owner of the house had helped select the new decor. Mrs. Valencia knew something about Grandma Witte's decorating tastes, and the missing woman would not have chosen the new colors and styles. Outside, there was also a new fixture: a doghouse!

Marie accounted for the missing plants by blaming the problems with the furnace during the winter. The plants died from the cold, she said.

And she explained that Elaine was still away on her vacation, visiting the Grand Canyon before moving on to the San Diego area to spend time with Eric, who had been assigned to Navy duty there.

The visit to Elaine's house didn't do a thing to ease Barbara's concern about her friend's safety and welfare. After the family returned to their home in Illinois, she began compiling a list of questions to ask Marie. On August 7, about a week after the disturbing visit in Trail Creek, she telephoned Marie and tried to get some straight answers about the old woman's whereabouts.

She asked what happened to Elaine's car; her method of travel on the vacation; who she was traveling with; when Marie had last talked with the old woman; when Elaine was home last; how she was getting her mail; how were her finances being handled.

During a later account of the replies, Mrs. Valencia said Marie told her Elaine couldn't drive any longer because of troubles with her arthritis, so she sold her car and let her license lapse. Marie also claimed Elaine had a traveling companion named Jeannie Frye. Marie said she thought Jeannie was a friend from Elaine's school days.

Mrs. Valencia asked Marie to get Mrs. Frye's

phone number from a personal registry that Elaine kept. Marie said she couldn't, Elaine took the booklet with her.

Marie also reportedly claimed the only personal mail Elaine had received since leaving on vacation was a card from Barbara. Everything else was junk mail, which had been disposed of.

Marie's responses to questions about how Elaine was financing her trip didn't shine any more light on her whereabouts than earlier conversations the two women had engaged in. She said Elaine took cash with her, and they hadn't spoken since before the Valencias' visit at the Trail Creek house in July. Marie apologized that she didn't know exactly where Elaine was. But she promised to contact someone at Great Lakes for information to help her get in touch with Eric. When she talked with him, she said, she would be able to find out if Elaine had arrived in San Diego.

Marie was doing the same beating around the bush that she had been at for months. No matter what questions Mrs. Valencia asked, Barbara wound up with a dead-end answer or an empty promise. At last she threatened that if Marie didn't get in touch with the police about the missing womann, she would take things in her own hands and notify authorities herself that something was amiss. A few days later, Barbara made good on her promise.

* * *

Marie was shaken by the conversation and by other questions from people who had been snooping around trying to get information about Elaine.

She confided to a couple of her acquaintances, including Kathy Klosinski and Linda Griswold, that she was sick and tired of being harassed by the police. They still seemed to believe she had something to do with Paul's death, and were even beginning to accuse her of doing something bad to Elaine. Marie told Kathy that a couple of law officers had come to her door one day and warned her that no matter what else happened, they always got their man. Presumably, they wanted her to get the message that they also got their woman. Marie was worried they would continue to poke around in her business, and she began to talk seriously about going to California.

In late summer Marie told Mrs. Griswold she was going to move west to be closer to her older son. Mrs. Griswold lived in Pines, a town of a few hundred people along the south edge of the Dunes Highway and Beverly Shores, and had run sled teams with Paul. She also ran the Ravenwood Kennel, and she gave Marie permission to leave the Winnebago there. Marie was afraid it would be vandalized if she left it at the house.

Marie indicated she still had some legal documents to complete before she would own the house, and speculated that eventually she would probably wind up renting it to someone. She asked her friend to keep an eye on the place while she was gone. Mrs. Griswold agreed to look after the house, and at Marie's request later disposed of a few additional pieces of unwanted furniture for her. The furniture was sold for $500, and she mailed the money — five $100 bills — to Marie at a California post office box.

Butch was the first to leave Trail Creek. He had been picked up shoplifting a tape cassette from a store in Michigan City, and his mother had to drive to the lockup to pick him up. Juvenile court authorities placed him on probation, but later agreed to drop their hold on him and permit him to move to California. Marie drove him to the O'Hare International Airport near Chicago, where he caught a flight to San Diego.

Butch moved into the RV park on San Ysidro Boulevard and enrolled in a nearby school. Marie told acquaintances that he was having troubles with the local schools and wasn't happy attending classes in Michigan City. She said she believed he would be better off starting over close to his brother.

At last, early in September, Marie loaded her

clothes and a few other personal items inside her Chevette. She locked up and drove away from Trail Creek. A neighbor's big, rumpled old yellow dog barked and took a halfhearted run at the vehicle, then lost interest as it pulled away.

Marie was headed west to join her sons and Eric's Navy buddies in San Diego. She didn't make the exhausting cross-country trip alone, however. The stress, worry, and guilt had also been working on Menkel. He went AWOL from the Navy, and he and another sailor pal who had been to the house on Johnson Road a few times drove to the West Coast with her.

Months later Menkel gave a curiously lame explanation for his flight from Great Lakes. He said he wanted to find out how much trouble he might be in over his involvement with the disappearance of Elaine Witte.

Seven

An Investigation

Skip Pierce had a gut feeling about Grandma Witte. He figured she was dead.

The premonition swept over him as he sat down with his friend, Roger Bernard, while the sheriff's deputy recounted his conversations with Max Trout.

Similar presentiments are common among police, especially for crime investigators. These flashes are as much experience, joined with a large dose of common sense, as they are ESP.

Coupled with the length of Elaine's absence, both Pierce and Bernard knew enough about the suspicious circumstances of Paul Witte's death to arouse their serious concern for her safety. Pierce assured his fellow officer that he would do some poking around and ask a few questions in an effort to dig up more solid information about Elaine's whereabouts.

Second-in-command and chief deputy of the

four-man Trail Creek police department, Pierce started off by passing on the information to his boss, Marshal Michael Chastain. A veteran of nearly three decades of small-town police work, the marshal had known Elaine for nearly twenty years. Never in all that time had he or any other law officer from the town ever had to make a domestic call or investigate any complaints of wrongdoing involving anyone living in the household.

Chastain drove over to the house to ask about her. A few days later, Pierce also stopped at 320 Johnson Road and asked about the old woman while investigating a report from Marie of a minor theft.

The replies from Marie and her son were disturbingly vague and often contradictory in details. But each of the lawmen was given basically the same story. Elaine had moved to California to be closer to her oldest grandson and to take advantage of the warm weather and easier living.

As Marie talked with Pierce, the veteran police officer listened carefully and watched her closely for any possible sign of nervousness. But she looked him in the eye, and neither her body language nor her speech betrayed any stress or discomfort. Marie talked in a normal tone of voice, with no hesitation or other indications that she was being careful in choosing her words. Elaine was on vacation, she declared. And that was that.

Nevertheless, neither Pierce nor his boss was satisfied with the too glib explanations. And when the husky deputy said he wanted to spend more time checking out Marie's story about Elaine's whereabouts, Chastain readily gave him the go-ahead. The Trail Creek marshal's department was small, but Chastain told his sergeant to spend as much time as he needed on the case. The marshal and the other two officers would fill in when necessary to carry out other duties while Pierce was busy looking for Elaine Witte.

The forty-six-year-old Pierce had spent about half of his working life in law enforcement. Born about thirty miles north of Trail Creek just across the state line in Benton Harbor, Michigan, he was a schoolboy when his family moved to Beverly Shores in 1956.

He was twenty-one when he began working part-time with the Beverly Shores police department. In 1962, however, he was inducted into the Army and assigned to a mechanized infantry unit in Germany.

Returning to northern Indiana after earning an honorable discharge in 1965, he worked for the Michigan City *News-Dispatch* as a linotype operator. But he missed the life of a policeman and soon found himself a part-time job in the field once more, this time with the Trail Creek town marshal's

Hilma Marie Witte, during the proceedings in LaPorte County Superior Court One to face charges in the murder of Elaine Witte, her stepmother-in-law.

Eric Witte, trailed by his mother, after his arrest for murdering
his father and helping dispose of his grandmother's remains.

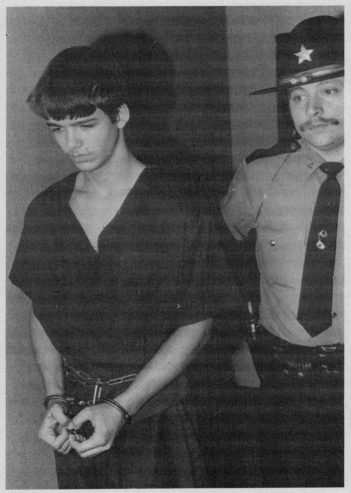

Hans Dieter "Butch" Witte, during the proceedings at LaPorte County Superior Court One in Michigan City.

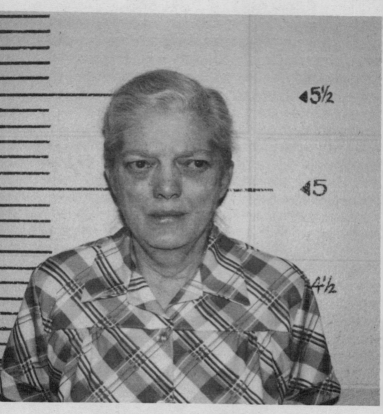

Margaret "Marcie" O'Donnell, Hilma Marie's mother, as she is being processed into the Indiana State Women's Correctional Facility. (*Courtesy of Indiana State Corrections Department*)

Paul J. Witte, steelworker, outdoorsman, and ill-fated husband of Hilma Marie.

Douglas Menkel, who admitted to being the lover of Hilma Marie and helping to dispose of Elaine Witte's body.

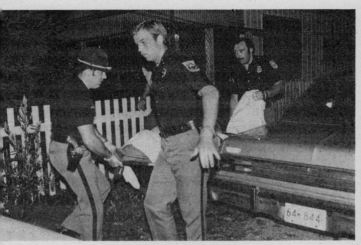

The body of Paul J. Witte being removed from his home in Beverly Shores. He was shot by his son Eric.

The house at 320 Johnson Road where Grandma Witte was murdered and dismembered.

Porter County courthouse in Valparaiso, where Hilma Marie Witte was tried for arranging the murder of her husband.

LaPorte County Superior Courthouse in Michigan City, where Hilma Marie Witte was tried for masterminding the slaughter of her stepmother-in-law.

Myron B. Crampton Security Center in Valparaiso, where Hilma Marie and her sons were held during court proceedings of the murder of Paul J. Witte.

William F. Herrbach, LaPorte County Chief Deputy Prosecutor, led the prosecution of Hilma Marie Witte and her sons in connection with the murder of Elaine Witte. Herrbach was later elected prosecutor. (*Courtesy of Bob Wellinski*)

Daniel R. Berning, Porter County Prosecutor, at the
time of Hilma Marie's trial for her husband's murder.

Scott King, the attorney who
represented Hilma Marie in
both of her murder trials.

Hilma Marie Witte, leaving the LaPorte County Superior Court One after her conviction for the murder of Elaine Witte.

Hilma Marie Witte, outside the LaPorte County Superior Court One after her sentencing for the murder of Elaine Witte.

department. In 1976, four years later, he was accepted on the department as a full-time officer.

Even then Pierce hadn't exactly broken into big-time police work. His duties in Trail Creek were similar to those in Beverly Shores. Much of his time during working hours was devoted to traffic enforcement and generally patrolling the town in a squad car. But he also handled his share of calls investigating thefts, burglaries, vandalism, rape and other sexual offenses, as well as a bit of everything else ranging from public intoxication, drug abuse, and domestic disturbances to stray dog complaints that are part of the life of both big-city and small-town law enforcement.

Trail Creek is like almost every other American suburb or small town, however, and Pierce occasionally found himself speeding to the scene of the stickup of a gas station, another small business, or an individual. A few times he worked with the FBI, the Indiana State Police, and the LaPorte County Sheriff's Department on bank robberies. He obtained some formal training in investigative techniques and other areas of police work when he attended the Indiana Police Academy at Plainfield, a few weeks after beginning part-time work with the marshal's department.

But he had never investigated a homicide; not even a suspected homicide. His first homicide investigation didn't begin shaping up until after he had his talk with Deputy Bernard about the lengthy and uncharacteristic absence of Elaine Witte from her home.

Pierce drove back to Johnson Road to talk with neighbors of the Wittes. He also chatted with some of Elaine's friends outside the neighborhood, including fellow members of the Indiana Bell Pioneers. Neighbors and friends told him that it wasn't at all like Elaine to go off on a vacation without telling them. And staying away so long without writing a single card or making a telephone call to the folks back home was unthinkable. Elaine simply didn't operate that way.

As he listened, Pierce dutifully recorded notes from his conversations in notebooks. Then he climbed back into his Trail Creek patrol car and drove away to interview someone else. He wound up with a collection of observations, suspicions, and rumors that helped him piece together a mosaic of the old woman's life and possible fate.

The conclusion Pierce drew from his talks was predictably grim. And he decided that it was time to confer with LaPorte County Prosecutor Walter P. "Skip" Chapala. Deputy Prosecutor Scott H. Duerring sat in on the meeting, and both he and his boss agreed there seemed to be a strong possibility that Elaine's uncharacteristic absence was due to a criminal act of some kind. Chapala and Duerring suggested Pierce continue the investigation and call on Indiana State Police Detective Boyd for help. Boyd had already met Marie Witte and her sons when he participated in the investigation of Paul's death.

The prosecutors and Pierce were well aware of interagency jealousies that frequently exist between different law enforcement agencies. Police work can be intense and stressful, and frustrations and personal likes and dislikes lead too often to disruptive quarreling between individual lawmen and women as well as between departments.

Detectives with a city or county police department may resent state police or federal agencies inserting themselves into an investigation and accuse them of taking over the operation or grabbing the glory for a big arrest. Veteran officers know that engaging in interagency rivalries and personal ego clashes is one of the surest ways to destroy an investigation. It squanders time and opportunities that can't be regained.

None of those things would be a problem for Pierce and Boyd, however. One reason was that, even with the support of Chastain and their fellow officers, Pierce knew the time he could devote to tracking down Elaine Witte was severely limited by the size of the Trail Creek marshal's department. He couldn't totally ignore his other work.

The other reason that the relationship between the two police officers would work was that Boyd was a crackerjack detective, an experienced professional who was good at his job and knew how to share authority and responsibilities when teaming up with investigators from cities and towns and county sheriff's departments. He got the job done without stepping on toes.

Pierce telephoned Boyd at the State Police Post in Lowell, and the veteran detective drove to Trail Creek for a talk. Then the two officers drove to the Witte house for a conversation with Marie.

Although Marie continued to appear calm, she may have been disturbed at seeing Boyd again. Boyd and Pierce had barely greeted her when she said she didn't know if she should be talking to them. But she agreed to talk after they pointed out they were merely asking for help locating her mother-in-law.

Marie repeated the story she had told before: Elaine was vacationing in California. But when Boyd and Pierce asked specific questions about how Elaine had traveled, who she traveled with, and exactly where she was staying, Marie's replies were vague and unsatisfactory.

The two lawmen began knocking on doors in the neighborhood, reinterviewing residents about Elaine's absence. They also reinterviewed the missing woman's friends outside the neighborhood.

At last they sat down together in the cramped

cubbyhole office Pierce shared with his colleagues in Trail Creek, and began mapping out a plan of action. On August 13, Pierce filed a formal missing person's report on Elaine, and information about the old woman was relayed to other police agencies in Indiana, Michigan, Illinois . . . and in California.

After the confrontation with Pierce and Boyd, Marie had no trouble making up her mind about leaving the house on Johnson Road. It would be months before she saw the police officers again; that would be in California.

When she arrived in southern California, she settled into the trailer at the RV park in San Ysidro. After the arrival of his mother and his Navy buddies, Eric began spending his evenings and weekends with them and Butch again, bringing along Schoonover and other sailor pals to visit the family and to play Dungeons & Dragons.

It was almost like old times. Marie began talking about selling the house in Indiana so they could buy their own home in southern California, somewhere near the organized jumble of Navy and Marine bases in the San Diego area where she would be permanently settled near her boys.

But there was still the troubling problem of the stubborn leftover chunks of Grandma Witte's skull and a few remaining pieces of her torso carried to

191

California in the portable cooler that had to be dealt with. For awhile Eric kept the cooler in a locked compartment in the back of the mobile home he was living in. Then he checked the cooler into a commercial storage bin in Chula Vista. A few weeks later after Menkel criticized him for renting the bin under his own name, Eric moved it again. He took it to another commercial storage facility, and this time registered it under a different name.

Once while some of the boys were idling away a few hours at the trailer playing Dungeons & Dragons, Eric asked Schoonover how he would get rid of a body. Coming out of the blue as it did, the question took the nineteen-year-old sailor by surprise.

"I don't know," he said. "Do you have a body?"

"Yes," Eric calmly responded.

Eric's reply was even more of a surprise than the original question.

Whose body was it, Schoonover asked.

Eric said it was his Grandmother Witte's. She had fallen down and accidentally killed herself, he explained in response to his buddy's continued questions.

Schoonover didn't understand why Eric's mother hadn't simply telephoned for the police or an ambulance, as most people would do if such an accident had occurred. Eric patiently explained that his mother was deathly afraid of the police.

The Navy pals nevertheless talked over the possibilities for disposal. Eric suggested that the remaining body parts might be left in a swamp where animals, decomposition, and other natural forces would soon return it to the earth. He also brought up the idea of dropping it in a trash bin so it would be carried away and disposed of by town refuse collectors. Menkel recommended placing the body in a boat, then sinking the boat.

Schoonover at last suggested that the most convenient and practical solution would be to discard the old woman's remains in a huge nearby landfill, where it would be unnoticed among the hoard of new refuse arriving there every day. Eric wouldn't tell his friend at that time exactly where the body was, except that it was in California.

Soon after that conversation, Schoonover was at the trailer one night when the boys left to get some take-out food, and Eric drove past a commercial storage rental business. The cooler with Grandma Witte's remains was in one of the lockers there, he told his pal.

A couple of nights later Schoonover got off duty late and arrived at the mobile home about 7:00 P.M. The trailer was full of sailors again, including Douglas Menkel, along with Butch and Marie.

193

Marie was in hysterics, trembling and crying uncontrollably.

"He did it for me. He did it for me," she moaned over and over. "It's all my fault. They're going to take my son away from me. They're going to take my Dougie away from me. And then I'll be in jail," she sobbed.

Eric tried to soothe his mother and assure her that no one was going to jail, and everything would be all right. Marie stopped sobbing for a moment. But about the time it appeared she was going to get control of herself, she choked up and burst into tears and moans again.

A day or two later the cooler was loaded into the pickup truck. Then Schoonover drove Marie to the Otay Mesa sanitary landfill in Chula Vista.

As sea gulls wheeled and screeched overhead like giant winged maggots and fat, gray Norway rats scurried through the piles of refuse, they dropped off the final remains of the old woman. The woman and the young man weren't yet out of sight before a landfill employee bulldozed the cooler with a Caterpillar.

Marie asked Menkel to drive her to the landfill the next day. She wanted to check and see if the cooler was still lying in the open or if the door might have been knocked off. She walked into the fill, stepping lightly over the piled-up mounds of new garbage and trash. When she returned to the car a few minutes later, she was satisfied. The cooler was nowhere to be seen. Grandma Witte had been dead almost exactly nine months.

While Marie and the boys were settling into their new homes and activities in southern California, Sergeants Boyd and Pierce were beating the bushes for information in northern Indiana, Michigan, and Illinois. They followed up every lead and tip on Elaine's possible whereabouts, no matter how tangential. They obtained subpoenas for bank and telephone records.

The bank records disclosed that Elaine's checking and savings accounts in Michigan City had been systematically drained while Marie was building up her personal account in the nearby town of Chesterton. Elaine's savings account was depleted first, with most of the funds transferred to her checking account. Then withdrawals were made from the checking account through drive-in windows and automatic teller machines.

The two sleuths also checked with Social Security authorities and learned that Elaine's checks had continued to be regularly signed with her name and cashed both before and after she was said to have left her home in Trail Creek for California. Boyd and Pierce asked for help from the United States Secret Service, and Larry F. Ziegler, a forensic document examiner with the agency, was assigned to study those signatures and those on other documents collected by the investigators for comparison.

Stationed with the Secret Service's Forensic Services Division in Washington, D. C., Ziegler was one of the best handwriting experts in the business. During more than fifteen years of training and experience in the field, he had become expert in handwriting identification, detection of forgery, and general identification of questionable documents.

Since the former Baltimore policeman began his federal law enforcement career and began specializing in the late 1960s, he had examined handwriting on threatening letters mailed to the President of the United States, federal judges, and other key government officials; documents tied to organized crime; also, suspected forgeries of government checks and other negotiables.

Most commonly, Ziegler makes his studies by comparing handwriting on questionable or threatening notes, documents, and checks with samples of the known handwriting of suspects. Microscopes and other equipment and techniques are used to scrutinize such components of handwriting as approach strokes, connecting strokes, terminal strokes, and pen pressure.

Pierce and Boyd didn't slow their probe of the Witte family while waiting for the results of

Ziegler's painstaking scrutiny of the handwriting samples. They continued opening up new areas of the investigation, and combed northern LaPorte County for clues.

The idea was even broached at one point of using an airplane and taking aerial photographs in an effort to pin down areas where minute changes in soil color or vegetation might indicate a body was buried. But information about the missing woman was still too nebulous, and the plan to take to the air was put on the back burner.

As they continued to probe the mystery of the old woman's disappearance, the detectives relayed regular reports to Duerring and to William F. Herrbach, who had been appointed a few months earlier as chief deputy prosecutor. Like Chapala, Herrbach was a second-generation law enforcement officer in LaPorte County. Chapala's father, Walter, had served as the county auditor and as the county prosecutor. Herrbach's father, Frank, was a highly respected and popular two-term LaPorte County sheriff in the late 1950s and early 1960s.

The sheriff had passed on his love and respect for the law to his son. The younger Herrbach earned a bachelor's degree at Indiana University before he was drafted into the Army during the Vietnam War. Volunteering for Officer Candidate School, he earned a commission and served a year in Vietnam as a company commander during his three-year stint of active service.

Returning home with the rank of captain, he joined the Army Reserve and entered law school at nearby Valparaiso University. After earning his law degree he went back into the Army, this time in the legal branch, defending GIs on a variety of charges. He remained on active military duty for another four years before returning to civilian life and joining the LaPorte County Prosecutor's staff.

Herrbach worked as a deputy prosecutor for six years before his appointment as chief deputy. He never regretted switching sides in the legal justice system. A law-and-order prosecutor, Herrbach decided early in his career that it would be difficult for him to justify defending not only certain crimes, but certain criminals as well.

As Herrbach began assuming a major role in directing the probe, George Baranowski, an investigator for the prosecutor's office, also joined the burgeoning inquiry.

By that time a reporter for the *News-Dispatch* had heard talk of Grandma Witte's mysterious absence and had begun to snoop around. Imaginative and innovative, Henry Lange was a veteran newsman who had spent twenty-five years with the Michigan City newspaper tracing the accomplishments and foibles of public servants and digging up other people's secrets. Before joining the *News-Dispatch*, he covered police and other area news for a local radio station. Over the years Lange had developed excellent contacts, and got along well with police and local politicians.

But when he started asking questions about Grandma Witte, his contacts in law enforcement and in local government clammed up. Neither Herrbach, Chapala, nor Pierce, whom Lange had known when they both worked for the same newspaper, would talk about the case. They wouldn't even admit there was a mystery or an investigation of any sort going on.

There was good reason for their intransigence, of course. Authorities themselves didn't yet know what had happened to Grandma Witte. And they didn't want to spook Marie or anyone else who might be involved in her disappearance with a newspaper story about the investigation. They were a long way from being ready to make an arrest. At that stage they didn't believe they could even justify requesting search warrants for the house, property, or vehicles at 320 Johnson Road.

So Lange talked with neighbors and friends of Elaine, who were more worried than ever about her uncharacteristic absence. Then he talked with his editors. Although there was general agreement that something was amiss and Lange had rounded up enough information for a story, it was decided to hold off. Neither the reporter not his superiors at the newspaper had any desire to hinder local law enforcement agencies, and they weren't in the business of fouling up important police investigations. Lange, however, continued to keep his eyes and ears open, watching and listening for tidbits of news about Elaine Witte.

The reporter didn't make any attempt at that time to talk to Marcie. She had been left behind in Michigan City, and she was terrified. Fear and conscience were stalking her and she tried to shout down her demons with her old standby, the bottle. She guzzled vodka and orange juice when she could afford it, and beer when money was especially short. Her frightened eyes deteriorated into a bleary wasteland. She stumbled around the apartment in an alcoholic haze. Even then, however, she couldn't totally forget.

On October 26, when Boyd and Pierce stopped at the apartment she shared with her friend, Jeannie, Marcie nevertheless stuck stubbornly to the same basic story her daughter and grandsons were telling. Marie's mother-in-law was in California, probably with the rest of the family.

The two tough lawmen didn't believe her frightened denials for a minute. But when they tried to pin her down on specifics, she was frustratingly evasive. Marcie stammered, backed up, and corrected herself. Her soggy whiskey eyes were wide with fear, and her sallow complexion was as yellow as a toad's belly. The miserable woman was wallowing in a quagmire of helplessness, and the terrible events of the past few months had overtaken her.

Marcie, along with her grandsons and her daughter, were trapped in a devilish netherworld inexorably bound together by guilt and the grim secrets they shared. Marcie didn't wear her guilt well, and the two lawmen weren't fooled by her boozy denials. They didn't give up. Even though they didn't obtain the information they were looking for, they managed to build a certain rapport with the confused and befuddled woman.

Boyd was no more successful in obtaining useful information when he drove a few miles into Michigan to question another relative of the Wittes. The woman apparently didn't know anything about what had happened to Grandma Witte. But Boyd's eyes widened when he turned to leave and saw a witch's hat and a witch's robe hanging on the back door. Both investigators had been hearing strange stories about eerie Satanic rites, witchcraft, ESP, and other darkling activities and abilities that were reputedly tied to Marie Witte and her boys. But on October 29, only three days after their earlier talk, Marcie contacted Boyd with a story that was even more bizarre.

Shortly before dawn the next morning Pierce was roused out of bed by a telephone call. His Indiana State Police colleague was on the line and said Marcie had admitted to him that Grandma Witte was dead. The detective wanted to get together at a Trail Creek restaurant for breakfast.

The call jarred Pierce wide-awake. Padding barefoot into the bathroom without bothering to turn the coffee maker on, he gave himself a quick shave, blotted the moisture from his face with a towel, and began pulling on his uniform. In less than twenty minutes after replacing the telephone receiver into the cradle, he was sliding into the driver's seat of his patrol car. Pulling out of his driveway, he steered toward the restaurant.

A waitress had barely poured hot coffee for the two lawmen and turned away before Pierce leaned over the table toward his companion.

"Where's the old woman's body?" he asked.

"There isn't any body," Boyd replied. "They got rid of it."

While Pierce absently spooned sugar into his steaming coffee cup, Boyd recounted what he had learned of the grisly dismemberment and destruction of Grandma Witte's corpse. Leaning over the table so that his face was close to Pierce's and interrupting his muted conversation only when the waitress approached to take their breakfast orders, Boyd laid out the macabre story of the murder and its aftermath.

Police would never find Grandma Witte, Marcie had told him, because she was shot to death with a crossbow, then cut up, chopped up, ground up and dissolved in acid. And her remaining body parts were scattered in areas of at least three states. Butch was the killer, and he, his mother, Eric, and others—including herself—had a hand in getting rid of the body, Marcie had related.

Marcie's confirmation that Elaine was dead was no surprise to either of the men. They had been virtually certain of that since beginning their investigation. But no one, not even the most experienced homicide investigator, could have anticipated the ghastly details linked to the disposal of the body. The story sounded more like something out of a Hollywood slasher film than real life.

Nevertheless, both officers realized that Marcie's nine-page, tape recorded statement represented the break in the case they were looking for. But the investigation wasn't wrapped up by any means.

After Boyd and Pierce left the restaurant, they conferred with prosecutors, passing on the startling new information and charting their next moves. Boyd also talked with his supervisor at the State Police Post in Lowell, and Pierce huddled with Chastain inside the cramped and littered marshal's office. Chastain and Pierce then had a private meeting with members of the Trail Creek town council. The council unanimously authorized Pierce to continue with the investigation and — importantly — agreed to back him up with funding from the municipality's modest budget.

Despite the optimistic new developments, however, investigators had little more than Marcie's word that Elaine was murdered. It was still too soon to obtain warrants for the arrests of Marie and her boys. But is wasn't too early to begin stepping up the pressure.

Boyd contacted officers with the San Diego Police Department's Homicide Division and the Naval Investigative Service and told them about the case. Officers with both agencies agreed to provide whatever assistance they could.

Then the two Hoosier policemen drove to the O'Hare International Airport at Chicago and boarded a flight for San Diego. The divorced father of two girls and a boy, Pierce had hurriedly tossed some trousers, a few shirts, socks, underwear, and a few personal grooming items into a single suitcase for the trip. Other passengers may have wondered about the solidly built man with the bull neck and close-cropped shock of hair if they could have peered into his carry-on bag and spotted the big Garfield doll that was stuffed inside.

Pierce's youngest daughter had given the stuffed cat to him for good luck and company. The small-town law officer had formed a habit of talking to the cartoon cat when he was troubled, alone, and needed to bounce complaints or ideas off someone. Garfield was a patient listener who never complained, and somehow it seemed to Pierce that things improved after their one-sided talks.

U. S. Naval investigators met Pierce and Boyd when they landed at San Diego International Airport-Lindbergh Field, and informed them that since learning of the homicide probe in Indiana they had kept Eric under close surveillance. After a brief meeting with the Navy investigators, Boyd and Pierce checked into a hotel. It was October 31, Halloween. To Pierce, the irony of the date seemed somehow fitting.

One slender crew-cut Navy sleuth, dressed in natty slacks, sports jacket with matching shirt and spit-shined shoes, indicated he had some initial doubts that Boyd and Pierce were really law officers.

"Are you guys packin'?" he finally asked, glancing through suspicious slitted eyes at their suit jackets. There were no telltale bulges to give away the presence of a shoulder holster or to otherwise indicate they were carrying weapons.

Boyd and Pierce were hurriedly putting their clothes on hangers and into dresser drawers, and they were unimpressed by the self-important strutting.

"No, we're unpackin'," Pierce grumbled. The burly small-town cop barely bothered to look up from his suitcase. He and Boyd had left their service revolvers behind. Carrying weapons on commercial airline flights is simply too much of a hassle, even for law enforcement officers. And both knew that if handguns were needed, their brother officers in California would be armed.

The Navy man still wasn't satisfied until he telephoned LaPorte and confirmed with a deputy prosecutor that Boyd and Pierce were indeed police officers from Indiana.

With the question of their identity at last settled to the distrustful Navy investigator's satisfaction, Boyd and Pierce swung into action. They met with San Diego city homicide detectives, with San Diego County Sheriff's Police and with agents from the U. S. Treasury Department, who were continuing to look into the probability that Elaine's signatures on her Social Security checks were being forged.

San Diego homicide detectives and Navy investigators, including the former Doubting Thomas, did everything they could to help the out-of-town lawmen. One of the Navy sleuths drove them to the trailer park in San Ysidro, and pointed out the trailer where Eric, Marie, and Butch were staying.

Local officers from San Diego helped maintain a near around-the-clock surveillance of the trailer and its occupants. They still had no arrest warrants.

Only Douglas Menkel had been taken into custody. Navy investigators and San Diego Police Department officers apprehended him on November 1 for being AWOL. And on the day the Indiana lawmen arrived in California he was briefly questioned about the murder of Elaine and disposal of her body. On November 2, he dictated an eleven-page statement to Navy investigators admitting his part in the cover-up. On November 3, he talked once more with police, this time with Boyd.

He related to the Indiana investigator that Marie told him Elaine was killed with a crossbow, but that Butch shot the old woman accidentally. Boyd passed on the information to prosecutors in La-Porte, but authorities weren't yet ready to request homicide warrants for the arrest of the Wittes. The investigation was paying off, but there was still considerable work to do before police were satisfied they had compiled sufficient evidence to prove probable cause.

Boyd's and Pierce's colleagues back in northern Indiana were also busy working the case. On the same day Menkel was giving his formal statements in San Diego, Baranowski obtained search warrants from the LaPorte County Superior Court for Elaine's house and for the recreation vehicle Marie left behind when she drove to California.

The LaPorte County Prosecutor's Office and other local law enforcement agencies had been busy while Pierce and Boyd were gone. Armed with the search warrant, they went through the house at 320 Johnson Road from top to bottom, looking for weapons, blood residue, and other evidence of the murder and disposal of a human body.

A platoon of detectives and technicians from the State Police Department, LaPorte County Sheriff's Department, Michigan City Police Department, and the Trail Creek Marshal's Office spread out through the house and yards searching for physical evidence to help prove the old woman was murdered and dismembered. The house was immaculately clean, but empty of almost all the furnishings.

Sergeant Matthew J. Jaworski, a field technician with the Northwest Indiana State Police Laboratory in Lowell, unhooked and removed the garbage disposal from under the kitchen sink. After disconnecting an electrical hookup to the junction box, he squeezed his upper body under the sink and dismantled the pipes connecting the unit to the sewer system, then lifted the entire device out. Jaworski noticed the garbage disposal appeared to be new, and the flooring under the sink was freshly painted. A new floor mat had been spread over the flooring.

Inspection of the kitchen appliance disclosed several strands of hair stuck inside. Additional hair was collected from the back porch.

In the basement Jaworski found a knife on a windowsill and added it to the growing collection of items the search team was gathering. Draperies were taken from window frames, and other furnishings were scooped up from the house and mobile home. The lawmen even collected paint chips from the basement floor, residue from the tile floor in the kitchen, and a red plastic apple containing white powder found in a kitchen cupboard.

After taking photographs at the scene, Jaworski eventually left with seventeen different items. One of the most intriguing pieces of possible evidence was a broadhead arrowhead Marcie said was imbedded in the inside wall of a closet. She complained she cut her finger on it while cleaning. Jaworski couldn't find it, so Marcie was taken upstairs and pointed it out to him. The arrowhead and the indentation had been expertly patched over with wood putty. Jaworski removed the whole board the arrow tip was imbedded in. All the potential pieces of evidence were taken to the crime laboratory for analysis.

On November 4, Marcie gave another statement to Indiana State Police Detective Sergeant Barry Rutherford. Two days after that, Marshal Chastain obtained a formal consent from Marcie to search the house she shared in Michigan City with Jeannie. Chastain and Jaworski conducted the search and found two gallons of muriatic acid. A single human tooth was later discovered and taken to the crime laboratory to be inspected.

Meanwhile, other law officers searched along county roads for the crossbow. They sifted through fire pits and burn piles where items taken from the house on Johnson Road were burned. A knife blade, the metal head of a hammer, chisel, hacksaw blades, scissors, keys, key chains, pieces of glass, bits of charred clothing, and other items were picked out of the ashes. The material was placed in evidence bags and sent to the Crime Laboratory for inspection and analysis.

But the crossbow was never recovered, and police later confirmed what they already suspected. It was burned. They were unable to find even so much as the smallest piece of charred wood or scorched metal. Failure to turn up the murder weapon made the arrowhead recovered from the closet a potentially important piece of evidence. It appeared to prove, at the very least, there had been a crossbow in the house.

Despite the flurry of activity, however, the situation in California appeared to have turned sour. Somehow, notwithstanding the close surveillance of the trailer, Marie and Butch had dropped from sight. No one with any of the various law enforcement agencies involved in keeping track of them knew exactly where they were.

Boyd and Pierce were rapidly running out of time and options. They were at a low point when they returned to their room. They were frustrated and discouraged. After traveling twenty-five hundred miles and spending a week in California, they had next to nothing to show for their efforts or for the expensive trip.

Boyd had talked once with Eric by telephone and another time in a face-to-face meeting. The young sailor was in class at the advanced corpsman's school at the huge Balboa Naval Hospital when military investigators summoned him to their office where the Indiana lawman was waiting. Eric's replies were carefully framed to be protective of his mother and younger brother.

But there had been no confrontations at all with Marie or Butch. The lawmen couldn't even sit down for a talk with Schoonover, who was off somewhere in the South Pacific aboard ship. None of the suspects in the affair had been taken into custody since Menkel was picked up; like Schoonover, he was a bit player who had stumbled naively into the tragedy. Neither sailor had anything to do with Elaine's murder or with the conspiracy to kill the old woman. All the information developed so far in the investigation indicated that neither of the young men was brought into the drama until weeks after the old woman's death.

Boyd picked up the telephone and checked the flights back to Chicago. His companion's bull neck was almost invisible in the weary slump of his shoulders as he listened to the telephone conversation. Then the dejected lawmen left the hotel to have a couple of drinks. They weren't feeling any better when they returned, and Boyd plopped down on his bed beside the stuffed yellow cat. The dejected policeman began having a little talk with his roommate's lucky charm.

"You haven't let us down yet, Garfield," the detective sergeant morosely mused to the doll. "But I guess it's time to pack it in."

The words had barely left Boyd's mouth before the telephone rang. He picked up the receiver and listened to the person on the other end of the line. The look of tiredness and depression which were scrawled on his features a few moments before, abruptly faded when he turned to Pierce.

"Marie and her boys have just been picked up at a bank in Chula Vista," he told his buddy.

The Secret Service had the mother and sons in custody. Federal charges were being filed against Marie and Eric by the U. S. Treasury Department for forgery and conspiracy to commit forgery, and they would be held in a federal lockup in San Diego.

Marie's arrest in California occurred almost exactly one year after she had begun helping herself to her mother-in-law's money.

Pierce had just enough time to peer at Garfield and shake his head in amazement before he and Boyd headed for the door. The lazy cat, or something just as welcome, had come through big-time.

A few hours later the Indiana lawmen were meeting with Butch in a juvenile lockup at the U. S. government complex in San Diego where he was being held. He was clearly upset, and his frightened eyes gleamed like newly snuffed coals.

Special Agent Steven Davis of the FBI had already talked with Butch after the boys and their mother were separated from each other and gotten a confession. At first Butch repeated the yarn his mother had concocted about Elaine being killed in an accidental shooting. Butch said he was playing with the crossbow in the dining room, when his mother told him to put it away. He was walking upstairs still fiddling with the weapon when Elaine emerged from behind a corner, startling him and causing him to discharge the bolt. It hit her in the chest. Butch said he didn't know anything about attempts to poison the old woman or to keep her drugged. He denied knowing anything about the events surrounding his father's shooting, and claimed he was in a soundproof playroom at the time.

Davis wasn't buying the story, and he continued to press for the truth. A few minutes later Butch confessed to the FBI agent that his grandmother's death wasn't an accident. He also agreed to talk with the Indiana lawmen, whom Davis said were on their way to the federal building.

A temporary guardian was hastily appointed by a local magistrate to protect the teenager's rights as a juvenile. And before any new questioning began, he was again read his Miranda rights against self-incrimination.

But Butch had made up his mind to talk. He said he was having trouble sleeping and wanted to get the story off his chest.

Confronting the subdued teenager in the spartanly furnished and bleak interrogation room, Pierce kept his voice and manner unemotional. He knew this was the defining moment of the biggest case he would ever work. There was no doubt about that. The deputy town marshal was neck-deep in an investigation that was being carried out by nearly a dozen law enforcement agencies that extended all the way to the U. S. Justice Department and the Pentagon.

But it wasn't time yet for musing about professional accomplishments; he was there to get the story of Elaine Witte's murder and its aftermath from her killer. There were times when Pierce's dark eyes had an easy mirth to them, a Jack Frost or Father Christmas crinkle of friendliness that somehow seemed to fit the winters in the Dunesland area where he had chosen to live. But there was no hint of that as he questioned the nervous boy. He was deadly serious, and his eyes had their most menacing "staring down a street punk" look.

Butch's round, smooth adolescent's face was stripped of all its usual surly defiance while he talked late into the night. The words tumbled from his mouth in a torrent of ugliness. When his audio and videotaped statement was transcribed, there were thirty-one pages. Then he gave another statement that was nine pages. He gave Boyd and Pierce the same basic story he told the FBI agent after deciding to tell the truth about Grandma Witte's murder.

He said he shot his grandmother because his mother made him do it.

It was a few minutes before midnight when Butch was finally through, and the weary boy was led back to his cell. The two police officers from Indiana were near the end of an exhausting day when they at last left the lockup and drove through the early morning neon streets of San Diego back to their motel. But they were exhilarated by the breakthrough and sat up for more than an hour talking before finally turning in.

Eric and his mother were locked in separate sections of the Metropolitan Correctional Center in San Diego. Marie refused to talk with the Indiana investigators.

After their meetings with the suspects, Boyd and Pierce boarded a flight for the return to the Midwest. Marshal Chastain drove to O'Hare International in his squad car to meet them in the terminal and chauffeur them back to LaPorte County. They had collected the lion's share of the information they needed to bring the killers of Elaine Witte to justice. Marcie's tortured admission had put them on the right track to unlocking the puzzle, but Butch's guilt-ridden confession was the key.

Eight
Negotiations

Henry Lange put in a routine day at his job as a police reporter for the *News-Dispatch* before at last heading for home, a hot meal, and a few hours of relaxation. When he finally crawled into bed shortly before midnight, he was exhausted and fell asleep in minutes.

Lange had been in and out of the Michigan City Police Department talking with the chief, detectives, and patrolmen; swung by the fire department; shuffled through a few criminal case files in the LaPorte County Superior Court Clerk's Office; peeked in for a few moments on a trial.

Then he returned to the newspaper and busied himself with the telephone, checking police and fire departments in Trail Creek, Beverly Shores, and other communities in the *News-Dispatch*'s circulation area, and calling the county sheriff in LaPorte to see what new troubles residents or visitors in the area had gotten themselves into overnight.

217

At last he wrote his stories for that day's edition of the afternoon newspaper, grabbed a sandwich and a bowl of soup at a cafe across the street from his office, and started all over again.

Lange was sleeping soundly at about 2:00 A.M. when his telephone rang. Half awake, he picked up the receiver and mumbled hello.

"Henry?"

"Yeah," he replied drowsily.

"You better get dressed and get on down to the courthouse," the caller advised. "There's something going on there I think you want to know about."

With that, the caller hung up!

The call had jolted Lange wide-awake, and moments later he was wriggling into his pants, buttoning his shirt, and lacing up his shoes. Scooping his billfold and keys up from a dresser top, he headed out the door and into the crisply cold early November night.

The streets around the courthouse, municipal library, newspaper, and other buildings were deserted when he arrived at the local government and business complex in the center of Michigan City's downtown area. Nearby buildings were so cloaked in shadow that Lange could barely make out the form of the northern Indiana Public Service Company's giant spool-shaped water cooling

218

tower that dominated the skyline along the lake-shore as he carefully guided his car into the darkened parking lot next to the courthouse.

The gray stone box-shaped hall of justice was ablaze with lights when Lange bounded up the steps of the building two-at-a-time and hurried to the second-floor courtroom. Several police officers and deputy prosecuting attorneys were already standing around inside, talking animatedly in stage whispers as they waited for the judge to emerge from his chambers. Lange recognized Herrbach, Baranowski, Chastain, and a few other people.

But the reporter didn't even have time to ask anyone what was going on before Judge Arthur A. Keppen swept through the door from his chambers with a rustle of black judicial robes and climbed into his chair. It was then, through the judge's crisp courtroom announcement, that the reporter learned why he had been roused out of bed at such an ungodly hour.

Judge Keppen had just convened a probable cause hearing, a judicial proceeding that starts the machinery of the law in motion to punish a crime. The hearing is required to legally establish before a judge or magistrate that a crime has been committed.

And this hearing was designed to show that Elaine Witte had been murdered in her home; then, over a period of months, Marie, her sons, and others had conspired to destroy and dispose of her remains.

Coincidentally, as the grisly story began unfolding in the near deserted courtroom, about a block away catty-cornered from the courthouse at the intersection of Michigan Boulevard and Franklin Street, one of the worst fires in Michigan City history broke out in the Commerce Square Apartment Complex. The fierce blaze was the handiwork of an arsonist who had been plaguing the city for months.

While the sirens of police cars, firetrucks, and other emergency vehicles shrieked outside, inside the courthouse Judge Keppen and others listened to a chilling account of wicked secrets, human degradation, and murder.

Baranowski, Chastain, and other investigators outlined for the court what they knew about the brutal slaying and dismemberment of Elaine Witte. In his testimony Chastain disclosed Butch's confession, obtained only a few hours earlier. During questioning by Herrbach, Chastain said that three of Elaine's neighbors reported the previous May that they hadn't seen her lately and were worried about her.

The town marshal patiently traced the investigation by Pierce and Boyd, including their conversations with Marie, their determination that Elaine hadn't been seen by anyone outside the family since December, and finally the flight to California that culminated in Butch's confession.

Chastain said that Butch admitted killing his grandmother in their home on Johnson Road by shooting her with a crossbow.

Chastain recounted how Marie had advised her son that it was time to kill his grandmother. "She gave him three choices: strangulation, suffocation, or the crossbow," the town marshal explained.

There was a moment of stunned silence as the mental image of the act clawed at the minds of the little knot of men assembled in the courtroom. When Herrbach resumed his questioning, however, the testimony became even more gruesome, as Chastain recounted Butch's grim story of how the old woman's body was cut up, ground up, and disposed of.

Chastain also testified about Menkel's statements and the roles that he and Eric played in helping to get rid of the body.

During questioning of Baranowski, the prosecutor's investigator identified the motive for the murder as money. Continuing to respond to questions from Herrbach, he traced Marie's looting of her mother-in-law's bank accounts and forging and cashing of the Social Security and pension checks. The investigator recounted the early morning conversation between mother and son when Marie told Butch that Grandma Witte had to be killed.

Throughout the testimony, Marie was identified as the conniving Circe who conceived, organized, and directed the murder and disposal of the body.

At the conclusion of the grim testimony, Judge Keppen ruled probable cause had been shown to indicate a crime was committed. At approximately 3:30 A.M., he swore out warrants for the arrests of Marie, Eric, Butch, and Menkel. Butch was charged with murder; Marie with being a accessory by aiding, inducing, or causing a murder; Eric and his friend Menkel with assisting a criminal after the fact. All the charges were felonies.

Lange had collected a half-dozen pages of furiously scribbled notes when Judge Keppen concluded the hearing. As Keppen walked from the courtroom, the reporter bounced a couple of quick questions at Baranowski and Herrbach, then dashed outside and hurried toward the roped-off perimeters police had set up around the burning buildings.

Shouting questions over the wail of sirens from trucks racing into the city from neighboring communities, the crackle of flames, and the shower of collapsing brick and stone, Lange began scribbling a new set of notes. Later he recalled the early morning flurry of activity as "one of the craziest nights I can remember."

222

The lead story in that afternoon's edition of the *News-Dispatch* wasn't about the destructive fire in the downtown area or about the firebug who set it. A screaming banner in type almost as large as the newspaper logo announced: "4 held for grisly murder." Similar headlines and articles were carried in other area newspapers, including the *LaPorte Herald-Argus*, Valparaiso's *Vidette-Messenger*, the *Gary Post-Tribune*, and the *South Bend Tribune*.

In an interview with a reporter for the *Herald-Argus*, Herrbach credited Butch's statement as being the key to the investigation.

"The only way you break a case like this is through an admission or confession," he remarked.

Later, he added an observation about Butch that he would repeat several times in court during trials and pretrial hearings: "He just did what his mom said."

The bizarre story was played prominently on most area radio and television newscasts, as well as in the newspapers. It stayed in the news, usually on front pages and in prominent spots on radio and television, for months. Like almost every other city of any appreciable size in the United States, Michigan City had its share of violent crime. For the most part, however, it was typically stupid and unimaginative violence: drug rip-offs gone bad, muggings, rapes, and bruising barroom fights over an insult or over a woman.

This was different. The story of Elaine Witte's murder could have been a dark tale crafted by Edgar Allan Poe, Clive Barker, or Stephen King. But it was no idle work of fiction. It was all true! Furthermore, residents of Michigan City and surrounding communities learned that the victim was one of their neighbors, and the accused killers had also lived among them.

There hadn't been such a notorious murder in LaPorte County for nearly a century, and a woman was also at the center of that case. Belle Gunness was in fact one of America's first and most prolific serial killers.

A big, powerful woman, Belle was twenty-two years old in 1881 when she immigrated to the United States from Norway under her maiden name, Brynhild Paulsdatter Storset. Americanizing her first name to Belle and marrying another Norwegian immigrant, she settled in Chicago. But a candy shop the hardworking couple opened burned down, then two houses, one after another, were destroyed by fire. Everything was covered by insurance.

A daughter died, then a son. Finally, Belle's husband died, leaving her with more insurance money. Curiously, both children and the husband had succumbed to acute stomach upset, a symptom of strychnine poisoning. No one, however, questioned the deaths.

By that time Belle had had enough of Chicago, and with her two surviving children and a young neighbor girl, she moved to a farm a couple of miles from LaPorte. Belle soon married again, but her new husband died. So she began advertising in the lovelorn columns of a Norwegian newspaper for mates.

Several men left their homes, most with considerable amounts of cash in their pockets, to meet the lonely lady in LaPorte. But they were never heard from again. Several men Belle took on at the farm as hired hands also disappeared.

On April 28, 1908, Belle's farmhouse burned to the ground. The remains of four bodies were found in the basement. Three of them were children. The other was the headless corpse of a woman. The LaPorte County sheriff decided that the female corpse was Belle's and the unfortunate widow had died in the fire with the children.

Then investigators began finding other bodies or portions of dismembered bodies and bones at the farm. Most of them were the remains of adult males. In addition to the horribly charred corpses recovered from the basement, searchers recovered the remains of twelve other victims and various additional body parts. At least ten men were buried under the hog pen, and two women or girls were interred in a garden a few feet from the house.

Historians eventually counted up sixteen certain victims for the American female serial killer, and another twelve possible murders. One of Belle's hired hands was arrested and charged with arson and murder shortly after the horror at the farm was first discovered. But after more than a year he was freed from custody and cleared of all charges.

By that time local law enforcement authorities were also hedging their bets that the headless woman found in the basement was not Belle. There were simply too many sightings of her reported in the area. Some people claimed to have seen her in LaPorte after the fire; others at South Bend; yet another at the train station in Decatur. Belle Gunness sightings continued, in fact, into the mid-1930s.

Belle Gunness was an unholy terror, but an old one. Grandma Witte's ghastly slaying was new and as fresh as the six o'clock news.

The story local residents began calling "the crossbow murder" was almost too outrageous to believe. Men and women talked about it in coffee shops, taprooms, factories, and offices throughout the Dunesland area. Anyone who had known any of the Wittes was treated as an instant expert on the case and shared in the family's doubtful celebrity.

With their worst fears confirmed, three of Grandma Witte's friends from the Indiana Bell Pioneers got together and organized a memorial service for her. On a chill Wednesday afternoon in early December about a week before the retirement club's annual Christmas Party, almost fifty people trooped mournfully into the St. John's United Church of Christ for the services led by the Rev. Paul Frankenfeld. The mourners were friends and people who had worked with Elaine at Indiana Bell. Elaine had apparently left no blood relatives.

Public disclosure of the murder also jolted Beverly Shores and Porter County law enforcement authorities into taking another, closer look at Paul Witte's suspicious shooting. Beverly Shores's new Town Marshal Richard Landis and Porter County Prosecutor Daniel Berning told reporters the investigation of the outdoorsman's death was being revived.

While Dunesland residents gossiped and conjectured about the ghastly slaying, law enforcement authorities still had a lot of investigating to do. Before the end of the day, warrants were prepared and sent on their way to San Diego county authorities requesting the arrest of Marie and her sons on the LaPorte County charges.

Authorities were hopeful that the Wittes would waive extradition, as most out-of-state criminal defendants do. If they refused, however, the Indiana Attorney General would be asked to initiate legal proceedings to have them returned to face trial.

Menkel was already being transferred to the brig at the Naval Training Center at Great Lakes for going AWOL. The warrant for his arrest was sent to Great Lakes, and plans were made for his transfer to the LaPorte County Jail in LaPorte.

Two days after making his confession, during a hearing in San Diego, Butch also waived extradition proceedings, and the prosecutor began arranging for his return to LaPorte County. Herrbach disclosed that although Butch was a juvenile, he expected to put him on trial in adult felony court because of the seriousness of the crime.

In the meantime, the imaginative teenager was back at his old habit of spinning tall tales. Butch was being held at a juvenile detention center in San Diego when he confided to a child psychiatrist that Elaine was murdered because she learned of a big dope deal Marie was involved in with the Mafia. The old woman was all set to blow the whistle to federal officers if she hadn't been killed, Butch claimed.

* * *

But from the very beginning, the prosecution in LaPorte and Porter Counties placed a priority on obtaining murder convictions against the person who orchestrated the killing plots against both Elaine and Paul. Herrbach, especially, was firmly convinced that Marie was the mastermind behind Elaine's murder. He was determined to see to it that when charges were finalized and balanced out against all the people connected with the slaying and the disposal of the body, that Marie would be properly dealt with. He expected to file much more serious charges against her, and was open to negotiations with the other defendants that could possibly lead to more lenient sentences in return for testimony and other help in convicting Marie of murder.

Although it can be extremely difficult to convict a defendant of murder without the body of the victim, it is not unknown in the United States. Herrbach was confident that even though both Elaine's body and the murder weapon were destroyed, he could obtain convictions. And he was determined to convict Marie of murder.

He had four witnesses, including Butch, Menkel, and hopefully, Eric, whom he expected to be able to call to testify that they had seen the body or parts of the body of Elaine Witte after her murder. Herrbach refused to immediately name the fourth witness in public statements about the case.

She was named a few days later when Marcie was arrested and locked up in the LaPorte County Jail on a charge of assisting a criminal, for her part in helping dispose of Grandma Witte's corpse.

The popular myth about criminals hanging tough and sticking together is just that — a myth. Marie's sons, her mother, even her lover, had either already provided damaging statements against her or eventually would. It was a rush of betrayal, a raspy chorus of accusation that started first with a solo, changed to a duet, then a trio, and finally a quartet; all anxious to minimize their own roles and point the finger of guilt at Marie as the ruthless female Svengali who lured every one of them into her evil enterprise.

The testimony of Marcie and the others would be critical to Herrbach's efforts to prove the *corpus delicti*. Although it is commonly believed by people outside the law enforcement and legal community that the *corpus delicti* is the body of the victim, the legal term actually refers to the "body of the crime." And to prove *corpus delicti*, it must be shown that a death occurred through criminal means.

It still helps the prosecution to have a corpse or portions of a corpse such as bones, other body parts, even hair. One of the most engrossing murder prosecutions of recent years became known in the press as "the wood chipper killing." In that case Richard Crafts, a former Eastern Airlines pilot from Newton, Connecticut, was convicted of murdering his Danish-born wife, Helle.

Investigators recovered only one gold-capped tooth and less than an ounce of bone fragments after the body of the Pan American Airways stewardess was sliced up with a chain saw and fed through a wood chipper in 1986. It was enough to prove *corpus delicti*, and convict her husband of the diabolical murder. Crafts was sentenced to fifty years in prison.

Herrbach didn't have even an ounce of bone or a gold-capped tooth. Not even the hair that evidence technicians lifted from the garbage disposal could be linked to Elaine. Although forensic tests determined that it was human, without a head there was nothing to compare it with in efforts to prove that it was Elaine's. And laboratory tests of draperies, bedclothing, and other items taken by police during the search of the house also failed to turn up any trace of blood. Nor were any narcotics or marijuana found.

And forensic dental tests on the tooth found in the house Marcie shared with her friend, Jeannie Frye, indicated that it had been removed from someone between the ages of eighteen and twenty-one. There was absolutely no medical or scientific possibility it could have come from a woman

Grandma Witte's age.

Nevertheless, the chief deputy prosecutor was confident that through his eyewitnesses and other evidence, he could obtain convictions for Elaine's murder.

And investigators weren't yet ready to give up on the idea of recovering bone fragments or other possible body parts from the elderly woman's corpse. Federal authorities in San Diego had the first crack at prosecuting Marie and Eric, so the northern Indiana sleuths had some time to continue their investigation and search.

The Navy continued to do everything possible to assist in the probe, and Naval Investigation Service agents arranged for Seabees to search the Otay Mesa Landfill for the cooler with Grandma Witte's final remains. Working in the blistering southern California sun, sailors maneuvered huge Caterpillars over the dump for days, digging up and moving tons of refuse in efforts to turn up the cooler. But the dump was simply too big, and the search was unsuccessful.

In Indiana, law officers from a half-dozen agencies continued the search for body parts or particles believed to have been dumped or burned at various locations in the Dunesland area. The former Witte property in Beverly Shores had been acquired by the Dunes National Lake Shore, and one of the park rangers discovered an old septic there.

During a joint search of the tank by the ranger, Pierce, Sheriff's Deputy Bernard, and officers from the town marshal's department in Beverly Shores, the team recovered a hunting knife, a set of nunchuks, and a couple of old walkie-talkies. Checking out the serial numbers on the walkie-talkies, investigators learned they were stolen from the Beverly Shores Fire Department about the time Paul Witte was killed. But there was no trace of Grandma Witte's remains.

Pierce and Bernard also tramped through some brush near an area where Eric and a friend of his from Beverly Shores were reportedly seen wandering around the previous summer, but came up empty-handed.

The detectives had already learned from their interrogation of some of the suspects that portions of Grandma Witte's flesh were mixed with potting soil before being disposed of. But Pierce's revulsion deepened when he heard another story that was even more gross and disturbing. One of his sources told him that the Wittes bought a hybrid timber wolf in Michigan to which they tried to feed the parts of the old woman's corpse. But the wolf refused to eat the meat, even after it was cooked, so they got rid of the animal.

Neither Pierce nor anyone else ever confirmed the report. But in light of other known aspects of the murder case, the tale of the wolf couldn't be discarded out-of-hand as being too weird to be true.

While the search for remains continued in La-Porte and Porter Counties, two LaPorte County Sheriff's deputies boarded a flight at O'Hare International for San Diego to pick up Butch and return him to Indiana. In the meantime, Menkel was also transferred from the Navy brig in Great Lakes to the LaPorte County Jail.

He was in handcuffs and dressed in jail-issue jumpsuit and white sneakers when he appeared at a plea hearing on charges of assisting a criminal. In response to questions from the judge, the somber Navy seaman replied that he didn't have any money, a car, or other property he could use to hire a lawyer. The judge entered a preliminary plea of not guilty for him, established bond at $10,000, set a preliminary trial date for early 1985, and said he would appoint a pauper attorney. Robert Beckmann was later named as the attorney.

A Michigan City lawyer, Steve Snyder, was appointed by the court as Butch's pauper attorney. Along with the job of defending Butch, Snyder also became the youth's official guardian. Atley Price, another Michigan City lawyer, became the second member of Butch's defense team.

Shortly after the teenager's return by commercial flight, Herrbach obtained a waiver and detention hearing before Judge Don Harner in LaPorte County Juvenile Court in Michigan City on a petition to permit the boy's continued jail custody and his prosecution as an adult. At the conclusion of the closed hearing, the case against Butch was transferred to adult court on charges of murder. His trial date was set for April 1, 1985.

Butch remained in the juvenile section of the jail, while Snyder began filing pretrial motions,

In one of the motions, Snyder asked for a change of venue to move the trial to another county, excluding the adjoining counties of Porter, Starke, and St. Joseph. He cited intensive publicity in the four-county northern Indiana area for prompting his request. Prosecutors responded by arguing that the press throughout the nation had already given widespread attention to the sensational case, so a change of venue to another county wouldn't make any difference. Judge Martin turned down the petition.

Snyder also filed a motion indicating he would base his defense on a claim of temporary insanity, and asked the court to appoint psychiatrists to examine Butch. Court appointment of psychiatrists is a requirement in accordance with the Indiana

State Criminal Code when an insanity defense is used.

Judge Martin appointed psychiatrists Chester McClure and George Batacan to carry out the examination. During his interviews with McClure, Butch reverted to the same old braggadocio and posturing he had tried with neighborhood girls in Trail Creek and his schoolmates. He still had some fanciful tales to tell. Butch advised the psychiatrist that he held a black belt in martial arts, and had captured an Indiana state championship in longbow archery. He claimed he had to live on the street for awhile after he was kicked out of his home by his mother when he was eleven years old. He also talked of reputedly working for a time as an enforcer for a rough gang of drug dealers and street toughs in Michigan City. Despite what appeared to be tall-tale telling, Dr. McClure concluded after his interviews that Butch was sane at the time Elaine was killed.

Dr. Batacan interviewed Butch twice, and concluded that he was a sociopath, an individual with an immature personality and a lack of moral judgment. Both psychiatrists were struck by the boy's unemotional, almost cavalier attitude when he discussed the murder of his grandmother and other traumatic family events.

Butch was disturbingly composed when he explained to Dr. McClure that he and his mother were playing a game of Dungeons & Dragons when she first suggested he murder his grandmother. He told the psychiatrist they often played the fantasy game.

It was determined by the court after considering the psychiatric findings that Butch was competent to stand trial for his grandmother's trial.

Herrbach had been skeptical from the beginning about the chances of an insanity defense working for Butch, and took a tough public stance, insisting that the only plea he would accept would be a plea of guilty to murder.

But there was other business to attend to before Butch could be put on trial. Early in February he and Menkel were flown back to San Diego to attend Marie's and Eric's federal court trials. Herrbach, Boyd, and Pierce, as well as bank executives and tellers from Michigan City, also flew west for the proceeding. Herrbach drew on his firsthand knowledge of the defendants' Indiana activities relating to the case to assist the U. S. attorney who headed the prosecution in California.

Eight men and four women were selected for the jury. But when a woman juror became ill before the trial started, she was replaced with a male alternate.

Federal prosecutors called twenty-two witnesses

to testify during the five-day trial, including Ziegler, other Secret Service agents, Butch, Menkel, and the bank employees. The defense called only one witness. On February 15, 1985, after only three hours of deliberation over two days, the jury returned guilty verdicts against Marie and Eric on eight charges each of forgery and conspiracy for signing and cashing Grandma Witte's Social Security checks.

A few weeks later, U. S. District Judge William B. Enright sentenced Marie to ten years in federal prison. The judge also fined her $10,000 and ordered her to pay $400 to a crime victim's fund and to make $1,335 in restitution for checks she cashed while she was living in the San Ysidro RV park. Eric drew a four-year prison sentence. Judge Enright explained that the Navy seaman was given a lesser sentence because the primary responsibility was Marie's.

After the trial, Boyd and Pierce returned to Indiana to continue the investigation, while extradition proceedings against Marie and her son were continued in the courts.

Navy investigators meanwhile had caught up with Schoonover in the Philippines when the *Leahy* pulled into Subic Bay on Christmas Eve. The lengthy Pacific cruise had already taken the ship to Pearl Harbor, Yokosuka, Japan, and

Hong Kong. The frightened sailor denied he knew anything about Grandma Witte's disappearance. "I have not been told by any of the Wittes that she was dead, or that they were the cause of her death," he declared.

By the time the Naval Investigative Service agents concluded their talks with Schoonover and he was free to return to his ship nearly three weeks later, the *Leahy* had left for the Indian Ocean and a stop at the port in Mombasa, Kenya. He was flown to the Indian Ocean to rejoin his ship and remained aboard during stops in Australia, back to Subic Bay, and finally to Pearl Harbor. In Hawaii he left his ship on leave once more to visit his family, and returned to duty after it was back at its home port in San Diego.

Schoonover had visited exotic ports and seen much of the world during the ship's cruise. But events in a midsized town in Indiana were gripping him in an emotional vise and appeared to be closing in.

Pierce also contacted the New York City Police Department for help locating another of the sailors who had hung around with Eric and his buddies and made trips to Indiana, for questioning about the case. NYPD detectives quickly tracked the Navy man down in Queens. He was the other Eric. But he didn't have much information, and wasn't a great help.

Pierce nevertheless continued years later to marvel about the exemplary cooperation between law enforcement agencies that marked the entire course of the investigation.

"Can you imagine the New York Police Department getting a call for help from someone in the Trail Creek, Indiana, marshal's department, and then moving out on the case just like it was one of their own?" he asked.

Pierce and his colleagues obtained assistance from yet two more police agencies when they learned that a gray 1983 Chevette had been found abandoned on a deserted road a few miles outside of Effingham, Illinois, and towed to the city police auto pound on November 20. Effingham police notified authorities that the vehicle was registered in LaPorte County to Hilma Marie Witte.

Boyd and Pierce quickly got in touch with Effingham police and asked them to impound the car. The Indiana officers told their Illinois colleagues there was a good chance it was used to dispose of the body of a murder victim. Then the two sleuths climbed into an Indiana State Police helicopter and were flown to Effingham.

The possible connection between Marie's car and Effingham appeared to be obvious. Someone driving across country from Michigan City to San Diego could easily route themselves through the south central Illinois community of eleven thousand people if they picked up Interstate 57 at one of the interchanges around Park Forest or Chicago Heights in chicago's south suburban area, then continued downstate on a near straight line. The driver could then swing west on Interstate 70 at Effingham, and drive west past St. Louis to the coast.

Illinois State Police met the Indiana officers at the airport in Effingham and drove them to the Effingham County courthouse. With assistance from local state and city police, Boyd and Pierce obtained a search warrant. Then, with the help of Illinois State Police evidence technicians and officers from the Effingham Police Department, they made a painstakingly precise search of the car.

The inspection created more questions than answers. The only trace of Elaine Witte was a letter she had written. Found in the glove compartment, it was innocently chatty, and dealt primarily with comments about a Sunday school. But a jacket, several belts, and a bagful of coins collected from various locations in the car added a frustrating new element of mystery to the investigation.

After returning to Indiana with the material, Pierce talked with Detective Larry Bittner of the

San Diego Police Department's robbery division and learned the car had been used in a house burglary there. Curiously, however, the burglary in which the coins and clothing were stolen didn't occur until after the Wittes and Menkel had all been arrested and were behind bars.

Any theories that Marie's car was abandoned in Effingham because it was utilized to discard bits and pieces of Elaine's cadaver were virtually overruled by news that it was used in a burglary after her apprehension.

It appeared more likely that another sailor or civilian had used it in the San Diego burglary, then driven it to the Midwest. Pierce released the coins and other evidence to Detective Bittner in San Diego.

In mid-February Schoonover again talked with Naval Investigative Service agents about the Wittes. The NIS officers opened the conversation by advising him that he was suspected of helping cover up the murder of Elaine Witte "after the fact" and assisting in the disposal of remains. This time he told a different story and confirmed that he had developed some suspicions about what was really going on. He admitted driving Marie and the cooler to the landfill, but he continued to guard some of his secrets. When the interrogation ended, Schoonover returned to duty, shaken more than ever, but still free of any criminal charges. The NIS officers passed on the results of their talk with the sailor to authorities in Indiana.

Then prosecutors worked out an early April Fools' Day surprise with Butch's defense attorneys. They reached a plea agreement permitting the boy to plead guilty to a scaled down charge of voluntary manslaughter for his role in Grandma Witte's murder. In return, he promised to testify against his mother at her murder trial. There would be no trial for Butch.

Plea agreements aren't always popular, but they are a necessary part of the legal process. Defenders of the practice point out that it is such an ingrained part of the court system that impossible gridlocks would occur in the already overburdened criminal courts if it was somehow abolished. There simply aren't enough judges, prosecutors, and other court officers—even courtrooms to take every case to trial. And some defendants couldn't be convicted without the testimony of accomplices or coconspirators.

Despite the plea agreement, however, Butch could face a maximum term of twenty years in prison. Taking Indiana's "good time" provision, which rewards convicts with one day off their sentences for every day of good behavior, he could actually serve as little as nine-and-one-half years.

Additionally, he would be credited for the time already served and still to be spent in jail during legal proceedings.

According to the plea agreement, if the maximum sentence was imposed, Butch couldn't look forward to release until he was about twenty-six years old or older. If the judge chose to do so, however, he could order the minimum term of only six years, which would enable Butch to be freed before he was twenty-one, once the "good time" provision was applied.

But even the maximum sentence offered a big improvement over the youth's outlook if he had been put on trial and convicted of murder. Then the most lenient possible sentence he could have hoped for would have been forty years. After that was cut in half with good time, he still could not have been freed before he was thirty-six years old.

Herrbach hadn't sought the death penalty for Butch, although it wasn't unknown among Indiana juries at the time to order capital punishment for juveniles. In nearby Lake County as pretrial proceedings in the Witte murders were underway, fifteen-year-old Paula Cooper and schoolgirl friends stabbed an elderly Bible teacher to death during a robbery in the old woman's home. Paula was pinpointed as the ringleader and sentenced to die in the electric chair, setting off an international furor among opponents of the death penalty that eventually led to a plea for mercy from

Pope John Paul, II. Four years later the Indiana Supreme court ruled that the Gary girl's execution would be unfair because she would be the youngest person ever executed in the state, and directed that she be resentenced to sixty years in prison.

Late in May, nearly five months since the arrest of Marie and her sons in California, she and Eric were ordered extradited to Indiana. U. S. District court Judge Wayne L. Peterson in San Diego issued the order. Marie and her oldest son had been held there in a federal lockup since their conviction on the forgery charges.

Once more Boyd and Pierce were driven to O'Hare, where they caught a flight for the West Coast. This time it was their final trip to San Diego, and they were accompanied by Bernard.

When the lawmen returned on another commercial flight, they boarded with their prisoners ahead of other passengers and took four seats in a middle aisle, along with an additional outside seat. Marie and Eric were seated in the middle, between Boyd and Pierce. Bernard took the aisle seat directly across from Boyd. Both police and prisoners wore civilian clothes.

Members of the Denver Police Department, including a female officer, met them at the airport during a ninety-minute layover in the Mile High City and escorted them to a secluded room. No one among the other busy travelers in the terminal appeared to notice anything special about the tight knot of men and women as they stepped briskly along the corridor. For the first time since the policemen and their prisoners began the flight back to the Midwest, Marie and Eric were handcuffed as soon as they entered the room. The cuffs were removed again before they reboarded for the final leg of the flight back to O'Hare.

Most other passengers on the jetliner appeared to be unaware that there was anything unusual about the four men and the woman who were seated together, although stewardesses and other crew members had been notified that police and prisoners were aboard. During her return trip to Indiana, Marie leafed desultorily through an inflight magazine, picked at the meals and snacks that were served, but mostly sat quietly with little animation.

There wasn't much conversation between the police officers and their prisoners, and while exchanging the limited amount of small talk that did occur everyone was careful not to discuss the case. Marie and Eric didn't even talk much to each other, except for brief snippets of conversation that any seatmates might normally exchange over food or reading material on a long flight.

Plainclothes officers from the LaPorte County Sheriff's Department in a trio of unmarked cars met the group at the airport and drove them back to Michigan City. Marie and Eric were driven in separate vehicles.

In Michigan City they were taken directly before Judge Keppen for closed hearings. Marie's hearing was all bad news for her. Herrbach had upgraded the charges against her for Elaine's slaying to murder and conspiracy to murder. Eric was also charged with the conspiracy to commit murder, in addition to the earlier count of assisting after the fact.

Marie first learned at the afternoon hearing that prosecutors were seeking the death penalty if she was convicted. It was a chilling revelation, and she was clearly shaken. But she got another nasty surprise when she learned authorities in Porter County had also charged her with murder in the fatal shooting of her husband.

In documents outlining the death penalty provision request, Herrbach cited premeditation, because Marie allegedly planned Elaine's death and was responsible for a previous murder. The prosecution had briefly considered citing a third basis for seeking the ultimate penalty, that Marie had hired Butch to commit the murder. But it was decided against making that assertion, because it was unclear if the argument was valid. No money had exchanged hands.

Herrbach disclosed that the new, more serious

247

charges were based heavily on statements obtained from Marie's youngest son. Although he was a strong believer in capital punishment, the late county sheriff's son had never prosecuted a death penalty case.

If Marie went to the electric chair in the old state prison located only a few blocks southwest of the courthouse, she would be the first woman ever executed by the state in Indiana.

In fact, only one woman had been executed in the United States since a U. S. Supreme Court ruling in 1977 permitted individual states to reinstate the death penalty. But the defendant must have been aware, as the court authorities were, that the execution of Margie Velma Barfield by lethal injection was carried out as recently as the previous November 2. Barfield died in North Carolina's execution chamber less than a week before the arrests of Marie and her boys in California.

Unlike Herrbach, Berning was not seeking the death penalty against Marie. He had decided that according to the current Indiana Criminal Code, which requires certain aggravating circumstances, it was not an option in the case.

After the hearings, Marie and Eric were driven to the LaPorte County Jail where Butch and Menkel were already being held. The mother and each of her sons were all kept in different sections of the jail. Marie was initially locked up in a holding cell by herself, then moved in with other women. Eric was lodged with adult males; Butch with juveniles. But Marie was also kept separated from her mother, and Eric was locked in a different cell from Menkel. Authorities didn't want them discussing the case with each other, and were taking precautions against the possibility the defendants might attack one another.

The pace of activity in the case picked up rapidly after the return of the mother and son to Indiana.

A few days after their arrival, Butch formally entered his guilty plea to voluntary manslaughter, an offense that under Indiana law usually referred to killings committed in a sudden heat of passion.

Butch was dressed in a baggy dark blue prison jumpsuit and white slippers, with his hands in cuffs that were attached to chains wrapped around his waist, when he appeared before Judge Martin at the ten-minute proceeding. The boy was flanked by his lawyers, Price and Snyder, as he stood before the bench.

"Did you, in fact, kill Elaine Witte?" Judge Martin asked the manacled and chained teenager.

Butch was calm and faced the judge with his head up. "Yes, sir," he replied.

Judge Martin accepted the plea and scheduled sentencing for about four weeks later. Butch, who had observed his sixteenth birthday behind bars, was returned to the jail.

At a press conference held by defense and prosecution attorneys after the brief proceeding, Snyder told a reporter he believed the plea bargain was fair to both sides. He said that although psychiatrists had determined Butch was sane when Elaine was killed, other factors were also taken into consideration in hammering out the agreement.

Snyder said Marie's domineering influence on the boy was the important factor, and described Butch as a pawn in the murder scheme. "He knows a lot of things are his fault, but this crime was not of his origin," Snyder declared. "It was at the direction of his mother."

The lawyer caused a bigger stir among the assembled reporters, however, when he brought up startling references to Satanism and witchcraft. He said the family had practiced occult religious rituals since Butch was very young.

Herrbach indicated the prosecution was also satisfied with the deal. "We are looking at a boy who committed a crime at the age of fourteen," he said. "He was sane, acting under duress at the time, under the domination of his mother. We believe the evidence will show the mother caused her children to commit these crimes."

Nearly four weeks later, on Friday afternoon,

June 14, Butch was ordered to serve the maximum sentence on the manslaughter charge, of a twenty-year prison term. It was the sentence recommended by the prosecution. He was given credit for 218 days already served, and turned over to the custody of state corrections officials to be assigned to a prison.

The youth's lawyers and Herrbach had already agreed on a recommendation asking that Butch be sent to the youth facility at Medaryville which was only about fifty miles south of Michigan City, or at the Indiana Youth Center at Plainfield, a few minutes drive west of Indianapolis in the central portion of the state. Court authorities in both LaPorte and Porter Counties were assured that wherever he was sent he would remain available to testify in the trials of his relatives.

A short time after Butch's plea bargain was worked out, Menkel entered into a similar agreement with the prosecution. The charge against him of assisting a criminal was scaled down from a felony to a misdemeanor, a much less serious offense according to the Indiana Criminal Code. In return, he agreed to testify against Marie.

Menkel was eventually sentenced to 422 days behind bars. But with the application of one day off his sentence for every day of good behavior behind bars, that was cut in half. He had already been jailed longer than that—seven months. He was released and returned to the Navy, although he was placed on legal hold so he would be available for the trial. Conviction on a felony charge of assisting a criminal could have brought a sentence of two to eight years in prison.

The Navy ordered a reduction in rank and a fine for going AWOL, and returned him to duty. He was eventually assigned to the USS *Seattle,* an armored cruiser.

In other developments, Marie hired her own attorney. She was being held without bail, normal procedure according to Indiana law at that time for someone accused of murder. Bail for Eric was set at $100,000, a staggering amount of money for the Navy seaman.

The troubles for Marie, her oldest son, and her mother continued to pile up. In Porter County, authorities filed charges of murder and of conspiracy against Marie, and a charge of attempted murder against Marcie, for allegedly attempting to poison Paul before he was shot. Prosecutor Berning disclosed that Eric would also be charged, but it hadn't yet been determined if he would be prosecuted as a juvenile or as an adult. Eric was fifteen when he shot his father.

A few weeks later, Porter County authorities made it official. After a hearing before Judge

Raymond Kickbush in Porter County Juvenile Court, Eric was waived to adult court. Berning filed new charges of murder against him. Berning said he was still studying the possibility of seeking the death penalty. Eric couldn't afford to pay a lawyer, and local Valparaiso attorney John Lyons was appointed by the court to represent him. Michigan City lawyer Steve Henry was named as his court-appointed attorney in LaPorte County Superior Court.

In the meantime Schoonover's ship returned to its home port in San Diego, and the executive officer told him he couldn't leave the ship until he talked with a police officer from Indiana who was going to telephone him. A couple of days before Marie's trial was scheduled to begin in Michigan City, Boyd telephoned Schoonover aboard the *Leahy*. This time Schoonover admitted knowing the old woman was killed, and provided other details helpful to the investigation.

No charges were filed against him. To an even greater extent than Menkel, Schoonover had been a bit player who was brought into the affair in the aftermath of the murder. He had nothing to do with the slaying or with the conspiracy to kill the old woman.

While shuttling between her jail cell and the courthouse, Marie was enduring problems that had nothing to do with the legal morass she was entangled in. She had been complaining of pain from her gallbladder ever since being extradited back to Indiana from San Diego, and was at last admitted to the LaPorte Hospital under close security measures. A couple of days later surgeons removed the cause of the problem. Local taxpayers, already burdened with the expense of the legal proceedings against Marie and her codefendants, were spared the approximate $3,000 cost of the operation. It was paid for with Marie's Social Security disability payments.

Marie also changed attorneys, hiring Scott L. King, an experienced criminal defense lawyer from Gary who was a former deputy Lake County prosecutor and assistant U. S. attorney assigned to the office in Hammond. Like Herrbach and Berning, whom he would oppose in two different courtrooms, he was a graduate of the Valparaiso University Law School.

As a prosecutor and defense attorney, he had already represented one side or the other in more than fifty homicide cases. King was a lawyer who thrilled to the challenge and excitement of criminal law and jury trials. He was recommended to Marie by an attorney acquaintance who practiced civil law, and agreed to accept the job for a reduced fee. Her defense promised to offer up more than its fair share of challenge and excitement.

Although the amount of the fee was never disclosed, King's agreement to represent Marie at a cut-rate price wasn't surprising. The crossbow murder was already one of the most high-profile homicide cases filed in Indiana courts in modern times, and it promised to continue attracting national publicity as it went to trial. Presentation of a strong, well-crafted defense, even if Marie was convicted of murder, could enhance the hard-driving lawyer's already notable professional reputation.

King didn't wait for the trial to begin before demonstrating just how spirited his defense of Marie would be. He launched into action by filing a flurry of motions during the pretrial jockeying. Among other things, he asked that the count of conspiracy to commit murder be dropped, that certain evidence collected by the prosecution be suppressed, and that the case be venued to another county.

Pretrial motions are a regular part of the give-and-take maneuvering between defense lawyers and the prosecution at almost every major criminal proceeding. It is the way the deadly serious game is played. Each side jousts with the other, as trial lawyers try to squeeze out any possible advantage while tilting over everything from how the jury will be selected, if a jury will be selected, where the trial will be held, just what evidence will be admitted, what questions can be asked of witnesses, even who the judge will be.

Some defense attorneys are especially good at using pretrial motions to lay the groundwork for later appeals. It can become good insurance in case their client is convicted.

King's motion for dismissal of the murder conspiracy charges against Marie on grounds of double jeopardy was a near classic example. Explained in layman's terms, American law, based on a critical clause in the Fifth Amendment to the U. S. Constitution, stipulates that a defendant can be prosecuted only once for the same crime. With his motion, King was contending that by pressing the two charges prosecutors were being unfairly given two shots at Marie for the same crime. If the judge rejected the request and Marie was convicted, the basis for the motion could be brought up later during the appeals process.

In his written motion, King said that based on information supplied to him by the prosecution through the legal process of discovery it was clear the two offenses are identical and conviction on both charges would violate Marie's Constitutional rights against double jeopardy. So he asked that one or the other of the charges be dismissed by the court, or alternatively that the prosecution be ordered to choose one of the charges to proceed with. Although the judge dismissed one of the counts to correct legal errors, he permitted the prosecution to refile and refused to limit the state to prosecution of a single count.

The defense lawyer tied his motion to suppress evidence to a challenge of the search warrants issued on November 2 for the house and the Winnebago. He contended that the search warrant for the house was issued on the basis of "hearsay," the statements given to investigators by Marcie and Menkel. Instead of presenting evidence to back up the statements, the prosecution merely provided more hearsay, the belief of some of Elaine's neighbors that it was unusual for Elaine to be gone for such a long time, he contended.

King stated that prosecutors claimed the statements of Marcie and the young sailor were credible because they had spoken "against their own penal interests." With their own words, they had implicated themselves. But the prosecutors were wrong in their contention for two reasons, he said. First of all, review of Marcie's statements prior to November 2, 1984, showed she wasn't accusing herself of any crime. "She stated that she had no knowledge of any scheme to kill Elaine Witte; that to her knowledge, Elaine had been accidentally slain by Hans (Butch) Witte; that she had no involvement in the death of Elaine and that she refused to assist in the disposal of Elaine's body," he contended in the written motion. "Secondly, the state ignores the fact that Indiana does not recognize admissions against penal interest as an exception to the hearsay rule," he declared.

King also noted Menkel's claims of engaging in telekinetic contests with others, and complained that the prosecution hadn't informed the courts of that fact. The implication was clear: How credible was someone who believed in telekinesis and other such paranormal abilities?

Duerring prepared and presented the argument against the motion. Marie didn't have a right to object to the search of the house because she wasn't the owner, and had abandoned it when she left to go to California, he contended. Furthermore, he argued, Marcie and Menkel corroborated each other's statements on many points even though they were thousands of miles away from each other when they were questioned.

"Statement by Margaret O'Donnell concerning the dismemberment of Elaine's body, the grinding up of Elaine's teeth, the fact that these certain body parts were placed in Margaret O'Donnell's freezer and also the work done on Marie's car all were corroborated by Doug Menkel's statement," he wrote. "Also the converse is true. Doug Menkel's statement taken in California was corroborated on all these major points by the statements taken from Margaret O'Donnell."

The petition to suppress evidence seized during the searches was denied.

King nevertheless managed to convince Judge Martin to establish bond for Marie, despite Indiana law that rules out bond in most homicide cases.

When King made his move to have bond set for his client, the prosecution was left facing an intriguing legal conundrum. If prosecutors opposed setting bond, the defense could request a hearing on the evidence the state had assembled in the case. And that could have led to calling all forty-five potential prosecution witnesses already lined up, with the result that the state would have had to reveal their case before the trial. It was a crafty, although perfectly proper, defense maneuver which could have led to a prosecution disaster.

Instead of opposing the request, the prosecution recommended the court set a whopping $200,000 as the minimum possible bond. At the conclusion of the thirty-minute hearing, the judge concurred. Herrbach and Duerring knew how to play the same courtroom games as the defense. And the experienced judge was also well aware of what was going on.

A clause in the Indiana State Criminal Code allows for bond to be set for murder defendants when the presumption of guilt is not great and there is a weak case. Courthouse sources indicated to reporters, however, that the fact Marie was not being accused of being the actual killer may have also affected the decision. Someone else, not Marie, pulled the trigger!

The amount of the bond, nevertheless, was far more than Marie would be able to raise. Even if she did somehow come up with the ten-percent cash or show proof of owning property worth $200,000 to meet the terms of the surety bond, she still had her federal prison sentence on the forgery conviction, and the murder charges in Porter County, to deal with. Marie remained behind bars.

When King obtained a bond hearing in Valparaiso, Butch and Marcie were called by the prosecution to testify. Marcie was being held at the Porter County Jail and Myrick B. Crampton Security Center in the county seat town on the attempted murder charges against her. Valparaiso lawyer Gary Germann had been appointed as her pauper attorney.

Butch told the court he remembered family conversations leading up to the murder of his father. He also testified that when his older brother shot Paul, it was at the insistence of their mother.

The teenager claimed his father beat him the night of the murder, and that he later heard a click and watched as Eric pulled the trigger of the handgun and shot their father in the head. In response to questioning by Berning, the witness extended his arms and held both his palms vertically in front of him in the classic position of someone using both hands to aim and shoot a gun. It was a position familiar to everyone in the courtroom who had ever seen a police or action film on television or in the movies.

Questioned by King about the conversations Butch reputedly overheard about the planned murder of Paul, the youth said he couldn't remember the exact words. Speaking in a soft, barely audible voice, he explained: "It was something on the order of, my dad had to be shot. My mother and my brother said that."

In response to other questions from King, Butch said that while living at 320 Johnson Road, he drank alcohol, smoked marijuana, and used methamphetamine and LSD. He used the street names, "speed" and "acid," for the two more powerful drugs.

When King asked who was living in the house at that time, Butch replied: "My mother, my brother, my grandmother, and I."

"Which grandmother?" King wanted to know.

Butch's reply was disturbingly unemotional and blunt.

"The one I killed," he said.

During lengthy testimony, Marcie also talked about her daughter's scheming, the early efforts to kill Paul, and of finally manipulating Eric into carrying out the murder. Marcie was escorted across the street from the lockup by a pair of local corrections officers to testify in the Porter County Courthouse. It was a warm and clear mid-July day, and merely getting outside the dreary jail for a few minutes was a treat for the distressed woman.

Nervous and speaking in a soft and halting voice, Marcie said Marie was scared of Paul, resented his abuse of the boys, and talked of wishing to poison him in some manner that would make his death appear accidental. Marie decided that arsenic would be one effective way of carrying out the murder. And the witness told of how both she and Marie slipped various pills and poisons, including rat poison, into the unsuspecting man's food and drink.

Marcie also recalled different discussions about shooting Paul. "I was wishing I was somewhere else," she testified. "I was terrified."

She also testified about her daughter confronting Eric with making a choice between his parents, of how Marie threatened that if he didn't kill Paul she would commit suicide. "Eric was a young boy and he said he would do what had to be done." Marcie stuttered. The witness looked at the lawyers or stared into her lap as she talked, doing her best to look anywhere but at the defense table where her daughter was quietly listening to the damning testimony.

In response to questions from Berning, Marcie said she was afraid to tell police the truth about the murder. She claimed she was threatened, and friends were threatened.

"We've heard the defendant's mother and her son testify that she was involved in the murder." Judge Douglas remarked as he concluded the hearing and denied the bail request. "You've never shown why the witnesses might not be telling the truth."

Appearing more scrawny than slim, and with the pasty complexion of a prisoner who has spent months behind bars, Marie showed no emotion in response to the ruling. Her eyes were hidden behind the round, oversize sunglasses that had become her trademark during the pretrial proceedings, and she was quiet and calm as she was led from the courtroom and helped into the backseat of a sheriff's department squad car for the half-hour drive back to LaPorte. According to some reports the already slender woman had lost about fifty pounds since her arrest.

With murder charges filed against Marie in La-Porte and in Porter Counties, King was fighting for his client on two fronts. And weeks before her first trial was scheduled to begin in Michigan City, he filed petitions in both jurisdictions to have pretrial hearings in the cases closed to the public. As justification for his request, he cited the possibility of potential jurors being influenced by publicity stemming from the hearings. King claimed continuation of the widespread media coverage would make it impossible to select an impartial jury, with the result that his client would be denied a fair trial.

Objections to King's effort to exclude the press from pretrial hearings were filed by five different elements of the news media, including four area newspapers and WIMS, a Michigan City radio station. Through its attorneys, the media contended that closing the hearings would violate the Constitutional rights of the news agencies and their reporters. The very process of jury selection itself was designed to ensure seating of an impartial jury, they contended. Arguing against the petition in Porter County, Berning also pointed out that jurors are screened for possible bias during the selection process.

Porter Superior Court Judge Douglas rejected the motion, ruling that King hadn't proven a need to close the hearings.

Judge Martin returned a similar ruling in Michigan City, after listening to two witnesses, the *Herald-Argus* City Editor David Jensen and David Frank, a Michigan City psychologist, who had conducted studies of juries. He was convinced jurors would not be influenced by reports of the case they heard or read outside the courtroom. Judge Martin said.

Herrbach and Duerring won another last-minute contest that was vitally important to the prosecution when Judge Martin ruled that carefully limited testimony could be called on at Marie's trial about Paul's shooting.

King argued the incident in Porter County had nothing to do with what happened to Elaine four years later, and that bringing up Paul's murder would prejudice the jury.

But the prosecution contended information about the shooting was necessary to show that Marie had employed a common scheme in both alleged murders. The motive in both murders was money, Marie ordered one of her sons to carry out each killing, the victim was sleeping when killed, and each slaying was planned, Duerring pointed out in the state's arguments. Information about Paul's shooting was a necessary part of telling the jury the whole story, and to let the panelists know that they weren't hearing about a normal family, the deputy prosecutor contended.

Virtually on the eve of Marie's trial, however, Herrbach dropped his request for the death penalty. Like his colleague in Porter County, after a careful study of the state criminal statutes, he arrived at the reluctant conclusion the death penalty wasn't an option for Marie under Indiana law. He had run into the same obstacle raised during the hearing on King's request for bond. Marie wasn't the actual killer; someone else was the triggerman.

The startling development marked the achievement of one of King's most critical goals: to avoid the death penalty and save his client from the electric chair. Now he was faced with the task of convincing a jury she was not guilty of murder.

The timing of the prosecutor's move had to be a relief for Marie. Less than a month earlier, the state of Indiana had carried out its second execution since the reinstatement of the death penalty. William Vandiver, an ex-convict from nearby Hammond, was electrocuted at the prison in Michigan City for the 1983 murder of his father-in-law.

Ironically, Vandiver was executed for a family murder that in several ways bore an eerie resemblance to the Witte slayings. The victim, Paul Komyatti, Sr., was stabbed more than thirty-four times, then dismembered, stuffed in garbage bags, and buried along the Lake Michigan shoreline. Vandiver had joined in at least one earlier attempt to murder the retired Hammond construction worker with rat poison. At the time of Vandiver's execution he was thirty-seven, the same age as Marie. And the victim's widow, Rosemary, his son, Paul, Jr., and his daughter, Vandiver's wife, Mariann, were all sentenced to prison for playing various roles in the crime.

Despite the disappointing prosecution setback, if Marie was convicted of murder she could still face a maximum sentence that might keep her behind bars the rest of her life. In November 1985, a few days more than a year after her arrest in San Diego, Marie was at last brought to trial for murder. Grandma Witte had been dead for twenty-two months.

Nine

A Prosecution

Some lawyers say trials are won or lost during pretrial maneuvering.

And it's true that the early jockeying between attorneys can be vitally important, but when the prosecution and Marie's defense team entered the courtroom for the beginning of her trial, there was no foregone conclusion. Attorneys were still facing a trial that was pickled with complexities, and the verdict was very much up for grabs.

Herrbach did most of the state's preparation himself, with the assistance of a couple of legal interns from his alma mater at Valparaiso who helped research case law. During the final six weeks before the trial's opening, the chief deputy prosecutor devoted his time almost exclusively to the case.

Reports in the press estimated potential prosecution witnesses at various numbers ranging from fifty to one hundred. By the time jury selection began on Monday morning, November 4, however, Herrbach had lined up twenty-two witnesses ranging from family members of the defendant and the victim to police detectives, forensic technicians, bankers, and retirees with the Indiana Bell Pioneers. The prosecution had pieced together a formidable case.

Even though there was no body, not even so much as a hair they could prove once belonged to Elaine, they had witnesses ready to testify they had seen at least portions of the remains. But Butch was the big gun in the prosecution's arsenal, and his testimony would be critical.

As the attorneys assembled in the second-floor courtroom to begin the deadly serious process of jury selection, Herrbach was confident in himself and in his case. His most serious concern was selecting a jury of men and women from the available cross section of homemakers, office workers, factory employees, retirees, salesmen, and farmers who could accept the testimony in the bizarre case as believable.

The panel would be hearing a story of an especially heinous murder of a harmless old woman committed with a medieval weapon, of hideous dismemberment, sex, and terrible family betrayal. There would be disgusting testimony about attempts to grind up body parts with a food processor, of mixing human flesh with potting soil, and dark hints of Satanism and occult rituals.

The prosecutor was concerned that the story to be told on the stand by Marie's two sons and other witnesses might be too deviant, so foreign and unacceptable to the jury of sober Midwesterners that they would reject it as counterfeit, a Hollywood-style horror fable concocted by over-ambitious imaginations. Butch and Eric had to come across to the jury as believable or the prosecution would be in trouble.

Butch was also the key to the defense's game plan. King planned to defend Marie by showing the jury that her youngest son not only committed the murder, but that he did so on his own. Butch had the motive, and Marie only became involved after Grandma Witte was already dead, when the natural protective emotions of a mother led her to try and cover up for her out-of-control son.

Marie had lost some of the wan and tired look of recent months, and she walked almost jauntily into the courtroom. Her drab jail clothes and the manacles she wore during preliminary hearings were gone, and she was dressed in a crisp gray business suit and white blouse for the first day of jury selection. At times during her incarceration and while attending preliminary hearings, her mouse-brown hair, which she parted in the middle, had appeared so stringy and dead that one courtroom observer described her as looking like "a wilted weasel." But another inmate at the jail gave her a permanent for the trial, and the turned-up ends were brushed into a healthy glisten just past her shoulders. She was flanked at the defense table by King and by Chicago attorney Paul Flynn, who was assisting him with her defense.

It took nearly three days of questioning before a panel composed of nine men, three women, and two alternates, was agreed upon. One potential juror was passed over after King asked if he was familiar with Dungeons & Dragons, and the man said he had a friend who was virtually obsessed by the game. King asked, "Do you think it's possible that someone playing the game can get carried away and lose sight of the fact that it is a game?"

"Yes," the man replied. A woman was also rejected after she revealed she once worked with Elaine.

Before opening statements and testimony began, however, one of the women jurors broke a leg. She was replaced by a male alternate. Six of the remaining jurors were parents of teenagers, including a male insurance agent with four.

Judge Martin told the jurors they could take

notes during the trial, but cautioned them not to become so involved with their writing that they didn't have time to listen to the testimony.

By the time attorneys were ready to present their opening statements, the spectator's section in Judge Martin's courtroom was so full that some people were sitting on the floor and others were standing in the hallway. Lured by reports of the case in the press, they were anxious to watch and listen from ringside seats while the heady human drama of greed, sex, and betrayal unfolded. Many of the spectators brought their lunch so they wouldn't lose their seats during the noontime recess.

The long, narrow courtroom was constructed without frills and designed with the bare basics needed to conduct the business of the court. A door directly across the corridor from the office of the court reporter provides public access to the rear of the courtroom. Rows of hard wooden benches are lined up rectangularly like church pews that march toward the front where they end just behind the defense table.

The prosecutor, his colleagues, and assistants are seated to the left, almost directly across from the jury box. The court reporter sits facing the defense table, and on a raised dais directly in back of him or her—at center stage—the judge presides over the affairs of the court. He is flanked on the bench by the stars and stripes of the United States and the white torch of liberty and stars on a blue field that compose the Indiana state flag.

When the trial at last opened, it began amid a rage of public pity for the hapless victim. There wasn't even a body left to bury, no coffin in which Elaine Witte could rest under the earth next to her husband. Spectators were especially anxious to get a look at the homemaker and mother who had lived among them and was accused of being the architect of the horrendous crime.

Mrs. Mary Bowyer, the mother of Paul and of Mrs. Valencia, was among the spectators. The seventy-five-year-old woman was living in Montgomery, Illinois. She and her daughter made the exhausting 180-mile round-trip drive from Illinois most days, but a few nights stayed in a local motel.

As he addressed the full jury for the first time, Herrbach portrayed the defendant as a greedy, ruthless woman whose evil was so corrosive that she lured her own sons into her murderous schemes. She dominated the boys, and her control was so powerful that they killed for her, he declared.

"You are about to be introduced to one of the most bizarre, grotesque, and disgusting murders to have happened in our community," Herrbach promised the rapt panel. "I believe that we will show that Hilma Marie Witte organized, schemed, and maneuvered the death of Elaine Witte."

Marie ordered both the murders of her husband and of her mother-in-law, Herrbach asserted. She even threatened to commit suicide if Eric didn't do as he was told.

Marie and her brood were described by the chief deputy prosecutor as an atypical family that worked together to commit a murder that was the most gruesome, inhuman act in the history of Trail Creek.

"It sounds like the state has a heck of a case," King told the jury when it was his turn to begin outlining the defense. "What can the defense say? I have a lot to say; this is not the yellow brick road the state would have you believe," he declared.

King traced his client's troubled childhood for the jury. He talked of Marcie's hospitalization in Florida; about Marie's marriage to Paul; how the hardy outdoorsman reputedly mistreated his wife and sons and rejected the sickly Butch as not being rugged enough for him. It was then that Marie began her pattern of protecting the boy, first, shielding him from taking beatings from her husband to ultimately covering up the events of January 10, 1984, the lawyer said.

The relationship between Marie and Elaine was like that of a mother and daughter, he told the jury. "Marie was the daughter Elaine never had, and Elaine was the mother Marie never had." They shared everything, including problems, and the boys weren't pleased about that, King declared.

Although Marie was a pushover for the boys, Elaine was strict about discipline and was especially tough when drugs were involved, he continued. King described Butch as an out of control scamp who was a school truant and thief; he was abusing drugs and alcohol before he even reached his teens. It was outrageous behavior that Elaine wouldn't tolerate, the lawyer said.

King also traced Butch's passionate attraction to the martial arts and his preoccupation with exotic weapons, including the crossbow. He told the middle-class Indiana jurors that Butch was deeply involved with such things as spiritualism, demons, monsters, and the various characters that are part of the alien fantasy world of Dungeons & Dragons. King contended that Butch became so wrapped up in the game that the line between reality and fantasy became so blurred that he was able to plot and carry out the murder of his grandmother.

Marie didn't browbeat or entice Butch into murdering his grandmother, the attorney claimed. The boy was so high on drugs and alcohol, and his sense of reality was so twisted and confused by the twilight world of D & D that he did it on his own.

King conceded up front that his client stole from her mother-in-law. Marie was ready to plead guilty to stealing, and, in fact, had already been convicted in federal court in California, he said. But she was a thief, not a murderer, he insisted.

He also conceded that his client had horribly mistreated the old woman's corpse. "We will not say she did not assist in the disposal of Elaine Witte's body," he said. "It was depraved and it was horrible, but it wasn't to protect herself. It was to protect her son." King said that if prosecutors decided to charge her with that depravity, or with taking money from Elaine after the old woman's death, the defense would respond with guilty pleas.

"But murder? And conspiracy to commit murder? We will deny that!"

Marie was an overprotective, loving parent, who was only trying to shield her sons, the flamboyant Gary lawyer claimed. He contended that she panicked when she learned Butch had killed Elaine. At first she thought the shooting was an accident, but even when she learned it was deliberate she was afraid to notify authorities because of Eric's rough treatment when police were investigating Paul's shooting.

King claimed police held Eric over his father's body and shook him in their attempt to make him confess the shooting was not an accident. He described the probe of Paul's death as one of the most fouled-up investigations he had ever seen.

According to the scenario laid out by the defense attorney, Marie was terrified that her younger son would be given the same kind of rough treatment her older son suffered at the hands of the police. And even though she later learned the crossbow killing was deliberate, she was desperate to protect her incorrigible son. So she helped him hide, then dispose of, the old woman's body.

At the conclusion of the lawyer's tale of a frightened mother's love and sacrifice, the faces of the jurors remained impassive. The battle lines, nevertheless, had been drawn!

Marcie was one of the prosecution's earliest witnesses, and was called to the stand after

Paul's half sister, Barbara Valencia, and Elaine's friends, Mrs. McCarten and Mrs. Voisenette, told of their concern and worry over the missing woman.

Mrs. Voisenette's testimony provided a glimpse of the difficulty that some of the witnesses, spectators, and others had in confronting the horror of Elaine's murder and dismemberment. During direct examination, Herrbach asked if she recalled the last time she had gotten together with Elaine.

"Possibly . . . well, it was just before she became ill," the witness replied.

The prosecutor established that their last meeting would have been about December 1983. Then he returned to her earlier statement. "You said Elaine became ill?" he inquired.

"No! I didn't want to use . . . I just said 'ill.' That isn't the correct word," Mrs. Voisenette explained. "That is, that was before I knew anything about Elaine. I did not talk to her or see her."

"All right, you are using the word to refer to a date that you believe Elaine died?" Herrbach asked.

"Right!" the witness responded.

That exchange didn't put to rest the witness's apparent difficulty in dealing head-on with the fact that her friend was so horribly murdered and mutilated. A bit later in her testimony, as she was discussing the last time she had contact with Elaine, either in personal conversations or in the exchange of cards, she remarked:

"I'm thinking it could have been the Thanksgiving prior to her being away, or not living anymore."

Mrs. Voisenette's appearance on the witness stand had dramatically illustrated the discomfort Elaine's friends could be expected to have in testifying. But Marcie's appearance was even more agonizing. It was a terrible ordeal.

Marcie had barely begun her testimony before revealing another marriage. She identified her husband as George W. Blade, although she was once again using her maiden name.

Questioned by Duerring, she reluctantly depicted her daughter as the architect of two murders. The fidgety witness also insisted no deal was made to give her a lenient sentence in return for her testimony. She said she agreed to testify against her daughter because she wanted the truth to come out.

"From the time Paul died four years ago, I made my peace with my Maker then, and I said if the day ever came that I knew that nobody else could be hurt I would, if I could, do my best to make it right.

"I was kept . . . I'm in jail now, but it's nothing to the prison I was in before where I had no life at all, no friends," she said, "I couldn't go anywhere or anything."

Marcie's halting explanation appeared to come from the heart.

After establishing information about her personal background, her reasons for testifying, and Marie's early years, Duerring turned to the events leading up to Paul's murder.

Before questioning turned to details of his slaying, however, the trembling fifty-nine-year-old witness's testimony was interrupted while Judge Martin gave special instructions to the jury. The jurist explained that evidence was about to be presented indicating the defendant may have committed crimes other than the one she was currently on trial for. He stressed, however, that the information was not admissible as proof that Marie was responsible for Elaine's murder, and that it was being submitted only to show a common scheme of plan.

It was an important distinction of law that had been strongly contested in pretrial maneuvering between the prosecution and defense. It was also a key element of the prosecution's case.

Responding to Duerring's lead, Marcie traced events at the house in Beverly Shores leading up to Paul's shooting. Asked why she didn't warn her son-in-law that Marie was attempting to poison him, the witness said she was too afraid.

"What were you afraid of?" the assistant prosecutor asked.

"I was afraid of being put in an institution for the rest of my life. I was afraid of going to the electric chair, and I was afraid of what Marie said her son would do to me," she replied.

Duerring asked what Marie said her son would do.

"She told me that Eric would kill me," Marcie said.

The witness's voice rose and fell as she testified, sometimes becoming so soft and indistinct that it almost completely faded out and Duerring had to remind her to speak up. Marcie fidgeted and shifted uncomfortably in her seat, occasionally swiping at the edge of an eye with a tissue. She avoided looking at Marie, who was seated almost directly in front of her and watching intently from the defense table.

Duerring asked if she recalled learning that the assassination plan had changed from poisoning Paul to killing him with a gun.

"Yes, sir," she replied. "About a week before Paul died, Marie and I went grocery shopping and when we came home Paul was at work, and Eric told Marie that Butch had taken the gun out in the yard and shot if off. She was very angry," Marcie said of her daughter, "because that was the gun that was going to be used and she didn't want it out where anyone would know anything about it." Marcie said the plan to kill Paul with a drug overdose was abandoned because it wasn't working.

The deputy prosecutor asked why Marcie didn't tell police the truth about Paul's death, when they questioned her immediately following the shooting. She said she was too afraid, because she had been threatened.

"Who threatened?" he asked.

"Marie threatened," she responded. "I watched the boys take karate lessons. I watched them learn to throw knives. I watched them throw tomahawks. And Marie told me what could be done to me, or what could be done to a friend of mine or a little boy that I helped to raise."

Duerring didn't pursue further information about the little boy, but asked if Marcie was threatened by anyone else.

"Eric," she said, "after his father died." Later in her testimony, she claimed Eric blamed her because she didn't do more to prevent Paul's murder.

Moving on to the night of the shooting, Marcie testified that Marie was furious when she returned home from the grocery store with Butch, and learned her husband was still alive. Speaking in a hoarse voice that was barely audible, Marcie said her daughter took Eric into a bedroom and they began arguing and yelling at each other. When they returned to the kitchen where Marcie was nervously tidying up, Marie told her son that Paul had to be killed that night or someone else would die the next day.

Duerring asked what Marie had meant when she said someone else would die if Paul wasn't killed.

"Paul had said earlier that if there wasn't a delivery of something that was promised the next morning, someone would die," she replied. Paul wanted to know where the antique furniture was.

But Eric continued to resist his mother's demands. He didn't want to shoot his father, because he was afraid Paul would get up from the sofa and attack him.

"Marie told him that his dad would not get up and get him, that he could shoot him and his daddy wouldn't get up. And Marie left, and she left Eric and Butch and myself at the house," Marcie continued in an increasingly shaky voice.

The witness recounted hearing the gunshot, and of playing with the idea that it may have been only a motorcycle backfire. And she recalled learning for the first time that the murder scheme had actually been carried out when Marie ran into the room screaming at her to get some towels because Paul was shot.

The deputy prosecutor asked why Marie hadn't simply gone ahead and divorced her husband if he was as abusive as family members claimed. Marcie replied that her daughter was afraid of losing the house and property. "Marie liked to live well," she explained.

Turning at last to questions about Elaine's murder, Marcie indicated that, with the exception of the eventual victim, at various times just about everyone in the troubled family living in the house at 320 Johnson Road was threatening to kill one another. Months before the murder, both Butch and Eric threatened her and Elaine, she said.

"All I could say was, 'It's Paul all over again, it's history repeating itself,' " she testified of her reaction when she heard her daughter scheming with the boys to have Elaine murdered.

Just as she had reacted to Paul's murder, fear prevented her from going to the police earlier about Elaine's murder. "I was too afraid of them. They didn't leave me alone. One of them was with me all the time."

Marcie stated that at first her daughter told her Butch accidentally shot his grandmother with the crossbow. Marie also revealed she had been slipping pills in Elaine's food for weeks so the old woman was so groggy and disoriented she didn't know what was going on before she was killed. Elaine may even have already been dead from the overdose of pills, the witness quoted the defendant as telling her.

"I told Marie I didn't want anything to do with it," Marcie asserted. But Marie responded that the old woman was already dead and the body had to be disposed of. If there was no corpse and no evidence there could be no crime, as far as the police were concerned, Marcie said the younger woman insisted.

According to the testimony, Marie's money troubles continued to torment her after Paul was killed, and she concocted various schemes to solve her financial woes.

Marcie said that in September 1983, Marie approached her and pleaded for $6,000, which she claimed she needed to save her from going to jail. Marcie explained to the court that when she was working for one of her invalid employers the woman's brother set up a $6,000 bank account to pay the household bills. Both her own name and the brother's name were on the account, she said.

Marie knew of the account and that her mother had access to it. But when Marie asked about the money, the witness said, she lied and claimed she couldn't get to it.

Later, she learned her daughter was attempting to forge Elaine's signature on checks. At Duerring's urging she elaborated about the methods Marie used to loot Grandma Witte's accounts and cash the old woman's Social Security and retirement checks. Most of the time, she said, Marie merely withdrew money from automatic teller machines.

But it was different when she had Elaine's checks to cash. "She had, I would call it, a makeup organizer that was plastic in the center, clear plastic. And she would open the lid and put it on her lap and put a flashlight between her legs that would shine up, and she would put one of Elaine's canceled checks on it and she would copy the signature," Marcie recalled.

While Marcie testified, she nervously locked and unlocked the stubby fingers of her hands in her lap or fitfully brushed imaginary specks from her skirt. And when she recounted some of the more grisly aspects of the horror that occurred at the house on Johnson Road, her eyes misted with tears and the cheeks of her booze-swollen face trembled in agony.

Once, when she was retracing Elaine's dismemberment, her voice choked and tears began streaming down her trembling cheeks. "This is not my daughter I'm talking about," she blubbered. Judge Martin ordered a fifteen-minute recess to give the emotion-wracked witness time to compose herself.

The testimony was shocking and disgusting, and spectators reacted several times with low moans of horror that drew stern looks of warning from court officers. At one point Duerring asked about Butch's role in the dissection, bringing a reply that made a woman juror lurch back in her seat and press her hand to her mouth while her face paled with revulsion. It was an involuntary reflex that was understandable under the circumstances.

Butch once accidentally cut his hand, and another time slashed his foot during the dismemberment process, Marcie testified. "And one time he came downstairs and he had stuff all over his hands. Like when you're cleaning a fish. You know how your hands will get." She quoted her daughter as telling the boy, "For God's sake," to wash his hands before smoking a cigarette.

The witness seemed oblivious to the appalling effect the gruesome anecdote had on the jury and spectators. She had already lived through the horror—close up.

She seemed equally insensitive when she recounted the day she was summoned to help her daughter and grandson in the basement. She said Marie had a small can of acid she was soaking bones in and had taken it downstairs and put a lid on it. When the witch's brew bubbled up and began to pour over the sides, Marie yelled for her mother. The witness said she refused to help, and her daughter and grandson took care of the mess by themselves.

Another time when Marie yelled from the basement for help, Marcie walked downstairs and found the mother and son pouring something into plastic bags. She described the substance as "an off-red liquid with white specks in it, with the most horrible odor I have ever smelled.

"I don't think I'll ever forget that smell as long as I live. And I saw her pouring this into the bags that went into the refrigerator," Marcie continued. She said she went back upstairs and became violently ill. A couple of the jurors looked as if they, too, were about to become ill, while they listened to the nauseating testimony.

The foul-smelling liquid was eventually mixed with potting soil and disposed of, Marcie explained. She said she returned to her apartment one day and found her daughter and grandson mixing it with potting soil, and ordered them to leave. It was beginning to smell up her apartment.

Marcie also told of watching as Marie was emptying containers that held grease from the deep-fryer into a burn pile. When the containers were thrown into the fire, she said, Marie spotted a toe. She quickly reached down and plucked it out of the pile.

Her daughter cautioned her that she had to watch real close so there wouldn't be any evidence left behind for the police to use. The toe was destroyed later with other leftover bits of tissue and bone.

"Did you see any other identifiable parts of the body besides that toe during this period of time?" the assistant prosecutor asked.

"Just after she was cutting up the bones in the containers and the white pieces in this awful-smelling liquid she was pouring," Marcie replied.

When the assistant prosecutor asked if anyone was at the house on Johnson Road when Elaine's body was being obliterated, Marcie explained that Jeannie accompanied her there one day. They picked up some shorts and tank tops from a downstairs bedroom and climbed into the hot tub, but only stayed a short time, she said. They didn't go upstairs or into the basement.

"Was she aware of what was going on, or did you tell her what was going on?" Herrbach asked.

Marcie didn't tell her roommate what was going on until later, sometime near the end of January or the first of February.

"She kept fighting with me because there was always somebody at our home. There was never any time that there wasn't someone in the apartment with us all the time," she explained. One night after they had been bickering, Marcie said, she got upset and screamed at her roommate: "For God's sake leave me alone. Elaine is dead and if they know I told you they'll kill me. Now leave me alone!"

Marcie had made a terrifying admission to her roommate. "I think Jeannie was as frightened as I was then," Marcie observed.

When King took his turn questioning the witness, his fierce and unrelenting cross-examination was met with frequent stammering, disconnected sentences, memory lapses, or embarrassing moments of silence while she stared into space.

"That's been a long time ago. I'm remembering as best I can," she responded several times.

As the cross-examination turned to questions about Marcie's boozing, it drew an admission that she had hit the bottle heavily before her brief interlude in the mental hospital in Florida twenty years earlier. She also conceded she was drinking heavily during the months that Elaine's friends and law enforcement officers were trying to find out what happened to her.

"In 1984, I drank enough that I wouldn't fall apart," she said. "I couldn't stand what was going on. I knew I'd be in trouble with the law, too, and I was afraid of the family."

Marcie at first denied she had previously admitted under oath that she took Valium and other prescription drugs, until King produced a deposition she gave to him earlier and read parts of it out loud. Marcie then agreed she had taken the drugs and drank heavily. But she firmly denied drinking had blurred her memory. "My memory is like anyone else's," she insisted.

King continued to point accusingly at glaring inconsistencies in her statements to the police and on the witness stand. He ripped ferociously at her testimony, comparing her remarks on the stand with statements she had given to police investigators.

Fixing her with an intent peering-down-a-gun-barrel gaze, the tenacious lawyer got her to admit she didn't see an arrow sticking out of Elaine's body after the old woman's death. Yet, the lawyer pointed out, in her statement to Boyd more than a year earlier she said she saw an arrow.

Stammering and squinting her eyes as if she was trying to peer into the past, she conceded she hadn't told Boyd the entire story behind Grandma Witte's disappearance during their first meeting.

"I didn't at first tell about seeing Elaine in the garbage can the night of January 10, 1984," she testified. "I didn't know what trouble I'd be in. I was afraid. I know how my daughter could manipulate things."

Eric had warned Marie that Marcie was the weak link, she said: "The boys told their mother that I was mentally incompetent."

Marcie's puffy, florid face twisted while she forced the words out in gasps. It was her third day of questioning, and it was an emotionally exhausting ordeal. She looked as if she wanted to lurch off the witness stand and run out of the courtroom.

King didn't let up, and he continued hurling fastballs and sliders at the shaky witness.

"You participated in discussions about her death?"

"I answered what I had to," she replied.

King asked if she acted out of fear. "That is definitely my testimony," she said.

That was when King brought up her assertion that no deal was made with the prosecution for her testimony.

"Yet, you've been charged with only assisting a criminal, never charged with conspiracy, a more serious crime?" he asked.

The lawyer's verbal assault was clearly designed to raise questions in the minds of jurors about Marcie's reasons for testifying against her daughter and her reliability as a witness.

The expressions on the faces of the jurors were

unchanged, but the unspoken accusation hung heavy in the silent courtroom. Was there an understanding between the witness and the prosecution to treat her leniently when it was her turn to be sentenced?

In other testimony, she talked about her brief commitment to a hospital for psychiatric care in 1964, and said Marie told her it was because she was unstable and mentally incompetent. But Marcie claimed the commitment was engineered by enemies who wanted her property lease.

Returning to the early relationship between her daughter and Elaine, Marcie said the older woman treated Marie like the little girl she had never had. Elaine gave Marie access to her bank accounts, loaned her money, and cosigned other loans for her, the witness said. Marcie also testified, however, about seeing her daughter tracing Elaine's signature.

When Marcie's exhausting marathon ordeal on the stand at last ended, her friend and roommate, Irma "Jeannie" Frye, was called as a witness. Herrbach took over the questioning.

Asked about drinking, she replied that she sometimes drank beer and Marcie drank vodka when they weren't on the job.

Jeannie remembered that during the autumn before Elaine's disappearance, Marie talked of the old woman's plans to take a vacation. She also said Marcie eventually told her Elaine was dead, and that she was afraid she might also be killed.

"Call the police," Jeannie said she advised her friend after learning that Elaine had been killed. "She said it was going to be the same thing as with Paul Witte." Marcie hadn't forgotten the investigation and immediate aftermath of the earlier murder in Beverly Shores.

Herrbach asked if Marie ever gave her instructions about what to say to the police if she was asked about Elaine. Jeannie confirmed that Marie had told her in September 1984 what to say.

"And what were you told at that time?" he inquired.

"I was told that if I didn't lie and tell the police Elaine had gone on vacation and I had gone with her and came back, that Marie could fry," the witness declared. "Marie told me this herself."

Jeannie testified about the freezer being moved into her house, and said Marcie later confessed to her that parts of Elaine's body were stored inside. She demanded Marie move the freezer, she said. But when the younger woman opened it once, there was nothing in there but junk food.

She didn't tell police about the freezer and the

dead woman because she was worried about her friend's safety, the witness said. "I was afraid for Marcie's life. Marcie told me she would be killed if I talked."

When Jeannie was asked if she ever saw Marie signing any of Elaine's checks or attempting to duplicate the old woman's signature, she replied that she had. They were sitting at a table in the Honey Bear restaurant in Michigan City when Marie took Elaine's checkbook out and began trying to copy the signature, the witness testified. But she said she never saw Marie try to cash one of the checks.

Despite her nervousness and frequent confusion, Marcie had managed to skirt disaster during cross-examination, and under direct examination had scored some telling points for the prosecution. Her roommate was an effective witness as well. But Butch's testimony was still the key to the prosecution's case. And true to expectations, his time on the witness stand would provide some of the most dramatic moments of the trial.

When Butch first entered the courtroom after his handcuffs and chains were removed outside, he looked like a typical teenager. Dressed in dark trousers and a sweater with a large bright horizontal stripe across the front, and with his dark hair neatly trimmed, he could have easily passed for an average schoolboy. But he wasn't typical and he wasn't in court because he had been caught stealing watermelons from local farmers or showing off to friends by speeding in his father's car. He wasn't a prankster. He was an admitted murderer.

Working patiently and methodically, Duerring led Butch through a grisly reconstruction of Elaine's murder and dismemberment, which the boy said was carried out at his mother's direction. Much of Butch's direct testimony had already been disclosed in depositions and press accounts.

Responding to the deputy prosecutor's questions, Butch said he watched his mother sign Elaine's signature to Social Security checks and cash them, both before and after the old woman was killed. Throughout his testimony he consistently referred to the victim as "Elaine," not as his grandmother. There was no trace of emotion in his voice when he talked of shooting her or of helping to cut up her body.

When Duerring turned to questions about Paul's death, Butch repeated his statements from the bond hearing, claiming he saw Eric shoot their father in the head. His mother ordered him not to say anything about what he saw, he added.

Marie listened intently and stared without apparent emotion at her youngest son while he ticked off the hideous accusations one by one. Butch demonstrated an equal lack of emotion, and his voice had a disturbing flatness to it as he calmly continued the gory recital.

"I wanted to help my mother out," he said while explaining why he agreed to her demand that he murder Elaine. When Duerring asked why he used a crossbow, Butch laconically replied that it was fast and simple.

Emotional fireworks exploded during cross-examination of the short-tempered teenager. It was important to the defense's case to discredit the youth. His direct testimony against Marie had been devastating. King didn't waste any time in going to work on damage control. But it wasn't until the second day of cross-examination that the dam burst.

King was reviewing the witness's statements about Paul's shooting, when Butch repeated his assertion that his father beat him with a strap the night of the slaying. The lawyer asked why he was beaten.

"That's really none of your business why I was beaten up that night," the teenager snapped.

King insisted that he answer the question. Butch refused again, citing his Fifth Amendment rights against self-incrimination. So the lawyer appealed to the judge to tell the witness to reply. The judge complied, and the sulky boy responded by claiming he didn't remember.

By that time, Butch had abandoned his earlier practice of courteously addressing his mother's lawyer as "sir." Now he was behaving like a defiant brat, and calling King, "Mister." He growled the word as the defense attorney poked and prodded at his testimony.

The experienced courtroom lawyer and the boy had been crossing verbal swords for hours, bickering over just about everything. Butch replied with combative remarks such as, "Mister, I told you two times already"; "I hope you got that clear"; "I answered that question once."

As the interrogation continued, Butch was becoming increasingly hostile. Tension in the courtroom became thick and ugly while King continued to chew away at the young witness's statements, comparing his current testimony to a deposition he had given two months earlier about Marcie's possible role in discussions leading up to Elaine's murder. Butch said he didn't remember Marcie being in on the murder talk before Elaine was killed.

"Do you remember those answers to those questions in September of this year when you were also under oath?" King demanded.

"Dig, Mister. You better fix . . ." Butch began.

"I'm not digging anything. Answer my question," King snapped.

Butch slid from his chair and lurched forward, jamming a finger in the startled lawyer's face. "Dig, punk!" he gritted.

"Answer my question," the lawyer stubbornly insisted.

Curling the lips of his anger-warped face in a Jimmy Cagney grimace, Butch snarled: "You best cool your shit!"

Surprised gasps at the profanity and threatened violence rippled through the courtroom. Sheriff's deputies and bailiffs rushed at the skinny teenager, grabbing at his arms and positioning themselves between him and the lawyer. King asked the court for a recess to give the youngster a chance to calm down.

When he lost his temper and went after King, Butch was playing into the hands of the defense. The startling performance didn't help his credibility and may have hurt it.

Judge Martin concurred that a time-out was a good idea. "Just take it easy, Butch," he soothed. Then the judge ordered a brief recess. When court resumed and Butch was recalled to the stand about ten minutes later, the judge advised him not to take the attorney's hard-driving questioning personally. "He's just doing his job. Okay?" the jurist pointed out.

When Butch resumed his testimony, he was once more referring to King as "sir." The sour, surly child's face was transformed by a good-natured grin as he replied to continued questioning.

King asked several questions designed to demonstrate that Elaine had threatened to send Butch to military school after finding drugs in his room and money missing from her purse. Wasn't the threat of military school the reason Butch wanted to kill his grandmother?" the lawyer inquired.

"No, sir, it isn't," Butch courteously replied.

King turned to statements the witness previously made to psychiatrists purporting to have roamed some of the toughest neighborhoods in Michigan City stealing, selling drugs, and working as an enforcer for a dealer named "Marvin." Butch claimed he was twelve or thirteen when he and another enforcer named "Darrin" worked as musclemen for the mysterious dealer. He said he sometimes armed himself with double-edge daggers, butterfly knives, razors, and handguns. He punched or stabbed people who tried to rip off the dealer.

"Carry guns?" King asked, keeping his face straight.

"Once or twice," Butch said.

Butch said he also sometimes dealt drugs, and did his own enforcing. King asked him to explain what he did as a drug enforcer. Butch said he once took back some drugs after chasing down a man who tried to run off without paying.

"Did you have to hit him or knife him or anything like that?" the defense attorney inquired.

"Yes, sir!"

"Which?" King persisted. "What did you do to him, according to you?"

"Mister, I cut his gut open if you really want to know," Butch replied.

"Yes, I do! Yes, I do! Tell us about that cutting," King urged. He asked how old the victim was and if it was a man or woman. Butch replied that the victim was a man, about twenty-five years old.

Mental images of the dreadful street assault and other enforcer activities Butch claimed to be responsible for were difficult to reconcile with the slight, pallid adolescent who was talking so tough on the witness stand. The boy looked like he was still too young to grow a decent mustache. And despite all the bluster and attempts to impress his audience, it was hard to imagine the baby-faced witness holding his own with the

301

tough drug dealers, pimps, hookers, and knife-men on the city's rough-and-tumble northside which old-timers still referred to as "The Patch."

One experienced news reporter, who knew the Harborside Homes public housing area that replaced the old "Patch," was unimpressed with Butch's blustering about terrorizing welchers and other careless street people.

"Those jitterbugs down there would have slit that little boy's throat and cut his head into four pieces," he whispered to a neighbor in the spectator's area.

Earlier, King spent considerable time questioning Butch about Dungeons & Dragons, especially about some of the darker fantasy roles such as those of assassins and thieves the teenager reputedly adopted during the games. And he brought out the popularity of the crossbow as a weapon in D & D.

Drawing on the witness's talk with his brother in the Winnebago, the lawyer brought up the possibility of some sort of dark ritual tied to human sacrifice figuring into Butch's motive for murdering his grandmother. The youth firmly denied there was any connection.

King also grilled the boy about his claims of amazing psychic abilities, such as moving inanimate objects with the power of his mind. Butch agreed he made those claims, but said he was merely joking around.

"Just joking around! Remember Mr. George Nague from the Swanson Center here in Michigan City?" the lawyer asked. Butch agreed that he remembered talking with the counselor.

"Do you remember telling Mr. Nague as you sat in his office with him that you could make the desk rise from the floor?" King wanted to know.

The boy said he didn't remember the incident.

Butch was also questioned about a statement made months later to a psychiatrist that the night before shooting Elaine he drank something he called "Everclear," a concoction of a jigger-and-a-half of whiskey and two shots of coke. Did Butch remember telling the doctor he had drunk fourteen or fifteen of the shots?

Butch said he didn't remember saying that, but conceded it might be a true statement.

"You may have had fourteen or fifteen jiggers-and-a-half of whiskey the night before you did this to Elaine?" the lawyer asked.

"Possibly," Butch replied.

King asked if he also claimed that he smoked about five sticks of marijuana that night.

"Somewhere around there, yes," the witness agreed.

It was amazing testimony. Drinking such a prodigious amount of alcohol in such a short time could be expected to cause many people to lapse into a coma and very likely kill them. And according to the witness he had topped the booze off with marijuana before at last winding up the lonely party and somehow making it up two flights of stairs to his bed.

Butch's immature braggadocio may have fit in well with the image he wished to create for himself, but it didn't help his credibility. Too many of his stories appeared to be preposterous and outrageously unlikely. Nevertheless, his direct testimony against his mother had been damning.

And the prosecution still had one more family member waiting to testify against her. Two days after the trial opened, Eric dictated a formal statement to Boyd, changing his earlier accounts. Significantly, he also agreed to testify against his mother.

Like his mother and brother, Eric had already spent several months behind bars and tasted the bleak future that was in store for him. Marie had manipulated her sons as children and teenagers, but even that couldn't compare with the total lack of control over their lives which they had come to endure. Their lives and movement were now governed by corrections officers, lawyers, and the police. Not only were Eric's Navy days over, but he was denied such plebeian pleasures as ownership of a house key, midnight raids on the icebox, and movie dates with teenage sweethearts.

There weren't many options left in his life when he made one of the few decisions still available to him and elected, at last, to cooperate with prosecutors.

According to the last-minute pact with the prosecution, Eric would plead guilty to assisting a criminal for his part in helping dispose of the body. In return, if the plea recommendation was followed by the court he would be sentenced to a five-year prison term. The more serious charge of conspiracy to commit murder would be dismissed.

The agreement, however, did not affect the even more serious charges pending against him for the shooting of his father.

Eric and Butch shared some matching vulnerabilities as well as the same slender builds and baby-faced appearance, but their performances as witnesses were radically different.

Sporting a wispy but neatly trimmed pencil mustache over his upper lip and wearing a suit with a conservative white shirt and necktie, Eric was unflappable on the witness stand. He underwent the same type of persistent prodding from King as his brother had. But he refused to permit the experienced defense attorney to rattle him. Eric's demeanor on the witness stand was calm, unemotional, and dust dry.

He never veered from his statements that his mother nagged him for months to murder Elaine, and it was only after his brother carried out the slaying that he became involved in helping to dispose of the body.

Eric conceded he lied during a confrontation with Boyd before his arrest in San Diego, as well as in later statements under oath. He said he finally decided to testify against his mother after his lawyer showed him statements from other prosecution witnesses. Eric blamed his earlier lies on a desire to protect his mother and younger brother. At that time he had resolved to try and take all the blame on himself.

During later questioning, he also claimed that during a conversation with his mother after their arrest she suggested various schemes for letting either Butch or himself take all the blame.

The prosecutor asked if Marie had ever suggested taking the blame herself.

"No, sir," Eric replied.

The sober, soft-spoken witness testified that he played Dungeons & Dragons, and read books about such exotic subjects as black magic, witchcraft, and mental telepathy.

Asked about his father's death, Eric said he remembered loading a pistol, standing over the slumbering man's reclining body on the sofa, cocking the gun, and aiming it. He even recalled the muzzle flash and his father's naked body lurching upward off the couch. He insisted he didn't remember pulling the trigger, and moments after seeing the flash of the gunfire he put the weapon down and ran from the house.

As Eric testified, it was apparent that there were radical differences between his story and his brother's account of exactly what happened in the house on Beverly Shores Drive the night that Paul was killed. Eric said it was he who was beaten that evening, about an hour before the shooting. And he claimed Butch got in trouble with his father because he hadn't properly trained a dog, not because a bat was loose. Butch didn't even own a bat, he had a ferret, Eric declared.

Butch had testified he saw his older brother deliberately pull the trigger of the gun and shoot their father. Eric insisted he didn't remember the last moment just before the gun was fired, and claimed his younger brother couldn't have seen the shooting because he was locked in a back room of the house at the time.

The conflicts between the statements of the

two brothers were important to Eric's future, because he still faced the murder trial in Porter County. If Butch did indeed see the shooting, Eric would not be the only witness who was in the living room with his father that night. And if he shot his father only an hour after being beaten, a case might be made for killing in the heat of anger. In that event, there was the possibility of a jury finding of some degree of manslaughter, offenses which carried much more lenient penalties than murder.

There was one important point the brothers agreed on in their testimony about their father's shooting, however. Their mother nagged Eric for months to kill him.

During cross-examination, King asked Eric about Jeannie Frye's drinking habits while she was living with Marcie. The sailor said she drank excessively while the women were living together, but not as heavily as his grandmother.

Nondrinkers know as drinkers do that too much alcohol can impair perception and memory, and Jeannie had provided some damaging testimony against the defendant. It was part of King's job to create doubt about her testimony if he could.

"In fact, do you recall an occasion where you were aware that one time between the two of them they polished off three cases of beer?" King asked.

"Yes, sir," the witness politely responded.

"When was that?" the lawyer demanded.

"Several times," Eric said.

During another exchange, Eric testified he made admissions in his first statements to authorities that were designed to protect his mother and brother and take the blame on himself. Then he switched his motivations in later statements to trying to save himself, he said.

"It didn't work, did it?" King asked.

"No, it didn't," Eric agreed.

When Eric's testimony was finally concluded, he was followed on the witness stand by Tammy Willis.

The twenty-year-old witness traced her relationship with Eric. Herrbach then asked if she knew Eric's family.

"I thought I did," she said. The reply brought embarrassed titters from the crowded courtroom. For days the jury and spectators had been listening to testimony about drinking, doping, black magic, thievery, and murder. Obviously the Wittes weren't "The Waltons." They were more like "The Munsters" turned suddenly homicidal.

Tammy told of sending flowers to Elaine after Eric left for the Navy, and of visiting at the house after he completed boot camp. She said bottles of prescription pills were all over the place. "There were some for Paul, some for Marie for her heart, and then there [were] some for Eric and some for Butch," she testified. The witness said she only recalled noticing the identity of pills in one of the bottles. They were Valiums.

None of the testimony of other prosecution witnesses, including various law enforcement officers, evidence technicians, bankers or bank tellers, and salespeople who had dealt with Marie matched the emotional impact of the family members. But the spectators' gallery was full of reporters and other court-watchers when Menkel was called to testify.

Marie's former lover had already settled his debt with the Navy over going AWOL, and was assigned to duty doing accounting work aboard a Navy cruiser, the *USS Seattle*, when he seated himself in the witness stand.

The chastened twenty-two-year-old sailor disclosed that he was still playing Dungeons & Dragons. He and about forty of his shipmates aboard the *Seattle* were in a D & D club.

Herrbach quickly moved the questioning to Menkel's relationship with members of the Witte family—especially Marie.

As soon as Herrbach indicated he was approaching the sensitive subject of intimate sexual relations, however, Flynn raised a defense objection. Lawyers for the defense and the prosecution huddled briefly with the judge at a bench conference out of hearing of the jury. Then Judge Martin announced that the objection was overruled.

When testimony continued, Herrbach asked the witness to explain how he and the defendant "became better acquaintances, or better than merely acquaintances."

Menkel shifted uncomfortably in his seat. Herrbach was staring at him. "Well, we had sexual relations," the sailor replied.

"And when did that start?" the prosecutor asked.

Menkel couldn't recall the exact date, but said it was sometime in June or July of 1985.

"Was that before or after you realized, or Marie told you, that Elaine had been killed and you were an accessory?" Herrbach asked. Menkel said it was before.

"Did at any time during that relationship—did she try to influence you through sex or anything like that?" the prosecutor continued.

"No," the sailor said.

"Was it a mutual relationship?"

"Yes!" he responded.

Turning from the question of sex and seduction, Herrbach brought up the experimentation with the paranormal.

Menkel told the jury that Eric appeared to have some special powers of extrasensory perception, ESP. "He told me a few things about myself that he couldn't just have known," the witness explained. "I mean, it could have been a lucky guess or whatever, but it was somewhat consistent."

Herrbach asked if he and Eric had locked horns in a telekinetic battle at one time.

"I thought I saw something that wasn't there. He said he was using telekinetic power," Menkel responded. "Marie and John said they could."

Menkel's description of what he saw inside the ice cooler when Eric lifted the lid once to wipe it off with a rag drew the most gasps from spectators. Asked by Herrbach if he noticed anything unusual, he replied: "Yes, it had a lot of white worms on it and some small flying black bugs."

The sickeningly graphic description of maggots on Grandma Witte's putrefying remains drew an immediate response from Marie's lead defense attorney. King leaped to his feet and asked for a mistrial.

"I know the state's out here to prejudice as much as possible my client and I think at this point they've succeeded, and I have to respectfully move for a mistrial," he declared. The court overruled the motion, but King persisted.

"We're not prejudicing one guilty person any more than we are another guilty person," Herrbach defended.

King promptly asked again for a mistrial, this time based on Herrbach's remarks about guilt. No jury had yet decided that his client was guilty, the lawyer pointed out.

The judge denied both motions for mistrial. After another brief bench conference, however, he instructed the panel to disregard the deputy chief prosecutor's reference to guilt.

During cross-examination by King, Menkel said John had told him he worshipped demons and he was afraid of some kind of occult retaliation because of his involvement in black magic.

The trial was already underway when Schoonover left San Diego and headed for Indiana to testify as a prosecution witness at the trial. The night before his appearance on the witness stand, he met with the prosecution team and Pierce and Boyd in a local motel room. He had decided to get everything off his chest and to truthfully recount his activities with the Wittes and his part in getting rid of Elaine's body.

The young sailor was dressed in a neatly

pressed Navy blue winter uniform for his court-room appearance.

Duerring asked if he ever saw Elaine's body. "I observed a cooler at the trailer park," he replied. Schoonover said a bag in the cooler was filled with something like wet garbage that was heavy and shifted around when it was picked up. It smelled like rotting meat, he explained. "I was not aware of what had been done to the body. But when I saw the cooler, I had a good idea."

The sailor told the jury about playing Dungeons & Dragon, about discussing how a human body could be disposed of, and of learning for the first time that Grandma Witte was dead.

Schoonover admitted he lied to Naval investigators in the Philippines the first time he was questioned about the case because he was afraid he would be arrested. But he insisted he told the truth when he talked with Detective Sergeant Boyd. He wanted to clear his conscience. "It came to a point in my mind that I was afraid of what would happen to me," he said. "I wanted to get my part over with. It was eating me."

During stiff cross-examination by King, Schoonover was questioned extensively about the possibility of promises by the state not to charge him with helping to get rid of Elaine's body. Schoonover, who was never charged with any criminal offenses in the case, said there were no deals or promises of deals.

A few other witnesses testified about such matters as Marie's purchase of the trash compactor and garbage disposal, and about her banking transactions both before and after Elaine's death. Much of the testimony from bank employees was designed to show how Marie's personal accounts soared and Elaine's dwindled as her accounts were systematically looted.

The final witness before the prosecution rested its case was Larry Ziegler, the Secret Service document analyst and forgery expert. Questioning began by establishing the witness's credentials and background. He briefly traced his career and recounted an apprenticeship program he completed in handwriting analysis while he was a Baltimore policeman; graduation from the Secret Service Questioned Document School; then attendance at various seminars conducted by the FBI, U. S. Postal Service, the Health, Education and Welfare Departments, and other federal agencies. Ziegler said he was currently an instructor at the Questioned Document School, which was conducted in Washington and at a facility in Glencoe, Georgia.

Then Herrbach got down to the serious business of the documents the witness had examined that were tied to Elaine's checks and banking accounts.

Ziegler testified that three bank withdrawal slips he examined were signed with Elaine's name, but the signatures were false. The withdrawals, totaling nearly $3,000, were made after her death, he said.

The documents expert was unable to determine that the withdrawal slips were forged by Marie, however. The problem with making an exact determination of *who* signed certain forgeries was illustrated during an exchange dealing with the $6,000 withdrawal slip placed in evidence from the January 9, 1984, transaction, the day before Elaine was killed. The signature was a tracing.

The witness pointed out that almost anyone could trace someone else's signature. "In fact, a true payee could trace their own signature for the purpose of disavowing it at a later date," he explained. "It's very rarely done in my experience, but, you know, that's a possibility."

He said that various other documents he studied as part of the investigation were also tracings. "These are either direct tracings and/or simulations of the true payee's writing. And once again, there weren't enough habits or characteristics belonging to, in this particular instance, Hilma Marie Witte," he said.

Ziegler explained that he had observed two different types of tracings during his career examining suspicious signatures and documents.

He referred to one as a direct tracing, which he said is usually made in either of two ways.

One of the easiest means would be to hold a copy of an authentic signature against a window pane and take advantage of the light coming in from outside to trace it onto another piece of paper, he said. Ziegler remarked that the signature could be duplicated the same way children are taught to make tracings in kindergarten.

The other method requires use of carbon paper, which forgers can utilize by placing it under a sample of the authentic signature then tracing over it with a draftsman's stylus, knitting needle, ballpoint pen, or other narrowly pointed instrument. After the carbon is made, the forger merely needs to go over the tracing with a ballpoint pen, fountain pen, pencil, or whatever medium he chooses to use. There are other methods as well, Ziegler said, but those are the easiest.

The testimony provided the jury and spectators with an intriguing mini-lesson in forgery. But the court was concerned with the specifics of Marie and her banking activities.

Ziegler testified that what appeared to be Elaine's signatures on seventeen government checks were not signed by her. He added that the signatures on the forged checks showed writing peculiarities that were consistent with Marie's writing habits. It was his opinion that two U. S.

Treasury checks issued in December 1984, which appeared to carry Elaine's endorsements, were forged by Marie.

It was Friday afternoon when Ziegler's testimony was concluded, and the prosecution informed the court it had completed presentation of its case. Judge Martin had previously planned to continue the trial into the weekend, but changed his mind. After cautioning jurors not to talk to anyone about the case, not to read or watch news accounts of the trial, he announced an adjournment until Monday when the defense would begin its turn at bat.

After listening to nearly ten full days of testimony by exactly two dozen prosecution witnesses, one of the big questions courtroom buffs had been speculating about since the trial began was about to be answered: Would Marie Witte testify as a witness in her own defense?

Ten

Verdicts

Early Monday morning Judge Martin overruled a defense move for a directed verdict of acquittal based on the contention that the prosecution had provided insufficient proof to back up its case. After the judge disposed of a couple of additional matters, the jury was summoned into the courtroom and King called his first witness.

It was the beginning of the third week of an emotionally grueling trial, but Marie appeared composed and alert as she settled into the witness chair.

According to American law, defendants in criminal cases may testify in their own defense if they wish, or they may exercise their right to pass up that opportunity. It is up to them, and the prosecution has no right to insist on their testimony regardless of how much the state might wish to question them. Furthermore, judges are careful to advise juries that the fact that a defendant does not choose to testify can not be considered evidence of guilt.

The decision on whether or not to testify has at times been referred to as a coin toss for defense attorneys. But the observation is rarely made by professionals in the legal justice system, because it is woefully inaccurate. It's not the kind of determination that can be left to chance.

Defense attorneys must carefully weigh the possible advantages against disadvantages before permitting their clients to take the witness stand. How will her appearance and demeanor as a witness impress the jury? Will she present a sympathetic picture, or will she come across as a cold, hard, conniving manipulator and liar? And how will she stand up under cross-examination, which can be fierce and brutal? Also, once a defendant has chosen to testify, her decision may open up whole new areas of inquiry otherwise closed to the prosecution because of various rules of law.

King was aware of those possible pitfalls. But when all the evaluating was completed and it was decision-making time, it seemed to be in Marie's best interests to testify.

Marie retraced her dreary childhood, including

her sexual molestation when she was five, her life and wedding at the nudist camp, and her later marriage and life with Paul, as King led her through the early stages of her testimony.

Marie said that after Paul proposed, she married him even though she wasn't in love. But she fell in love with him later, and the early years together were pleasant until he had his accident and turned mean. He screamed at the boys and sexually bullied her, she claimed.

Then King brought her to the night of her husband's fatal shooting. According to her halting, tearful account, she wasn't in the house when Paul was killed. Marie said she went out early in the evening to visit a friend, and after returning home she left again with Butch to go to a store.

When she got home she remembered that she had forgotten to pick up some caramel corn Paul wanted, so she left again, this time by herself. She said she drove to the Bumble Bee liquor store to get the snack food, and when she returned home Eric was standing in the driveway with a pistol in his hand. Marie crumpled a tissue and dabbed at moist eyes as she recalled the dreadful scene.

" 'Mommy, Mommy, I tripped and fell.' " she quoted her boy as crying. "Then he kind of paused and then he said, 'And Daddy was shot.' "

Marie testified she took the weapon away from her distraught son and hurried inside, summoned an ambulance, then began pressing towels to the terrible wound in her husband's head. Tears flowed down her cheeks as she recalled that while she was soothing him, calling him "Honey," and trying to assure him it was going to be all right, he reached out and tenderly brushed her arm.

"The next thing I remember is the policeman moving me away from Paul," she said.

A short time later the police moved her into Paul's bedroom, she continued.

"You say Paul's bedroom?" King asked.

She explained that Paul slept in the bedroom, and she slept on a lovechair in the front room. She had been sleeping there on-and-off for several years, Marie continued.

Eric was outside with one of the dogs when she and the others were ushered into the bedroom, and she didn't know he had returned inside until she heard yelling. " 'Why did you kill your father?' 'Why did you kill your father?' " she said someone was demanding.

Marie said she tried to get out of the bedroom to her son, but was prevented from leaving for awhile. When she was eventually allowed to go to Eric, he appeared to be in shock.

"His face was expressionless. He had a kind of blank . . . like there was . . . just no expression, and when I called his name it was like he didn't hear me," she testified.

Continuing the emotional account, Marie told of taking Eric to the hospital emergency room. She said that after doctors looked the boy over, they told her he was in shock and she should try to keep him calm and make sure he had something to eat and drink. They told her to contact them if he appeared to be having any more problems.

King asked his client if she had known after coming home that night that her husband was going to be killed; if she had talked with her sons or her mother about killing or otherwise injuring her husband; if she had mixed drugs or poison in his food or knew of anyone else in the house doing that; or if she had ever thought of killing him.

Marie answered "No" to every question.

"Was there ever a point in your life during that period of time where you felt hatred toward the man?" the lawyer asked.

"Yes!" she replied. But she said she didn't hate Paul the night he was shot.

King moved on to the period when Marie and the boys moved into the house on Johnson Road with Grandma Witte. Marie referred to the old woman as "Mom" during her testimony.

323

She talked about Butch's problems in school, with neighborhood children, and at home. Asked about the boy's testimony about being kicked out of the house and living on the streets, she said it wasn't true. No one in the courtroom showed any obvious signs of surprise at her response indicating Butch's life on the street as an enforcer and drug dealer was a figment of his overactive imagination.

Butch had other means of obtaining spending money, according to her testimony.

One day someone at Krueger telephoned her and told her Butch was giving money away at the school, she said. When she confronted him and demanded to know where the money was coming from, he eventually admitted stealing it.

"He was taking it from Elaine and myself. We had money under the rugs, you know, kind of like money that you put aside for something." Marie also said he took money from dresser drawers and from their purses.

Depicting herself as a devoted, concerned mother, she said she tried to correct Butch's stealing, drinking, and other misbehavior by taking away his television, stereo, and telephone privileges. For awhile she even went to school and sat in the classroom with him in efforts to improve his performance as a student, she said. His grades improved after she began accompanying him to class.

According to Marie's story, she and Grandma Witte were desperate to find some way of disciplining the boy and improving his behavior. A few days before the slaying, the two women had a long talk about money missing from Elaine's checking accounts which they believed Butch was withdrawing from automatic teller machines. Marie claimed Elaine offered to help send the boy to military school where he could get the male supervision he needed. Elaine, in fact, indicated she would pay a big portion, possibly even all of the cost.

Continuing her story, Marie said they agreed she should confront Butch the next day about the missing money, and advise him of the decision to send him to military school. Elaine didn't want to be present when Butch was told about the plan. Marie said when she confronted her son he denied using the ATM card, and they wound up in a nasty quarrel. Finally she took Elaine's savings passbook from a drawer, traced the old woman's signature on a withdrawal ticket and ordered her son to get into the car.

Marie had planned to take Marcie shopping, she said. So with Butch in tow, she picked up her mother, then drove to Citizens' Bank where Elaine had her account to make a withdrawal. Marie had spilled a can of Tab on the withdrawal slip, so she had her mother make out another one for the same amount — $6,000.

Marie said she deposited half the money into Elaine's checking account and took the rest in cash. She said that as she drove away from the teller lane, she turned to her son and told him: "Read it and weep, buddy. You are on your way. You are going to military school."

A short time later she deposited the cash in her own checking and savings accounts at the Chesterton State Bank in Chesterton.

The witness claimed she told Elaine later that evening about withdrawing the $6,000, and the older woman agreed it was the right thing to do if it would get Butch into military school.

Elaine was killed the next morning. Every eye in the courtroom was on Marie as she described the last morning of the old woman's life.

The thirty-eight-year-old defendant occasionally wiped at tears that slowly welled from her eyes and spilled over the sharp planes of her slender face during her sometimes halting testimony. But the tears came in a flood when she gave her version of first learning the old woman who had been a substitute mother for her was dead.

Marie said she planned to catch a South Shore train in Michigan City at 7:00 A.M. the next morning for the trip to Chicago to attend the Social Security hearing. She got up about 5:00 A.M. to get ready for the trip and a bit later saw Butch in the dining room with the crossbow. She told him to put it away because it wasn't his, then returned to her bedroom to fix her hair and get dressed.

She was almost ready to leave the house when she called for Butch. He didn't reply, so she walked upstairs looking for him. Walking into Elaine's bedroom, she found him standing beside the bed, crying.

"I'm sorry! I didn't mean it. I didn't mean it," he bawled. Elaine was lying on the bed with a crossbow bolt in her chest.

There was absolute silence in the courtroom for a moment. Then King asked what happened next.

"I went over to see if she was all right, and she was dead," Marie replied. She said she told Butch she was going to call an ambulance, but he was hysterical. He grabbed her arm, and screamed at her that he didn't want her to call anyone. He repeatedly told her, " 'Remember what happened before?' "

Marie eventually agreed not to call anyone, but it was obvious something had to be done with the old woman's body. Marie testified that her son told her he would take care of the problem and she returned downstairs. But a few minutes later he returned and said he needed help upstairs.

When she got upstairs she found that Butch had dumped Elaine upside down in the trash can and needed help moving it. But when they lifted it, the lid kept popping off. Finally Butch tied some rope through the handles and secured the lid so they could lug the can outside and put it in the closet of another of the bedrooms. Then, she said, they made up the bed and left for Chicago.

Marie told of attending the hearing and of returning to Michigan City. She said they stopped briefly at the house and discovered the furnace had broken before she telephoned her mother.

Most of the gory details of the dismemberment, destruction, and disposal of Elaine's remains were quickly passed over during the direct examination. But Marie admitted helping to get rid of her mother-in-law's body and looting her bank accounts after the shooting. But she staunchly denied she plotted the murder, and insisted she only helped with the disposal of the body because she wanted to protect her son.

"Did you ever discuss or plan with anyone, hurting or killing Elaine Witte in any way?" King asked.

Marie held her head up straight and looked directly at the lawyer as she replied. "No, sir," she said firmly.

"Did you ever administer any sort of drug or poison to Elaine Witte at any time?"

"Never!"

Marie insisted she never tried to get either of her sons to kill their grandmother, and she never threatened her own mother.

"I loved them. I'm hurt by what they have done," she said of Marcie and the boys. "I think they need psychiatric help."

King announced that he was through with the witness. If there was anything easy about Marie's appearance on the witness stand, that part was over. It was the prosecution's turn to cross-examine the witness, and Herrbach wasn't gentle.

The chief deputy prosecutor began his questioning by establishing that despite the years of abuse Marie claimed she and the boys suffered at Paul's hands, she never filed for divorce.

As testimony moved on to the second slaying, she again explained that after Butch told her he had killed Elaine she let him talk her out of calling an ambulance or the police. Instead, she said she agreed to help him dispose of the corpse because the boy was afraid of facing the same kind of rough treatment from police his older brother had undergone after Paul's shooting.

She said she didn't remember whose idea it was to get rid of the body, but admitted buying the microwave, garbage disposal unit, and trash compactor used in the efforts to cook, grind, and crush it.

But she balked at being portrayed as a manipulator of young men, when Herrbach asked if she would admit using Menkel to crush Elaine's teeth.

"I did not use Doug," she declared.

"You had Doug do it, did you not?" Herrbach persisted.

"I asked Doug for help, and Doug helped me on his own," she said.

Herrbach asked if she would admit to having Menkel help dispose of Elaine's body parts. She replied that she asked him what to do and he told her. Then the prosecutor asked the same questions about Schoonover.

"I did not use Jeff," she said. "Again, I asked Jeff, 'Jeff—'"

Herrbach cut her denial off in mid-sentence. "That's your answer?" he asked, the tone of disbelief obvious in his voice. Marie responded that she didn't know how to give him a truthful answer to the question.

Herrbach accused her of planning to get rid of all the evidence so the police couldn't prove there was a murder or tie the murder to anyone. She denied the accusation and claimed she only helped dispose of Elaine's remains because Butch had already started cutting it up. There was no plan, she insisted. The dismemberment of Elaine's body was something that just happened.

As the cross-examination continued, Marie admitted lying to Barbara Valencia, to Elaine's friends, and to the police about the whereabouts of the missing woman. She admitted lying to bank employees when she cashed Elaine's checks, lying to Gerald Gallion when the house was remodeled, and lying to Mrs. Bentley when the car was sold. But she denied initially lying to Menkel. And she claimed that she didn't give Mrs. Griswold permission to sell the furniture, except for a pool table.

When Marie at last concluded her testimony it was nearly three o'clock Monday afternoon. Judge Martin adjourned the trial for the rest of the day. The proceeding had moved into its third week and was rapidly winding down.

Shortly after 9:00 A.M., Tuesday, King called Dr. Chester F. McClure to testify. He was the first of two psychiatrists who would be called as defense witnesses.

Dr. McClure had met twice with Butch at the LaPorte County Detention Center the previous January to determine his competency to understand the charges against him and to assist in his own defense. The psychiatrist recalled Butch's boastful claims of being a black belt and of winning a state championship in long-bow archery. And he testified that Butch told him Marie suggested while they were playing Dungeons & Dragons that he kill Elaine.

Continuing to trace his conversations with the boy, the psychiatrist said Butch talked of being the leader of a group of Michigan City street toughs called the Angel Gang, and once broke several ribs and cut the Achilles tendon of another youngster he beat up.

During their meetings Butch didn't show the signs of remorse that would normally be expected of someone in his situation, Dr. McClure added.

"He was what we call a rather flat affect. That is, he did not have much facial expression as he talked, and I designated that he was quite unemotional during the relating of these facts," the witness explained.

During cross-examination by Herrbach, however, Dr. McClure told the jury that he concluded the teenager was sane during the interviews and at the time of the slaying, although he was under extreme pressure from Marie.

Even though Dr. McClure didn't diagnose

Butch as a sociopath, when he was asked a few minutes later about the term during redirect examination by King, he elaborated on the definition of a sociopath for the jury.

"Sociopaths are (in psychiatric terms) in a limbo as far as the law is concerned," he explained. "In psychiatric terms they are persons who do not learn from their mistakes and they—neither the psychiatrist nor the courts—really look at this as a mental illness. Half of the men at the prison are sociopaths."

Continuing, he said they are people who lack empathy with others. "When you and I harm someone, we feel badly about it," he said. "There seems to be a lack of ability to empathize or feel for the other person in the sociopathic personality. . . . He has an ability to act a great deal. He's commonly known as a con man."

Sociopaths tend to be liars, he agreed in response to a question by the defense lawyer.

The other psychiatrist, Dr. George A. Batacan, also interviewed Butch twice during January. A medical director of the Adult Psychiatric unit of Kingwood Hospital in Michigan City, the witness told the jury he had diagnosed the youth as a sociopath. Dr. Batacan defined the term as a person with an immature personality and a lack of moral judgment.

As he did when he talked with the other psychiatrist, Butch had woven a fanciful story for Dr. Batacan of living on the streets after his father died.

Dr. Batacan talked extensively to the teenager about Dungeons & Dragons, and King asked if Butch had described Elaine's shooting with the crossbow in terms of the game. The witness said he didn't, although he provided a step-by-step chronicle of events leading up to the killing.

Referring to two basic character alignments Butch had outlined as being observed in the game, "neutral good" and "neutral evil," King asked if Butch had described what his feelings were at the time Elaine was shot.

Dr. Batacan said Butch told him he had "neutral feelings."

Butch apparently hadn't branded his feelings as either "neutral good" or "neutral evil," but it seemed the question had been planted in the jury's mind: With all the assassins, monsters, and other characters in Dungeons & Dragons and the battling between good and evil, could Butch have believed he was merely killing off another player when he shot his grandmother with the crossbow? Could her death have been as easily accomplished in real life as was the killing of Marie and Tammy's characters in the fantasy world of Dungeons & Dragons?

Dr. Batacan also remarked about Butch's absence of visible emotion while discussing the horrendous things that had happened in his life. He said Butch told him he never liked his mother.

When Herrbach had his opportunity to cross-examine the witness, he quickly moved to the question of Butch's emotions at the time Elaine was killed and to whether or not he might have been influenced by his fondness for Dungeons & Dragons. He asked if Butch's remark about feeling "neutral" when Elaine was killed was linked to the roles in the fantasy game, or if he merely meant he didn't have any guilt feelings one way or another about his grandmother's death. Batacan said Butch indulged in fantasies tied to the game, but he did not live those fantasies.

If King had scored a point earlier that tended to blame Dungeons & Dragons for playing a major role in Elaine's death, rather than Marie, it had apparently been nullified. Based on the psychiatrist's examinations and conclusions, Butch didn't kill Elaine because he was living a fantasy role tied to the game.

The defense lawyer had one more chance at the witness, during redirect examination. He asked Dr. Batacan if he accepted the things Butch told him as being true. The psychiatrist said he did. King asked if he accepted Butch's statements about being a twelve-year-old enforcer for a drug dealer.

"At the time I accepted it as a statement of fact on his part because I don't believe that there is an age limit," Dr. Batacan responded. "I don't know that there is an age limit as to what is supposed to be an enforcer or not."

One of the bankers who had appeared on the witness stand earlier was briefly recalled to clarify testimony about some of the transactions involving Elaine's checks and accounts. Then King called Sergeant Boyd as a witness.

King warmed up by establishing Boyd's credentials. The lawman stated he was a sixteen-year veteran of the Indiana State Police Department, and had worked as an investigator for all but about five years of that time.

Then the defense attorney got down to the serious business of the interviews Boyd had conducted and the statements he had taken from the defendant's sons in California and in Indiana.

King conducted a grueling examination, jumping from one statement to another while stringing together a bewildering scatter of dates, names, and phrases that flashed and flickered through the courtroom like heat lightning. He asked questions about statements on November 6, November 7, November 14, and January 10, rapidly shifting from one to another.

Boyd was once permitted to leave the stand to

fish out copies of statements and reports from his files and help refresh his memory. But he refused to become confused by the barrage of questions, and he and King traded some sharp exchanges.

"Well, your object is to get a complete statement, correct?" King demanded at one point while going over interrogation techniques.

"My object is to get the truth!" the state police detective replied. Boyd knew how to handle himself on the witness stand.

The lawyer and the police investigator clashed again over Butch's statement of November 14, when Boyd couldn't immediately come up with a written record or transcript of certain remarks the detective had made at the time.

"Mr. King, if I kept copies of everything that I said, there'd be mounds of paper in here," the policeman declared.

"All right, Sergeant! You know I've got copies of everything, too?"

"Yes, sir, I know."

"I think that's an occupational hazard," King observed.

"It surely is," the witness wearily agreed.

At the conclusion of Boyd's testimony, a couple more witnesses who appeared earlier were recalled briefly and asked additional questions by Herrbach.

Menkel testified that Marie had told him Paul mistreated her and she had thought about various ways to kill him, including poison and by gunshot. The prosecutor asked if she ever mentioned who the killer should be.

"As far as who would do it, she said that Eric would be most likely because it would be hard to prosecute a juvenile," the sailor replied.

King moved quickly during cross-examination to repair the damage. Responding to his questions, Menkel agreed that Marie told him Paul's death was an accident. The talk of murder, judging from the witness's response to the defense questioning, was only that: Just talk!

It was 1:30 P.M. in the afternoon when Menkel's second session on the witness stand was ended, and testimony in the lengthy proceeding was concluded. Judge Martin adjourned the trial for the day. He explained to the jury that he wanted to work on his final instructions and give them an opportunity to return to court the next morning refreshed and ready to listen to final arguments.

Early Wednesday morning on November 20, three-and-a-half weeks after the trial got underway, attorneys began their summations to the jury.

Herrbach characterized Marie as a ruthless, money-hungry schemer who manipulated her own sons into murdering their father and step-grandmother. "This is not a complicated case," he said. "The motive is as old as crime itself: greed!"

Crisp and precise, the chief deputy prosecutor recalled testimony about the looting of Elaine's bank accounts before and after her death. And he said Paul died because Marie was worried that if she got a divorce she would lose everything. The two murders were so much alike they were like a signature or a fingerprint, he said.

Even after setting up Grandma Witte's murder, Marie could hardly wait before ridding herself of the old woman's treasures and begin spending her money, according to the prosecutor. He pointed out she remodeled the house and bought a car and a Winnebago camper. "Marie was caught with her hands in the cookie jar," Herrbach declared.

Herrbach scoffed at the defense's contention that Marie was protective of her youngest son, pointing to her testimony laying the blame for Grandma Witte's slaying on him.

He accused the defendant of setting up premeditated murder and said she was so cool that she didn't even bother to call off the Social Security hearing after the old woman was killed. Marie was able to represent herself so well at the

339

hearing, only a few hours after the slaying, that she was able to get her payments restored, the prosecutor pointed out.

Returning to the relationship between the defendant and her youngest son, he asked: "What do you do with a sixteen-year-old boy who never had a chance, who had a mother like Marie to raise him?"

In the defense's summation, King painted a far different picture of his client. Instead of a malignant woman of almost supernatural evil, he depicted her as a loving mother who was being victimized by liars. And he claimed the prosecution failed in its effort to demonstrate that Marie was a manipulative woman who took advantage of people and used sex to manipulate one of her eldest son's friends into doing her bidding.

The lawyer's summation also seemed to confirm that he had deliberately prodded Butch on the witness stand so the youth would lose his temper and betray his real character. King pointed to discrepancies in the testimony of the brothers and of their grandmother, Marcie O'Donnell, about the night of Paul Witte's shooting.

King suggested it was Butch who had looted Grandma Witte's bank account by using her ATM card, prior to the old woman's murder.

And he reiterated his contention that Butch had the motive for murder. The teenager had been caught drinking alcohol, using drugs, stealing, and skipping school, and the old woman wasn't going to put up with his misbehavior any longer. Butch believed his grandmother was going to pay to have him sent away to military school, King told the jury.

"This kid was capable, and, in fact, did shoot Elaine Witte for his own reasons," the lawyer declared.

The only contrary evidence to that assertion, he claimed, was the testimony of the brothers and their maternal grandmother. And that was the word of liars, he insisted. "You cannot believe these people beyond a reasonable doubt," he declared.

"What they have done in this case is parade before you liars and people who did make deals. I don't care how much Mr. Herrbach sugarcoats it."

At the conclusion of the summations, Judge Martin ordered a recess for lunch. When court reconvened, he issued jury instructions, and the panel began deliberations.

If Marie had any supporters other than her attorneys, they were keeping their partisanship to themselves. Based on the courthouse gossip and talk in nearby cafes and bars, Marie had already been judged by her neighbors. Regardless of what the jury might decide, they had made up their minds: She was guilty as sin!

A few minutes after 7:00 P.M., following a break for dinner, jury foreman Delbert E. Miller signaled that verdicts had been reached.

Members of the prosecution and defense teams were notified and hurried into the courtroom. Dressed modestly in a matching gray blazer, gray skirt, and checkered blouse, Marie appeared composed and looked neither to the left nor to the right as she walked quietly inside and took her seat at the defense table between King and Flynn.

News reporters and a few other persistent spectators who were determined to see the trial to the end settled onto the hard benches in the sparsely filled courtroom.

The jury announced they had found the defendant guilty on both counts: murder and conspiracy to commit murder. As the verdict was announced, Pierce and Boyd, the two rugged veteran police officers who had worked so hard on the case, reached over and gave each other a congratulatory hug. "It was just like the movies," Pierce later recalled.

The defendant appeared to be fighting back

tears as she listened to the verdict. When court was adjourned, she exchanged a few half-whispered words with her lawyer, gave him a nervous peck on the cheek, then was led away to be driven back to the county jail.

Outside the courtroom, Paul Witte's mother and sister were in tears. "I'm not crying for me," Mrs. Bowyer told a reporter. "Look what she's done to my grandsons. My son's gone! My grandsons are gone!"

Henry Lange and several of his colleagues from the media were skipping between Paul's relatives, prosecutors, and King, trying to talk to all of them at once before they drifted away from the courthouse.

The defense attorney told reporters he and his client were "obviously disappointed." He also indicated he would probably file an appeal based at least in part on defense contentions that admission of testimony about Paul Witte's death made it impossible to obtain a fair trial.

Herrbach said he would ask for the maximum penalty, one hundred and ten years in prison, including sixty years on the murder charge and fifty years for conspiracy to murder. The court would be asked to order the terms served consecutively.

Minutes before adjourning the court, Judge

343

Martin had scheduled sentencing for four weeks later, December 20. In the meantime, Marie and King would be busy in Valparaiso. Her trial on charges that she masterminded the murder of her husband was set to begin in Porter County Circuit Court on December 2.

Eleven
The Second Trial

After the sensational and grisly testimony of Marie's trial for engineering Elaine's murder, her second trial was largely anticlimactic.

King's effort to have the trial moved to another county was rejected, and it began on schedule, December 2, in the old Porter County Courthouse in the center of downtown Valparaiso.

It was true there had been months of publicity over the sensational case. Testimony during Marie's recent trial in Michigan City about Butch's claims of occult powers and references to the possibility of human sacrifice as a possible motive for Elaine's murder had also helped fuel fears of Satanic and black magic activities in the area.

Only a few weeks before the trial was scheduled to begin, police rounded up fourteen teenagers in Chesterton cemetery. The youngsters were carrying a copy of The Satanic Bible, a Ouija board, and a ceremonial knife. Some of the youths told police they were looking for the grave of another teenager who had died a violent death.

A few days later the outer walls of Krueger Junior High School which Butch once attended was spray painted with crudely sketched crescents, pitchforks, and other occult symbols.

A reporter for the *South Bend Tribune* tied the ominous occult activities occurring in northern Indiana and Marie's trial in Michigan City all together in the same disturbing account published on November 25. It was less than a week before jury selection for Marie's trial in Valparaiso got underway.

But newspaper reporters weren't prosecuting or defending Marie in court. That was the job of Berning and King. Their immediate task was selecting an impartial jury composed of people who weren't prejudiced by either the strange rumors flashing around the Dunesland area or by stories they may have already heard about Marie's homicidal ways.

And like King, Berning had picked jurors for high-profile criminal trials before. A native Hoosier, the small-town county prosecutor followed a couple of uncles into the legal profession. After completing high school in Fort Wayne, he attended Wabash College in Crawfordsville. Then, like Herrbach, he enrolled in Valparaiso University Law School.

Although he planned to return to his hometown in Allen County after graduation in 1977 and work as a law clerk for a judge there, he changed his plans after talking with a friend he played basketball with at the Valparaiso YMCA.

The friend was the chief deputy with the Porter County Prosecutor's Office and tipped him off that there was a job opening as an investigator. Berning took the job and quickly began moving up through the ranks, becoming a deputy prosecutor, then in 1979 taking over his friend's former job as chief deputy prosecutor.

In March 1982, about six months after Paul Witte was shot to death and a little more than three years before his widow would be put on trial for reputedly masterminding the slaying, Berning was elected Porter County Prosecutor.

Berning wasn't a prosecutor who put a lot of faith in the popular practice in some of the larger jurisdictions around the country of calling in psychologists and other specialists who supposedly had special insight into the mental processes of prospective jurors and how they might treat the evidence in a case. He relied on his experience, and the personal gut feeling he was left with after asking a few basic questions during the venire selection of the jury. That technique served him well enough in the half-dozen or so homicide cases he had already personally prosecuted.

Despite the widespread publicity about the Witte slayings, nervousness over the weird goings-on in the graveyard, and gossip about the possibility of organized groups of Satanists at work in the area, a jury of six men and six women was selected the first day.

There were some dramatic differences in the setting for the trial in Valparaiso and its earlier counterpart in Michigan City. More than half the seats in the spectator area were empty when the jury was seated and the proceeding moved to the prosecutor's opening statement.

Only a few faithful reporters from the area media in Valparaiso, Gary, LaPorte, Michigan City, and South Bend were bothering to cover Marie's second trial. The national media, including the Chicago press, lost major interest in the case after the drama and titillation of the more sensational first trial. There would be no titillating or grisly testimony about murders with exotic medieval weapons, ground-up or acid-soaked bodies of old ladies to be disposed of in cross-country dumpings, or young sailors in Marie's trial for her husband's murder.

* * *

In his opening statement, the prosecutor covered much of the same ground Herrbach went over during the first trial. Even Berning's style was much like that of the chief deputy prosecutor in the adjoining county. They were both well-prepared and methodical, and built their cases for the juries with building-block precision.

A slender six-foot, three-inches-tall, Berning is confident and precise in the courtroom. In the court of law or on the basketball court, he plays to win. And he had the same devastating trio of Marie's family members waiting to testify against her in Valparaiso that Herrbach had called in Michigan City.

The testimony of the brothers again differed in regard to Butch's location when their father was shot. Butch said he was in the living room and saw the shooting. Eric said his younger brother was locked in another room and couldn't possibly have seen their father shot.

Eric conceded that he intended to kill his father when he took the pistol from the cabinet on the night of the shooting. But he said he may have changed his mind and discharged the gun accidentally while backing away from the dozing man. He couldn't remember pulling the trigger, he told the somber, silent jury.

Marie again sat motionless and blank-faced

349

beside her attorney, while her sons and mother repeated their dreadful testimony.

King's effort to present two psychiatric reports from prosecution witnesses relating to Butch and his Grandmother O'Donnell was rebuffed by the judge, and the defense called only one witness.

This time Marie did not testify. If she had chosen to become a witness, the prosecution would have been permitted to bring up her conviction in LaPorte County. The decision to pass up the opportunity to take the stand in her own defense ruled out any possibility of damaging cross-examination about her role in Grandma Witte's slaying.

King argued during summation, as he had in Michigan City, that the murder was committed by one of Marie's sons, and she was involved later only in attempting to cover up the crime. He claimed Eric killed Paul to protect himself and other family members from the victim's violence.

"Baloney," the prosecutor responded during his summation. "Why would three family members come in and frame the defendant?" he demanded. Berning claimed to the jury that Marie was the mastermind, and used her oldest son to get rid of the husband she no longer wanted.

The lanky prosecutor also addressed testimony by witnesses depicting Paul as abusive to his family. "The natural inclination is to feel sorry for the children and maybe even Marie Witte," he reminded the jury. "But remember, what is abuse to some people is discipline to others.

"The question is, did Eric Witte knowingly kill Paul Witte, and did Marie Witte induce him to do it? Did she attempt to poison Paul Witte? He isn't here to tell his side," Berning declared.

Despite the conflicts in the accounts of two of the major witnesses in the Porter County trial, the result was the same. And this time the proceeding took only three days, not three weeks. After six hours of deliberation the jury returned their verdicts: guilty of murder and guilty of attempted murder.

There were no tears or outbursts from Marie when she heard the jury's decision. She accepted the verdicts calmly, and once more was returned to jail to await sentencing. As she did in LaPorte County Superior Court, she faced a possible maximum combined sentence on both counts of 110 years in prison. Judge Douglas scheduled her sentencing hearing for January 3.

* * *

On December 20, she appeared before Judge Martin in Michigan City to be sentenced for Elaine's murder. As a convicted murderess, the neat business suits she wore for her trials had been stored or given away. She was dressed for sentencing in an oversized blouse and prison pants, and manacles and chains were locked around her waist and wrists.

When it was his turn to plead for a more lenient sentence, King began by pointing out that his client continued to maintain that she was innocent of the crimes she was convicted of.

With that out of the way, he asked the judge to order concurrent sentences on the convictions instead of stacking them one on the other. He backed up his request by recalling his pretrial motion for dismissal on the grounds that prosecution on the twin charges of conspiracy and of murder constituted double jeopardy. The way to avoid the issue, he said, would be to order concurrent sentences.

Continuing, he addressed the hideous means that Elaine's body was disposed of. "As I told the court and the jury during trial, at no time did we make any effort, nor do we now, to minimize my client's involvement in that aspect of this case. And it was an aggravating thing. It is something that is troubling to anyone involved in this profession to hear accounts of something happening to this wonderful elderly lady, to her body after the fact of her death," he said.

Then he returned to his earlier criticism of the plea bargain agreements extended to other players in the grisly drama.

He pointed out that Eric offered advice about how to dispose of the body, and helped transport and get rid of the remains. Yet he wound up with only a five-year prison sentence for assisting a criminal and wasn't even charged for conspiracy to commit murder.

Menkel was deeply involved in disposing of the remains, even helping crush the teeth of the old woman, yet he served only 211 days behind bars on a misdemeanor and was allowed to return to duty with the Navy.

Jeffrey Schoonover wasn't charged with any criminal offense and never lost so much as a day's pay from the Navy, despite his involvement in the disposal of the body.

Butch, who committed the murder, was given a twenty-year term for manslaughter. "In ten years, at age twenty-five, that sociopath will be unleashed, at least initially, into this community," King declared.

And Marcie got off with a charge of assisting a criminal, not the more serious offense of conspiracy, even though by her own account she was deeply involved in the conspiracy.

"Now, make no mistake, I have as a deputy prosecutor and as an assistant United States attorney, realized the necessity of making deals, and sometimes very distasteful deals," he said. "But in this case, I have to confess to the court, I have never seen the use of dealing, plea bargaining, to the extent it was utilized in this case."

He said he was sure the prosecution would ask for a sentence of 110 years. "They want vindication from this court, they want the court to underwrite, to justify the deals that they've made," he said. "I don't think the court, in whatever sentence it is going to give, is going to give a sentence with that in mind." It would not be justice, he asserted, "to dump Marie into a cell without any hope of ever seeing the light of day outside a penitentiary."

When Herrbach at last had his chance at bat, he asked the court to impose the maximum sentence. He cited the meanness of the crime and the absence of contrition and insisted that aggravating circumstances were proven that justified a stiff sentence.

"I would ask the court to remember the testimony of Eric Witte that his mother even asked him as early as 1982 to kill Elaine Witte. That after he refused, and even moved out of the house, that she continued and asked her other

354

son to do the killing that she for some reason did not want to do," Herrbach pleaded.

"And then we have to remember, not only did this mother use her children to commit the crime in this case and dismember and dispose of the body, but she also killed a person who was seventy-four years of age, a senior citizen of our community, a person whose only crime was taking the defendant and her family into her home and giving her money on occasion to live on," he continued.

"But that wasn't good enough for the defendant. It wasn't enough money.

"When we were talking of the murder of a senior citizen, your Honor, we weren't talking of an act that occurred in a matter of seconds. We're talking of a cold, calculated conjuring of a plan and waiting until this senior citizen was at her weakest moment, lying in her castle, asleep in her bed," the prosecutor told the judge. Elaine's body hadn't even been left intact so she could have a normal funeral.

He asked the court to consider the "cold viciousness" demonstrated in the killing and dismemberment in determining the sentence.

"I suppose the real sad part of this particular crime is that, yes, John "Butch" Witte may be a sociopath. But we know also that a sociopath's character is learned from their parents, as the psychiatrist testified," he declared. "And a child becomes what they learn at home."

The prosecutor pointed out Marie hadn't shown any signs of repentance or remorse. The final slap in the face was her testimony attempting to blame her youngest son for the terrible act she put him up to.

He asked the judge to impose the maximum penalty and order that they be served consecutively instead of concurrently.

Herrbach's statement was a terrible indictment, but Marie listened and watched stone-faced.

King was given a final opportunity to plead for mercy for his client, when Judge Martin asked him if he wished to present a brief rebuttal. The defense asked once more to carefully consider ordering concurrent sentences.

When Marie was at last called before the bench for sentencing she declined an invitation by the judge to speak.

The jurist's presentencing remarks to the woman standing before him were harsh and uncompromising. He said that aggravating circumstances as outlined in Indiana law to justify the most severe sentences were proven. Marie caused the death of a person over sixty-five years old. Furthermore she stole money from the victim both while Elaine was alive and after her death. There were other aggravating circumstances as well.

"But Mrs. Witte, all those aggravating circumstances pale to insignificance when you consider the primary one, which is that you caused the destruction, not only of Elaine Witte, but you caused the destruction of your own son, your own son, your youngest son by forcing him to commit the actual killing," the judge scolded.

"This act, the act of killing Elaine Witte was horrible enough. But the final act of causing the destruction of your own son by making him do what he did is heinous almost beyond comprehension."

Judge Martin sentenced Marie to sixty years on the murder charge, and another thirty years for conspiracy to murder. He ordered the sentences to be served consecutively.

Marie was advised she would be given credit for 216 days already spent behind bars. The judge confirmed that the sheriff had recommended additional credit for good behavior, referred to in correctional and legal parlance as "good time." Then he added the court's recommendation for "good time" credit as well.

Marie would not even begin serving her new sentences until completing the ten-year term she faced on the federal court conviction for forging and cashing Elaine's Social Security checks. And she still faced sentencing in Porter County for engineering the murder of her husband.

* * *

On Friday morning, January 3, Marie was again led in manacles into a courtroom to be sentenced for using one of her sons to carry out the murder of another family member. This time she was in the Porter County Courthouse in Valparaiso, about fifty miles southwest of Michigan City. She was dressed for the somber occasion in loose-fitting green prison pants and shirt, with white tennis shoes.

Berning told the judge he was sorry he couldn't ask for the death penalty. Consequently, he requested the court to do what he termed "the next best thing," and impose a long sentence that would insure Marie was never released from prison. "I think it's appropriate that she never sees the light of day again," he declared.

King repeated his contention that Eric was responsible for Paul's slaying. "We do not know, and in light of the events of the past week, may never know Eric Witte's motivation," he declared. The defense lawyer complained that prosecutors in both trials had minimized the roles of the actual killers of Paul and Elaine Witte.

The previous Monday, only a week before Eric's murder trial for the slaying of his father was scheduled to begin, another plea bargain was agreed upon. He was to be permitted to plead guilty to a scaled-down charge of voluntary manslaughter. Berning planned to ask for a twenty-year prison sentence.

After the attorney's statements, the judge sentenced Marie to concurrent fifty-year prison terms on the charges of murder and of attempted murder. But he ordered that the sentences were to be served consecutively to the terms imposed in LaPorte County.

Convicted in three jurisdictions, Marie had amassed a staggering total of 150 consecutive years of prison sentences. Based on the Indiana Criminal Code and Corrections Department regulations in force at the time, the thirty-eight-year-old woman would have to serve a minimum of seventy years of the sentences imposed by the state courts before becoming eligible for parole.

In May 1986, Eric was sentenced by Porter Count Superior Court Judge Roger Bradford to a twenty-year prison term.

In LaPorte County Superior Court Eric and his Grandmother O'Donnell were each given five-year prison terms on their guilty pleas to assisting a criminal for their roles helping dispose of Elaine's body. All of Eric's sentences, including his four-year term stemming from his federal court conviction in San Diego, were to be served concurrently. He would become eligible for parole in about ten years.

Marcie, who had observed her sixtieth birthday behind bars, also faced charges of attempted murder for trying to poison her son-in-law. In March 1986 she was permitted to plead guilty to a scaled-down charge of assisting a criminal. A few weeks later Judge Douglas sentenced her to a six-year prison term. It was ordered served concurrently with the sentence from LaPorte County. She could become eligible for parole within three years.

Despite her plea not to be locked up with her daughter because she was afraid of Marie, she was transported to the Indiana State Women's Correctional Center near Indianapolis to serve her term.

Attorneys for Marie appealed her convictions in both Indiana courts.

Early in December 1987 the Indiana Court of Appeals upheld her convictions in Paul's murder. The court, however, ruled she should not have been ordered to serve her Porter County sentence consecutively to her term for the LaPorte County slaying.

After Judge Douglas ordered her sentence in Porter County be served concurrently with the first sentence, the date of her first parole eligibility was also altered. Her earliest possible re-lease date was set at 2029, when she would be eighty or eighty-one years old.

Major points in the appeal of her conviction in LaPorte County focused on Judge Martin's ruling permitting evidence of her husband's shooting to be introduced in her trial for Elaine's murder, and claims that especially gruesome tes-timony about the old woman's dismemberment and disposal of the body was prejudicial and shouldn't have been allowed.

Marie's attorneys asserted that the two crimes were so separated in time and method that evi-dence relating to Paul's slaying should not have been permitted in her trial for Elaine's murder.

Early in 1990, in a three-to-two ruling, the In-diana Supreme Court affirmed her convictions in the slaying of her stepmother-in-law. The high court determined that the two crimes met the re-quirement for exception of the general rule that evidence of independent crimes is inadmissable.

Writing in the majority opinion, Justice Richard Given stated the two crimes were similar because each involved a conspiracy within the family to murder another family member.

In the dissenting opinion written with the con-currence of Chief Justice Randall Shepard, Jus-tice Roger DeBruler claimed the crimes were dissimilar because the motives were different; Paul was reputedly murdered because he was abusive, and Elaine was killed for her money.

The dissenting justices wrote that admission of the evidence relating to Paul's shooting was highly likely to have led to Marie's conviction. They added in their dissent they believed she should be given a new trial, or at least have her conviction and sentence on the conspiracy count set aside.

The court in its majority opinion also rejected the argument of Marie's attorneys that Menkel's testimony about seeing "a lot of white worms" and "some small flying black bugs" on the garbage bags containing Elaine's remains was unnecessary and was used solely in order to prejudice the jury.

"Relevant evidence which logically tends to prove a material fact may be admitted although it is gruesome and cumulative in nature," the court ruled. "In the case at bar, Menkel's testimony was admissible to show the macabre way in which [the] appellant and her two sons disposed of Elaine Witte's body and their indifference toward her gruesome death." The justices concluded that permission to submit the evidence was well within the discretion of the court.

Epilogue

As this book was written, Marie Witte was serving her prison sentences at White Institute, the Indiana State Women's Correctional Center near Indianapolis.

Several months after her imprisonment there she received two letters from a wealthy retired oilman from Greenville, Texas, who wrote that she was his "dream girl" and said he wanted her to come live with him.

Marie contacted King and told him about the curious communication.

According to the Gary defense lawyer, Donald Lee Laisure, Sr., asked her to grant him power of attorney. The oilman reportedly reasoned that would enable him to hire a high-powered lawyer to obtain her early release. Once Marie was free of prison bars she could settle down with the Texan and they could begin building a life together.

Marie wasn't the first woman behind bars that Laisure had contacted or written to with romance on his mind.

Sometimes known by the nickname "Flash," he is noted for his many marriages and his more recent habit of wooing women imprisoned for notorious crimes. One of his brides was Susan Atkins, a Manson Family member who helped kill pregnant Hollywood actress Sharon Tate and later boasted of tasting the blood of her victim.

Laisure was fifty-two when he and Susan were wed in 1981, and on his marriage certificate he noted that he had been married thirty-five times before.

Predictably, perhaps, the marriage lasted barely more than a year before Laisure experienced the agony of yet another divorce. In a letter Los Angeles Deputy District Attorney Steven Kay carried to one of Susan's parole board hearings, Laisure accused her of stabbing him twice during a jealous fit while he was visiting her at the prison.

Marie apparently was unimpressed by the eccentric multimillionaire. King said she sent one of the letters to him and asked, "Who is this nut?"

Margaret "Marcie" O'Donnell died at 8:25 P.M. on July 27, 1990, at the St. Elizabeth Hospital Medical Center in Lafayette, Indiana, of lung cancer and respiratory failure. She had suffered from emphysema for years. Marcie was sixty-four years old, had been released from prison, and was living a few miles outside the small town of Monon in White County.

Marie was transported from the prison for a memorial service for her mother at St. Joseph's Catholic Church in the farming community of Reynolds, a few miles south of Monon. Marcie was cremated. Obituary information provided to the mortuary listed survivors as a daughter, Marie Witte, of Indianapolis, and two grandchildren. There was no mention of her other survivors.

In February 1992, Eric petitioned the Indiana Parole Board for clemency and a recommendation to Indiana Governor Evan Bayh for a reduction of his twenty-year prison sentence. He said he had arranged for a job as a researcher with a public relations firm in Valparaiso if he was released early. Eric was imprisoned at the Westville Correctional Center near the Purdue University North Central campus where his mother once attended night school.

At a hearing before the board, he recounted the tragic events of his childhood. He said his father was abusive, and he was brainwashed by his mother. "My family is nuts," he observed matter-of-factly. "Dysfunctional is not the word."

The board rejected his petition. According to state correctional regulations, he can petition once a year for clemency. In the meantime he remains imprisoned at Westville. Eric's anticipated release date is July 1995.

Butch was also serving his time in the Indiana State Prison system. Herrbach says that of the major players in the tragedy, he believes Butch is the most normal.

"He's the one who broke the case. He said he can't live with this anymore, that he wanted to come forward and tell what happened. And that indicates to me that he had some sense of responsibility, and some sense of right and wrong," the prosecutor told this writer. "Whether prison has removed that ability from him or hampered it in some way, I don't know. But I think that he's probably more normal than the rest of the family is."

William F. Herrbach was elected in November 1990 as the LaPorte County Prosecutor. He was also an advisor to the Drug and Narcotic Unit of LaPorte County and took a leading role in the formation of the LaPorte County Homicide

Team. After Marie's trial, he prosecuted two death penalty cases. He won convictions in both trials, but the jury declined to recommend the death penalty in one.

Herrbach works out of a law office catty-cornered from the Superior Court building in Michigan City. Several drawings of the Witte trial rendered by a courtroom sketch artist are mounted on one wall of his private office.

In 1990 after thirteen years with the Porter County Prosecutor's Office, Berning left public service to go into private practice. He set up offices in a red-brick building about a block from the courthouse, where at this writing he was practicing family law and handling some personal injury cases.

Skip Pierce was appointed by the Trail Creek Town Board as marshal after Chastain left in 1988 to take a job as a patrolman with the police department in the nearby town of Long Beach. A few months after the Witte case was concluded in the courts, Pierce assisted in the investigation of a Trail Creek house fire that killed a man, his reputed mistress, and another couple. Patricia Anna Johnson was eventually convicted of setting the fire that killed her husband of twenty-three years, Eugene Johnson, Terry Ward, and Ron and Beverly Kirby. She was given an eighty-year prison sentence.

Pierce is a member of the LaPorte County Homicide Team which draws talent from the Indiana State Police, the LaPorte County Sheriff's Department, local police, and town marshal's departments for difficult murder investigations.

He continues to work out of a cramped concrete block office at the end of Sarah Jo Avenue that is filled with file cabinets, books on Indiana criminal codes, a police radio, a desk, four chairs, an electric typewriter, stained coffee cups, and dozens of cigarette stubs. The walls of the cluttered office are decorated with framed service awards and certificates from law enforcement courses and seminars he had attended. A bottled coyote head preserved in formaldehyde is jammed in among several books on a narrow shelf. Pierce is at home there.

Sergeant Arland Boyd is continuing with his job as a homicide and major crimes investigator at the Indiana State Police Post in Lowell, and at this writing had a collaboration agreement with a Hollywood producer to work on a movie about the Witte case.

Scott L. King continues to practice criminal law and to maintain an office in Gary.

* * *

Early in 1986 Judge Martin appointed a La-Porte lawyer as administrator of Elaine's estate. If Grandma Witte left a will it was lost or destroyed. In the absence of a will or eligible heirs, her estate reverted to the state of Indiana.

In April 1986 her house and two-and-a-half acres of property were sold at auction for $26,750, about half the appraised value. After deduction of costs, the money was scheduled for eventual deposit in the state's common school fund. Interest from the fund, which at that time stood at nearly $200 million, is loaned at low interest rates to school corporations to build schools.

A couple from Beverly Shores, Leo Firme and his wife, Mary Fox, outlasted two other active bidders to become the new owners of the property. Ms. Fox was editor of the *News-Dispatch*'s religion and life-styles pages. Her husband was a sales manager. They told a reporter they planned to have a Catholic priest bless the five-room house.

**ORDINARY LIVES DESTROYED BY EXTRAORDINARY HORROR.
FACTS MORE DANGEROUS THAN FICTION.
CAPTURE A PINNACLE TRUE CRIME . . . IF YOU DARE.**

LITTLE GIRL LOST (593, $4.99)
By Joan Merriam
When Anna Brackett, an elderly woman living alone, allowed two teenage girls into her home, she never realized that a brutal death awaited her. Within an hour, Mrs. Brackett would be savagely stabbed twenty-eight times. Her executioners were Shirley Katherine Wolf, 14, and Cindy Lee Collier, 15. *Little Girl Lost* examines how two adolescents were driven through neglect and sexual abuse to commit the ultimate crime.

HUSH, LITTLE BABY (541, $4.99)
By Jim Carrier
Darci Kayleen Pierce seemed to be the kind of woman you stand next to in the grocery store. However, Darci was obsessed with the need to be a mother. She desperately wanted a baby—any baby. On a summer day, Darci kidnapped a nine-month pregnant woman, strangled her, and performed a makeshift Cesarean section with a car key. In this arresting account, readers will learn how Pierce's tortured fantasy of motherhood spiralled into a bloody reality.

IN A FATHER'S RAGE (547, $4.99)
By Raymond Van Over
Dr. Kenneth Z. Taylor promised his third wife Teresa that he would mend his drug-addictive, violent ways. His vow didn't last. He nearly beat his bride to death on their honeymoon. This nuptial nightmare worsened until Taylor killed Teresa after allegedly catching her sexually abusing their infant son. Claiming to have been driven beyond a father's rage, Taylor was still found guilty of first degree murder. This gripping page-turner reveals how a marriage made in heaven can become a living hell.

I KNOW MY FIRST NAME IS STEVEN (563, $4.99)
By Mike Echols
A TV movie was based on this terrifying tale of abduction, child molesting, and brainwashing. Yet, a ray of hope shines through this evil swamp for Steven Stayner escaped from his captor and testified against the socially disturbed Kenneth Eugene Parnell. For seven years, Steven was shuttled across California under the assumed name of "Dennis Parnell." Despite the humiliations and degradations, Steven never lost sight of his origins or his courage.

RITES OF BURIAL (611, $4.99)
By Tom Jackman and Troy Cole
Many pundits believe that the atrocious murders and dismemberments performed by Robert Berdella may have inspired Jeffrey Dahmer. Berdella stalked and savagely tortured young men; sadistically photographing their suffering and ritualistically preserving totems from their deaths. Upon his arrest, police uncovered human skulls, envelopes of teeth, and a partially decomposed human head. This shocking expose is written by two men who worked daily on this case.

Available wherever paperbacks are sold, or order direct from the Publisher. Send cover price plus 50¢ per copy for mailing and handling to Pinnacle Books, Dept. 773 , 475 Park Avenue South, New York, N.Y. 10016. Residents of New York and Tennessee must include sales tax. DO NOT SEND CASH. For a free Zebra/Pinnacle catalog please write to the above address.